Hillsboro Public Library
Hillsboro, OR
A member of Washington County
COOPERATIVE LIBRARY SERVICES

MOTHER TONGUE

MOTHER TONGUE

MY FAMILY'S GLOBE-TROTTING QUEST

TO DREAM IN MANDARIN,

LAUGH IN ARABIC, AND SING IN SPANISH

Christine Gilbert

AVERY
an imprint of Penguin Random House
New York

an imprint of Penguin Random House LLC
375 Hudson Street
New York, New York 10014

Copyright © 2016 by Christine Gilbert
Penguin supports copyright. Copyright fuels creativity, encourages diverse voices,
promotes free speech, and creates a vibrant culture. Thank you for buying an authorized
edition of this book and for complying with copyright laws by not reproducing, scanning,
or distributing any part of it in any form without permission. You are supporting
writers and allowing Penguin to continue to publish books for every reader.

Most Avery books are available at special quantity discounts for bulk
purchase for sales promotions, premiums, fund-raising, and educational needs.
Special books or book excerpts also can be created to fit specific needs.
For details, write SpecialMarkets@penguinrandomhouse.com.

ISBN 9781592407927

Printed in the United States of America
1 3 5 7 9 10 8 6 4 2

Book design by Meighan Cavanaugh

To Cole and Stella—

this is what we did when you were babies.

CONTENTS

....

INTRODUCTION

··

Halfway down the street, I stop walking. The crowd of Barcelona holiday shoppers flows past me, and I let them, the weight of my shopping bags cutting into my hands. Christmas lights twinkling overhead light the path through the looming architecture of the Gothic quarter as I stand gripped in a wave of déjà vu. *I've been here before.* I feel like I am seeing a lithograph of my past, the paper-thin memory of a place laid carefully over the scene that lies before me.

I have been here before, of course, I know that. I am constantly seeing buildings and streets that jog some buried half memory. But this feeling is different. Somehow I have brushed up against a sense memory of that time. For a moment I remember my last visit, years ago, and how it felt to live in my skin then and how different it feels now to be just another city dweller out buying Christmas gifts on a chilly December evening. The city hasn't changed—I have.

A decade ago, my husband, Drew, and I honeymooned in Barcelona. It was our first time in Europe—our first time abroad, really, unless you count a few trips to Canada. We stayed in a hotel that cost way too much, cuddling in a tiny room with a double bed, peering out at the world over a wrought-iron balcony, just north of La Rambla. The whole city seemed black and white to me then. It was a rainy week in October, the gray stones slick and gloomy. But we were desperately in love, both with each other and with Spain, and nothing could dampen our spirits. We walked around this same Gothic quarter like the stunned Americans we were, holding hands, admiring the architecture, swooning over quaint cafés and stylish Catalan men and women with their dedication to trim cuts and knotted scarves. Later we collapsed in Café Zurich, ordered strong coffees, and marveled at our lives. Could there be anything more romantic than Europe?

The kinetic sensation of being young and newly married came back to me all at once. I wish I could travel through time and whisper into my ten-years-younger ear, *You will live here one day.* Maybe in some way I knew, because no matter what we did in the years after, no matter where we went, the magnetic pull of Barcelona was irresistible. Ten years later, via the most indirect path possible, we would return to the romantic land of our first days as newlyweds, this time to rent an apartment, buy groceries, and settle into domestic life. We are still in love, with each other and the city, but it is oh so different. We're older. We have two kids now. We have seen the world.

On that first trip to Barcelona, my most vivid memories were of the wild curves Gaudí created, sculpting buildings like they were made of melting candle wax. Now, I see the people. It's the "bon dia" to my neighbor as we briskly left our apartment this afternoon, the half smile to the woman wheeling her grocery tote behind her, the familiar road leading up to the bakery where the young woman with the severe bun gives us baguettes each morning. There's the fruit stand with a display of *mandarinas* on the sidewalk next to the meat shop with a full Iberian leg of ham in the store window, then the wine shop where they refill one-liter jugs with *tinto*. I barely look up anymore at the imposing architecture. My focus is all street level, straight ahead, walking quickly toward the bus stop, *la parada*, so we could swipe our metro cards, squeeze past the bundled masses, and slide into our seats.

Today we were going shopping.

"¡AY, GUAPA!" THE WOMAN CALLED to my daughter from across the bus, waving her hand. She was wearing a scarf tied artfully around her neck, a kind of quadruple knot that I had not yet mastered, with a fitted trench coat and an oversized leather purse. When her waving failed to attract Stella's interest, she quickly closed the distance between us, shuffling down the aisle, the movement of the bus propelling her forward. "¡Muñeca!"

My daughter sat on my lap, unfazed by the compliments. *Beautiful. Doll. Blondie.* Stella's legs poked out from beneath her pink peacoat, her tiny hands rested on her lap, and she stared straight ahead, eyes fixed on some point in front of her and slowly losing focus. The gentle shaking of the bus was lulling her to sleep.

The people here call Stella *bien seria*, "very serious," because she is so stoic and self-contained. Until recently, I hadn't taught her to smile and engage with strangers—I would just hold her, talk to her, point things out, make her engage with the world. But make her interact with strangers? Pass her around? Let everyone smile and coo at her? I grew up American, and that was reflected in my parenting. I was focused more on her than on her relationship with others. But I was learning that socially adept children were highly prized in Spain. I was finding out that, like so many other things, raising kids varied wildly by culture. What I always thought was an innate quality of the Spanish—that they were warmer, friendlier, and more social than Americans—was actually a cultivated quality. They valued it and made it a point to shape their children in this way. It would influence their social landscape for life.

This emphasis on friendliness was also part of why I had fallen so in love with Spain. That natural warmth was so inviting.

"Hola, joven," I said to the woman, imitating something cheeky I had heard in the market. *Hello, youngster.* I was becoming a more friendly version of myself in Spain, more likely to break the ice and start conversations.

"¡Ay, tu hija es tan hermooooossssaa!" she cooed, leaning over Drew and our son, Cole, to get a better look at Stella. *Your daughter is so beautiful!*

"¡Gracias!"

She smelled like rose soap—like *jabón de rosa*, I thought to myself, the Spanish translation bubbling up unbidden. We had been here for about a month, but it wasn't my first brush with Spanish. I noticed over time that the more I used the language, the more it stayed with me. By now it was a constant passenger in my head, a never-ending closed-captioning *en español* that ran like an internal dubbing of my thoughts. *I live here now*, I thought. *Ya vivo aquí.*

"A ella le gusta sentarse con su mamá," the woman said. *She likes to sit with her mama.*

"¡Síííí, por supuesto!"—*yes, of course!*—I said, dragging out the *sí* emphatically, the same way I had seen Spanish women talk to one another. Always imitating, always watching for the response. Nearly identical to how my children were learning.

Rose Soap Woman smiled at me, and I felt like I had passed some unspoken social test. When we first came to Spain, we had hoped that we would find a new family, starting with a Spanish *mamacita* who would lavish affection on our children. Little had we known we were getting a city full of them. Drew and I grinned at each other with knowing looks: Our daughter was an *abuela* magnet.

Stella finally looked up at the woman and allowed her head to be patted. I tried to get her to say hello:

"Dile 'hola,' Stella," I said, waving her little hand at the woman.

"Hola," my daughter offered meekly.

"¿Cuál es su nombre?" the woman asked. *What is her name?*

"Stella."

"Hmm?"

"Stella." The woman still looked puzzled.

Drew jumped in. "*Es*tella."

She broke into a smile. "Ah, *Estella*."

"Sí." I smiled, too.

"Y tu hijo?" she asked, running her hand over our son's blond head. He shook his head impatiently.

"Cole," I replied.

"Col?" she asked, again looking puzzled.

"Sí."

Everyone wanted to call Stella "Estella," and sometimes she'd get mistaken for *chela*, the Mexican slang for beer. Cole, on the other hand, *is* a Spanish word, at least how it's pronounced. It's Catalan as well, which is the second language in Barcelona (or first, depending on who you ask). Cole is pronounced like the Spanish word *col* and means "cabbage." We accidentally named our son after the slightly smelly vegetable they put in *cocidos* and *ensaladas*.

Meet our children: Beer and Cabbage.

Apparently it didn't matter, as the *abuelita* quickly launched into a story about her three children and eight grandchildren (who all lived outside the city, sadly) and her hand injury that had only recently healed.

I nodded and Drew offered, "Sí, sí, vale, vale," the usual Spanish murmurs of agreement.

The bus stopped and we said our good-byes as she departed. After the bus had started rolling again, I leaned over to Drew and whispered, "If we have another baby, we are naming her Alejandra—or Javier if it's a boy—something so Spanish no one ever asks us twice."

He grinned. "Agreed."

WE GOT OFF THE BUS at Plaza Cataluyna, where the Generalitat had turned the main plaza into an ice skating rink and the emblematic retail store El Corte Inglés broadcast holiday cheer across a city block with a multistory light display on its stone walls. Around the corner, toward La Catedral, an oversized Christmas tree flashed holiday messages in three languages:

Merry Christmas

Bon Nadal

Feliz Navidad

The holiday crowd swarmed around it, snapping photos and making their way toward the real attraction: La Feria Artesanal Santa Lucía. It was Barcelona's most popular Christmas market and our best bet for finding Catalan holiday accessories.

My daughter wanted to walk, so we hung back with her as she wobbled along, releasing Cole to dash off and explore while Drew kept an eye on him.

"Look, lights," Stella said, pointing to the strings of white Christmas lights hung throughout the market, making a post-rain halo around each stall.

"Sí, luces," I replied.

"Moon!" she said, pointing to the patch of sky above us, framed by the looming church in the distance.

"Sí, muy bien, Stella, la luna," I said, taking her hand.

"La luna," she repeated to herself.

Cole, trotting around ahead of us, sprinted to see the *caga tiós*. This was his first Christmas in Barcelona, and Cole was especially delighted by the scatological twist Father Christmas took in these parts.

"Mama, come here!" Cole said to me excitedly, pointing to a display full of Christmas logs. Each one had two little legs that propped it up at a forty-five-degree angle. On its head was a red hat, the traditional Catalan *barretina*, with a face drawn on the cut end and black eyes affixed to the wood. This was *Caga Tió*, giver of nougat, hazelnuts, and candy.

If we had lived in the countryside, we would have ventured into the woods to find the perfect round log and immediately covered it in a blanket to keep our new friend warm. Back home, I would have applied some googly eyes and a red hat. However, since we lived in *la Zona Franca*, on the fourth floor of an apartment building, where there were no moss-covered forests to hunt for gift-giving wood, we were left to purchase one. Once we'd found our *caga tió* and brought it home, we would follow tradition and tell the story of the original *caga tió*. Then throughout the month of December, the kids would tend to the log, making sure it was cozy in its blanket and hat, feeding it orange peels and giving it water to drink.

Drew leaned in to the stall to talk to the owner, who was sitting on a stool arranging wreaths. They conferred for a long while, until Drew nodded and turned around to us.

"I got him down to twenty euros," Drew told me.

"What is that?" Cole asked, pointing to the one closest to his eye level.

"That's a *caga tió*, Cole."

"Why?"

"That's what it's called."

"Why?"

"It means 'pooping log' in Spanish."

"Why?"

"Well, we take him home and feed him and keep him warm, and then on Christmas Eve, we sing a song and ask him for presents. Then we hit him with a stick until he poops out candy."

Cole looked at me blankly. After a pause, I asked him, "Do you want to get one?"

"Yeah!"

Drew and I laughed. He turned to Stella. "What do you think, Stella? Yes?"

"Ya!" She clapped her hands in excitement.

It seemed insane to spend twenty euros on what was essentially a piece of wood with a face painted on it, but we were embracing the tradition wholeheartedly.

"Okay, let's do it." I nodded at Drew and he paid for our *caga tió*, then stuffed it in his backpack.

"Come on, kids, let's keep looking," I said, and took Drew's hand. My husband now had a massive piece of wood in his backpack, the cartoonish little face and red hat poking out of the top.

"How's it look?" Drew asked me, turning away from me so I could see.

"Good, he looks snug. Very Catalan."

"I want a sword! And an ax!" Cole said to Drew, and ran ahead to another stall.

"Oh, cool. *Una espada*. Maybe for Christmas," Drew said.

"Espada," Cole repeated, and lightly touched the wooden blade.

"Come on, Cole, the *caganer*!" I said, pointing to a stand with a large statue of a Catalan man squatting on the top. High above the market traffic, he perched, wearing the same red *barretina* as our *caga tió*, plus a white shirt, red belt, and black pants. He had his pants pulled down to his thighs, his round bottom was bare, and he was taking a massive poo.

Cole stood in awe for a full minute.

"Mama . . ."

"Qué hace el hombre?" I asked him. *What is that man doing?*

He looked at me wide-eyed, a hint of a giggle tugging at his dimples.

"He's pooping!" I said.

"Why is he pooping?"

"He's the *caganer*. He poops to make us laugh."

Cole laughed and covered his mouth. Stella copied him, covering her mouth and issuing a loud, fake guffaw. Then she turned to Cole and clumsily tried to hug him.

"Aw . . ." I said, and Stella repeated me. "Awww."

"Look, Mama, I'm hugging Stella," Cole said, leaning down to embrace his sister. He hugged her so tight, she leaned back with one foot off the ground, like that iconic photo of the sailor kissing the nurse on V-J Day.

"Drew, look," I said.

"I know," he said. "They are killing me with cuteness today."

"Okay, guys, let's go get something to eat," I said, clapping my hands. "Say good-bye to the *caganer*."

"Bye, *caganer*!" Cole shouted.

As we walked away, Cole kept looking over his shoulder at the larger-than-life shrine to silliness. From this angle we could see the soft-serve swirl of poop that lay just below his bum, a graphic and entirely ludicrous sight in the middle of a Christmas market.

We should have headed to the official *pessebre* next, the nativity scene, where the *caganer* is most commonly found. He's usually placed somewhere in the back, quietly doing his business while Mary takes care of baby Jesus. Sometimes he's dressed as a celebrity or noted politician. It's a reminder of our human frailty and to not take ourselves too seriously, even during the holidays. It's also completely hilarious to Catalan children.

Instead we made a beeline to a nearby plaza that had a small playground with a gate next to a café with outdoor seats. It was nearly ten p.m., but people were just starting to come out for the night. We led the kids into the playground, closed the gate, and found our seats.

A waiter came by, and Drew ordered: "Quiero una caña y patatas bravas."

"Y una caña para mí," I added.

They delivered our beers and spicy potatoes and while the kids played, Drew and I considered what to order for the kids.

"Stella really liked the calamari last time," I said.

"Okay, and we'll get Cole a crepe."

"Sounds good. By the way, your poop log is making a break for it."

"Oh, shit. But literally. Ha!" Drew chortled, pushing the log back into the backpack and attempting to force the zipper shut.

We both took a sip of our beers and gazed around in contentment. The plaza was just an open space between buildings. The alleyways leading off to the Gothic quarter or back to La Rambla were dark and twisting, all gray cobblestones with the flames of lanterns lighting each restaurant, the tables half full, waiters in crisp white shirts moving efficiently inside and out.

Dinner was later here, close to midnight in some cases. Kids were a part of public life and it wasn't unusual to see children out with their parents late into the evening. Barcelona was a haven for parents of young children who still wanted to go out. Our children got to play on a slide and seesaws while we drank one-euro beers. When they got their fill, we'd scoop them up and bring them to our table to eat.

I set my beer down and gazed at my husband. "Drew, how the hell did we get here?"

He just grinned back at me.

CHRISTMAS EVE DAWNED with a touch of misting rain, and I couldn't find anything in our apartment.

"Drew! *¿Dónde están los zapatitos de Cole?* And what are you wearing?"

Even though we were alone, we made it a habit to use some

Spanish with each other. It had started out as more serious attempts to teach Cole the language, but quickly we realized it wasn't at all necessary, considering that we were living in a Spanish-speaking country. Few people here spoke decent English. In a report commissioned by the EU on English speaking, only 20 percent of Spain residents spoke English well enough to hold a conversation (compared to nearly 95 percent of Norway, where fluency in English is so common, it might as well be an official second language).

Instead, there are a number of second languages here, including Catalan, which is spoken across Catalonia, including in our home of Barcelona. Then there's also Basque, Valencian, Galician, and Occitan. Occitan sounds similar to a mashup of French and Italian. The existence of these official second languages (plus a half-dozen unofficial ones) means that while most Spain residents don't speak English, they are often still bilingual.

In fact, it was this multilingual atmosphere that attracted us here long-term: the lack of English and the commitment to bilingual education. In Barcelona we spent our days immersed in non-English languages, which made our own language study so much easier—not to mention the communal feel of being surrounded by like-minded people who thought that speaking multiple languages was a worthy life goal.

"What?" Drew shouted back.

"*Zapatitos*—the shoes!" I hollered again.

"Aquí, ya los tengo."

Like most bilingual couples I knew, Drew and I had our dominant language, but we flipped between languages. The kids were still sorting out which language to use when. Water was always *agua*, but it paired with English for: "I want *agua*." Sometimes, the whole thing felt chaotic. Especially when we were running late and the kids were successfully applying divide-and-conquer strategies to keep us one step behind as they avoided getting dressed, brushing their teeth and having their tiny feet shoved into those damn *zapatitos*.

"Drew!" I yelled.

"Ya vengo," he said, scooping up a giggling Stella in one arm and prying a marker out of her hand before she could draw on her face any more. Just then Cole came sprinting out of his room, completely naked, with a plastic light saber over his head.

"Oh my God, we're never going to make it," I said, half-exasperated and half-amused.

"It's okay, we'll just be late. Is that a Spanish thing?" Drew said, setting Stella down to grab Cole. "Let's pretend it is *very* Spanish."

Two hours later, we arrived at our friends' house, an American and Argentine couple with two kids slightly older than our own. Their kids were attending school in Barcelona, so they were learning Catalan and already spoke Spanish from their dad. We got right down to business: That *caga tió* wasn't going to poop out presents without a little help.

The key to getting your *caga tió* to poop is twofold: First you must sing a song, then you must beat it with a stick. The song is in Catalan, and it goes like this:

Poop log,
Poop turrón [a nougat Christmas candy]
Hazelnuts and cheese
If you don't poop well,
I'll hit you with a stick,
Poop log!

Poop log!
Log of Christmas,
Don't poop herrings,
They are too salty,
Poop turrón,
They are much better!

Log of Christmas,
Poop turrón,
Pee white wine,
Don't poop herrings,
They are too salty,
Poop turrón,
They are much better!
Poop log!

Of course, after a glass of wine, this is even more hilarious. We gave the traditional song our best effort, but mostly just sang "¡Cagaaaa tióóóó!" with gusto while helping the kids hit the log with sticks.

There's a bit of Christmas magic here, where the parents

have to slip the presents under the log's blanket while the kids are distracted, which I failed to do discreetly. Drew took photos, our friends sang the song, I pulled out presents for the kids, and Cole and Stella had their first taste of Christmas in Barcelona.

I SLIPPED BACK IN TIME and considered that older version of me. I had loved Barcelona when we honeymooned here but couldn't see any way to live overseas. I couldn't have imagined raising my kids bilingual. But now, all I had to do was stay. Everything seemed so simple now. But we sure did take the long way to get here.

(PART 1)

CHINA

One

Drew lay on our hotel bed in Cairo, propped up on his elbow, holding up his face in the palm of his hand, our sleeping son next to him. I was pacing the length of the oversized room. The former grandeur of this building was apparent from the ample quarters, the hand-laid tile, the elaborate crown molding, but it had been long neglected. Everything was slowly grinding itself back into the ground, little cracks expanding across the plaster, the tiles, the joints between walls. Still, at fifteen bucks a night, it was an affordable hotel and well located, even if it was just a shell, an artifact of another time. I imagined those days: plush bedding, leather couches, artwork, and the twinkle of refined light fixtures. Instead we had lonely double beds with thin blankets, a folding chair, and a light spot on the wall where a mirror or painting once hung.

The dust was everywhere, a constant companion in Egypt,

something we noticed when we arrived at the airport, and it had followed us ever since. There was a broom leaning next to our door when we arrived, as if the futility of the task had been realized, and the struggle abandoned.

There was a wide balcony attached to our room that trembled when you crossed it, but it gave a bird's-eye view of the city from sixteen stories above. I stood in the door frame and looked out.

"Okay, so we're doing it?" I said to Drew.

"Mm-hmm," Drew said slowly.

I turned around and regarded my husband. He looked like he was about to join our son for a nap.

"Drew, it will be great. We'll live in China, in Beijing, and learn Mandarin. Then we'll go to the Middle East—maybe Jordan or somewhere, I'm not sure yet—and learn Arabic. I don't know how much Cole will learn, but I am sure he'll pick some up. Then we can go to Mexico or Costa Rica, live on the beach, eat tacos, and learn Spanish. I mean, just *think* about it."

"Uh-huh."

"We would get fluent in three different languages, in just a couple of years. And beyond that, we'd also be learning about three massively different cultures, back to back. The implications are huge. I feel like we would understand the world better." I took a deep breath. "Look, it's Asia, the Middle East, and Latin culture. Boom. You know?"

"Right."

"I mean *who* does this? Have you ever heard of someone else doing something like this?" I didn't wait for him to answer. "It will be amazing!"

"Okay." Drew yawned.

"No, really. I need you to get excited about this," I said.

He pushed himself off the bed and sat up. "I am!" He stretched his arms and gave me a grin.

"Okay, good. Because we are doing it." I kept pacing. "Are you going to learn the languages with me?"

"Ah—no." Drew smiled sheepishly.

I did my quick circuit around the room again, then resumed my position at the open balcony door and looked down toward the street below. A man was selling hot shawarma, carving meat off massive spits with a flick of his wrist and then piling it high into pitas. A gaggle of people stood around awaiting their orders. Egyptian families strolled past, the mothers in full *abayas*, the extended hijab that flowed over the entire body. Their little children bounced around them as they leisurely crossed the square.

I bit my nail and turned around again. "So when should we go to China?"

THIS MAD, IMPULSIVE IDEA for a language immersion project hadn't occurred to me overnight. In my mind, it was all about Cole. I had first started thinking about multilingualism when I was pregnant with him and researching everything I could possibly read about, from home birth to vaccines to raising the baby bilingual. I ended up with a C-section scar, a fully vaccinated child, and a vague idea that we two all-American monolinguals should somehow raise him bilingual, if that was even possible.

But after Cole's birth, we got distracted. Drew and I were filming a documentary project together that took us around the world, hitting Colombia, Thailand, India, Greece, Spain, and finally Egypt. Everyone back home kept asking us how all this travel was changing our son, and our honest answer was: probably not at all. During our travels, we had seen Cole pick up little words here and there, like "kap koon" for *thank you* in Thailand or "hola" in Spain, but he didn't retain those words once he stopped hearing them every day. And while it was fascinating to watch him adapt to each culture so effortlessly, we knew as a one-year-old he wouldn't remember any of it. Without encountering Spanish, Thai, Hindi, Greek, or Arabic again, for a sustained period, he would grow up to be an English-only speaker like us.

I had heard that there is a window when a child is very young during which exposure to a second language can lead to native mastery of that second language. For example, if we moved somewhere *right now* where Cole would hear, say, Hindi every day, he could grow up to speak Hindi just as well as he spoke English.

These were the thoughts percolating in my head around the time I ran into the research of Ellen Bialystok. Her research showed that there was a cognitive benefit to being bilingual, that speaking a second or third language could stave off the effects of dementia by four to five years. My grandfather had died from complications surrounding dementia a few years earlier, so when I read these results, I took notice.

My grandfather had been an English-Finnish bilingual. The last four to five years of his life were maybe the best he ever had. He played a lot of golf in those four years. He made the three-day trip in his red Cadillac from his lake house in Massachusetts to his condo in Florida and back multiple times in that period. We had long conversations over the phone, and I told him that I would take him to Finland with me. We hadn't been close when I was young, but in his last years (though we didn't know they were his last years), I really got to know him. If he hadn't had those extra five years to live, thanks to his bilingualism, I might never have really known him.

My grandfather's dementia was likely a hereditary condition, but unlike him, I don't have bilingualism to delay the effects. It's possible that acquiring a second language later in life could help, but Bialystok only studied lifelong bilinguals who spoke both languages fluently. If there was a window for mastering a second language to native-like fluency, it had probably closed for me. But it wasn't too late for my son.

FOR OUR DOCUMENTARY, the filming was done. Drew would be doing the bulk of the editing, so, true to form, I was feeling my familiar tug toward the next big project. I started seriously thinking about languages and how to raise my child bilingual. Drew and I could do our jobs from anywhere with a wireless

Internet connection. Cole was squarely in his second-language-mastery window, but growing fast. If we wanted him to learn another language fluently enough to pass for a native speaker—and then maybe to ward off the dementia that was likely coming for me and him from my grandfather's genes—we'd have to act fast. Suddenly, the way forward seemed clear. What had before been just a few isolated details now connected in a way that could not be unseen. It felt like fate. I wasn't prone to magical thinking, but somehow I was letting that feeling drive me.

We'd move abroad. Somewhere with a tough language, one that Cole would really only be able to master if he lived there from toddlerhood. And I'd learn it too, so I could speak to him in the language at home—and reap whatever brain-protecting benefits I could from later-in-life language study.

And if knowing two languages was better than knowing one language, surely knowing three or four would be better than knowing just two. So—once we mastered the first foreign language, we'd replicate the experiment twice more. We'd become fluent in three new languages in just a few years by devoting ourselves completely to them and immersing ourselves in those cultures and countries. It was a brilliant plan.

First, I had to convince my husband.

Somehow I was always the one pitching an idea and cajoling Drew into coming along. Ten years prior, I had scooped Drew up from his man-cave attic apartment in Connecticut, where he was working as an animator, and convinced him to move cross-country together to Seattle after only three months of dating. The timing was right; we both wanted new jobs and a new start, so we decided to take the leap. But when I showed up at his apartment the morning of the move, it was a disaster. Years' worth of his artwork, drawings, and illustrations covered the floor, like newspaper on the bottom of a hamster cage. His fish tank was green with a long-forgotten dead fish and one floating baby doll for effect. He had saved every empty beer bottle from the last six months of drinking and had haphazardly lined them up on the counters, on the windowsills, and against the baseboards. I would need a shovel to dig him out of this mess. It wasn't until later, when we started our cross-country road trip, that I began to realize what was going on. He was nervous. He didn't pack because he was procrastinating, avoiding the enormity of the life change we were embarking on.

He told me stories on that ten-day drive, stories about not taking his SATs or applying to any colleges until a full semester after he graduated high school when he realized, *Oh right, everyone really has left.* He was comfortable with routine and liked having things stay the same. As a third-generation Vermonter, he had it in his bones. I realized that this was part of why we worked well together. He was the anchor that kept me from floating away.

Now we were seven years into our marriage, parents to a young child, and had many cities under our belt. We had lived in Seattle for five years, Dallas for two, and been back to Boston for one. We'd briefly moved to Madrid, traveled to Central America, and had a baby in Oregon. After Cole was born, we continued traveling and filmed the documentary that eventually landed us in Egypt. Two years into our travels, he had joked that I just had to tell him what day to arrive at the airport and remember to pack his passport for him.

Still, this project would be different. It wasn't the same as strong-arming him into spending three months in the tropical paradise of Thailand, where if Drew got homesick, hated the food, or what have you, change was only a plane ticket away. This would be a years-long commitment. I'd be busy with language classes all day—and I hoped he would join me in trying to learn the languages, too. I'd be taking him to places we'd never talked about living, and I'd need his full support along the way.

"So why *THREE* LANGUAGES?" Drew asked.

I sat down on the bed next to him, careful to not wake Cole. I pushed my hair behind my ear.

"Well, if we're going to do this, let's just check off the big bucket-list item," I said.

Drew laughed and lay back down on the bed. "I knew you were going to say that. You can never do anything just *a little bit*."

"I know, but this might be our only shot to do something big like this." I lay down next to him for a second and talked quietly over Cole's dozing head. "We've talked about learning Spanish for years. I've always wanted to be someone who spoke a bunch of languages. How do those people get there? They just make the decision to do it. So if we're going down this path, let's go all the way. And think about how many doors it will open for Cole.

He won't even have to work to learn these languages, he'll just grow up speaking them all from living there."

Drew gave me a look. "Sure, he won't have to work for them. But we will."

I got up. The tile floor was cold under my bare feet. The hotel was so quiet it felt like we were the only guests. The sun had set at some point during our conversation, and now I felt a chill in the air. I walked to the balcony and closed the door.

"True," I said. "But I'm tired of traveling to places and only learning traveler-Spanish or restaurant-Thai. Aren't you?"

I had to get Drew on board with this, but I couldn't force it. Otherwise the entire project would be a nonstarter. We were talking about how to raise our son and deciding to embark on a quest to learn these languages and travel to interesting places— yes—but also we'd be raising Cole in a way that would change him. He wouldn't be a normal American kid. He'd be that kid who spoke four languages. I couldn't even wrap my brain around what that would be like, to hear my son eventually getting so good at Arabic that I couldn't keep up with his slang, or listen to him switching between English and Spanish effortlessly. It was a grand experiment, but it was also a little scary. Would I be introducing an emotional distance between us and Cole? Would I feel like an immigrant mother who loses touch with her child as the child assimilates and absorbs the new culture faster than she can? Would it be unnerving or exhilarating?

"Okay, so"—Drew sat up—"how will it work?"

I smiled. He had opened the door. "We'll just do what we did in Guatemala." I sat down next to him again. "We'll go somewhere that doesn't speak a lot of English, enroll in a local school, try to only speak that language all day, really immerse ourselves in it. After a few months, we'll be conversational, and by six months we'll have a level of fluency."

"Really?" Drew asked dubiously.

"Well, Spanish for sure, yes. I think in six months we can be pretty fluent. I mean, we'll have accents, but I'm talking about being able to talk without stumbling over our words. For Arabic and Mandarin we'll have to see, but I think being proficient in six months is a reasonable goal."

He mulled it over again. "So six months each. China, the Middle East, and Latin America, huh?"

"Yes," I said, trying to force my heart to slow down.

"Hmm . . ."

I grabbed my laptop and started looking up images of Beijing for Drew: the Forbidden City, Wanshou Temple, the Summer Palace, Tiananmen Square, Dongyue Temple.

"What's that?" he asked, intrigued by one photo.

"It's, um, Beihai Park, it looks like. In the winter."

Inspired, I made a new search for images of Beijing in the winter. The images leapt off the screen. The Great Wall covered in snow, making a white line through the misty hillside. The red-tiled roof of the Summer Palace peeking out beneath a blanket of fresh snow, frozen branches of ice-covered trees framing the scene. Chinese tourists huddled outside the Forbidden City, teenagers skiing cross-country across the snow by the Olympic stadium, and families ice-skating while holding hands.

"Ooh," Drew said as I clicked open one particularly striking image. It was from Harbin, a city north of Beijing, about eight hours away by train. It was an entire palace and forest carved in ice, built nearly to scale, three times taller than the heavily cloaked visitors in the picture. I sensed his excitement.

"We could go to Beijing in the winter," I offered.

"I would love that. But would you?"

We had been chasing the summer for several years now. My childhood in New England had not left me enamored of the cold. The last winter we were there, before we drove cross-country, I would sit in my frozen car, violently shivering as I tried to force my keys into the ignition with stiff fingers so the car would begin to warm up while I cleared off the snow. I would drive the entire thirty minutes to work each day tensed up in my frigid car, only warming up as I arrived at the office. I had sworn to myself, "Never, ever again."

Drew, on the other hand, remembered those winters—times of skiing, snowball fights, and hot chocolate—with fondness. Over the years, he had pitched cold-weather destinations to me, and I had evaded and dodged as best I could. I kept promising him a winter season, eventually. If he was willing to follow me around the world on this crazy project, I could stand a few months of winter for him.

"It's okay, I'll just bundle up. It'll be great. Think of how beautiful Beijing will be!" I leaned against him, giving him a better view of the computer.

He looked again at the ice castles and squeezed my shoulders. "It looks great."

We were doing this.

Two

We soon ran out of time on our thirty-day Egyptian visas, so I booked a cheap direct flight to Thailand, where, with Drew's tacit approval, I began seriously planning for our project. Thailand was the perfect place to stop traveling for a few months, because we could rent a furnished apartment easily, the Internet was fast, the food was delicious, and the people were friendly.

This morning, I was on a mission. We needed supplies. I needed a whiteboard, textbooks, an Internet connection, contacts who'd lived in Beijing, and much more. But first, we had to get a motorbike and helmets.

In Thailand, even the kids rode motorbikes. Unlike other places where the Vespa was the cool bike to own, in Chiang Mai it was the Scoopy, 110 cc of pure, adorable, motoring cuteness. We rented the latest model from the repair shop down the street.

It was powder pink, with a large decal of a cartoon skull that had a pink bow perched on its head. It looked like something a teenage girl would love, but Thais of both genders loved the color pink—in fact, pink was the official royal color of the king.

We found a sprawling helmet shop just north of Tha Phae Gate. Hundreds of helmets lined the store shelves—helmets with panda ears, helmets with ladybug decals, helmets depicting cartoons like Pokémon. It was easier to find one for Cole (yellow with the creature from the 1988 Japanese animated film *My Neighbor Totoro*) than it was for us. Our giant melons were too big for most of them, and we ended up leaving with too-small blue helmets that sat atop our heads like mushroom caps.

Thus awkwardly outfitted, we could navigate the city on wheels and pick up all the things that would let me start planning what I was calling our "fluency experiment."

Chiang Mai is arranged around a central moat that is one mile long and makes a square around the old city. If you missed your exit from the main highway, you had to circle painfully around the city again to make your way back, or try to navigate some winding *soi*, or lane, and hope you could loop around. It was something of a joy to get lost, at least to me anyway, and on this day, we had predictably missed the shopping center that had the whiteboards, markers, Post-it notes, index cards, and other supplies I needed to turn our $150-a-month studio apartment into Language Learning HQ. Drew was driving. I sat behind him, Cole strapped to my chest in his baby carrier, his Totoro helmet banging against my chin when we went over bumps.

"Drew, turn there!" I shouted over his shoulder, pointing at the *wat*—temple—on our right. Drew swerved the bike a little, then kept driving.

"What are you—"

"Er—hold on," he said, and kept driving straight.

"Okay, take that one!" I said to him, pointing over his shoulder again at the next *soi*. He ignored me.

I had long learned to expect this when driving with Drew. He had adult ADHD, which I had come to understand as not an inability to focus, but an inability to *not* focus on everything. He explained it to me as a lack of a filter. Everything that came into his purview demanded his complete attention, and he had no way to dampen down some of the signals and focus on others. In Thailand, this was doubly challenging. Driving around the old city meant the distraction of a crowded visual landscape. The ornate temples and gardens were pushed up next to guesthouses and open-air restaurants. Rows of motorbikes lined the sides of buildings, *tuk-tuks* (motorized rickshaws—a motorbike with a half carriage attached) roamed the streets, and tourists walked the broken sidewalks, stepping over potholes and cracked cement. In the sky was a rat's nest of telephone wires. Billboards and flashing signs were mounted everywhere. I was used to it. Half the time, I didn't even register the madness before me. But for Drew, driving in the city was sensory overload, and my suggestion that he take a right turn was impossible. He was already juggling a dozen other demands on his attention.

I could have done the driving, of course, but instead I insisted that he drive us everywhere. Years before, I'd gotten in the habit of doing all our driving, and then one time when Drew had to take the car through Boston, he was so overwhelmed by the city he nearly had a panic attack trying to simply drive to our new apartment and park the car. From that moment forward, I refused to drive when we were together, convinced that he could simply learn to do it through practice. I was right and wrong. He will always have ADHD; his attention will always be grabbed by whatever crosses his path, without fail, which means we'll get lost, miss turns, and sometimes get into fender-benders. But he did get better. Familiarity took some of the edge off, and over time he relaxed and drove around Boston like a pro.

We weren't quite there yet in Thailand.

"Drew!" I said as he kept driving straight, missing every opportunity to turn.

"I know!" he said with regret. He was powering through.

I sighed. It would take us ten minutes to loop around to make a second pass at the right turn. I forced myself to release my momentary annoyance that he didn't just listen to me and enjoy the ride. It was quite nice on the motorbike: the wind, the gentle motion, getting to see the city as you putter by at ten miles per hour.

Still, these little pressure points with Drew, the times when I'd try to steer and he'd reel the opposite way, the chafing that it caused, was something we'd had to learn to handle in our marriage. It meant I did all the planning. Drew and I used to share it. We tried. The last time was in Greece when he offered to handle booking our flights. We showed up at the airport in Athens and discovered that our flight was scheduled for two weeks later. Drew had neglected to change the default date on the search form, so hyperfocused on the task of booking the flight that he zoomed right past that part. He was beyond mortified. I was mad. But in that moment, with a cranky baby on my hip, all of our luggage in hand, and no flight, I had to make a decision. I could decide either to have a really big fight, or to not have a really big fight. It was that simple. So I chose to skip it. We'd gone through that fight before. And Drew had never once yelled at me in our entire relationship. He raised the bar so high for being a patient spouse that I had no choice but to try to meet it. So we laughed. Drew handed me the credit card and I got a refund minus fees for our flight, looked at the departure monitor, picked a new destination, and scheduled us to fly to Santorini later that afternoon. What could have been a disaster turned into one of the most beautiful trips we've ever taken, on a gorgeous island we might not have otherwise seen.

However, that marked the end of Drew's planning days for good. Now he was in charge of odd jobs like driving, carrying the luggage, killing spiders, waiting in line to get paperwork, changing diapers, and running to the grocery store. His ADHD makes him a great traveler—social, friendly, easygoing. But one thing was absolutely clear: If we were going to learn three languages, travel to three countries, set up a home in each one, and somehow immerse ourselves in the culture and become fluent . . . well then, it was all going to rest on my shoulders. That wasn't just the deal we made; that was the result of years of trial and error, of marital negotiation and relationship rigging. The system was there for a reason, and I knew it was best to not mess with it.

We rounded the final corner, flanked by other motorbikes, and Drew put on his signal and made the turn. We made it. We had traveled to the opposite end of the world and navigated Thai traffic, on a motorbike, with a baby, all to arrive at a mecca of sorts: Office Depot. I was in planning-preparation heaven.

I passed Cole to Drew as he was taking off his helmet and headed inside. It was just like the Office Depots in the States, except imagine cramming an entire store in about a quarter as much space. On the far end, they had given up on any semblance of aisles or stacking things and just left the office furniture in random piles.

I ran over to the whiteboard section, and involuntarily grinned. For about $10 USD I could get a five-foot-wide whiteboard. I pulled out two and brought them to the front. Drew was just walking in with Cole.

"Drew!" I said as I buzzed past him toward the markers. "Everything is so cheap here!" Markers, notebooks, planners, and pens sailed into my basket. In the end I wound up with an impressively high bill and more things than I could possibly carry.

"How are we going to get this home?" I wondered aloud. Drew gave me a look as we dragged full bags of office supplies out to the bike.

Luckily there was a *tuk-tuk* nearby, with a driver sitting sleepily at the helm, who was willing to drive us across town for $4. We piled the *tuk-tuk* full of our stuff, I climbed in with Cole, and straddling two giant whiteboards, we made our way back to the apartment. From the back window I flashed a huge smile at Drew as he trailed us in the pink, bubbly scooter.

BACK IN THE APARTMENT, I got to work. Drew took Cole down to the swimming pool, and I set up my planning headquarters. I printed out Bialystok's interview from the *New York Times* and taped it to the whiteboard. She was the starting point, and everything emanated out from there. Her research had found that bilinguals gained a four-year reprieve from the symptoms of dementia, while trilinguals gained five years. She didn't study people who spoke more than three languages, or "higher-order polyglots," but I had to assume it would be higher.

I wrote the three languages across the whiteboards: Arabic, Spanish, and Mandarin. I had settled on these three because they represented huge populations of the earth. Besides Hindi and English, they were the three most spoken languages on the planet. As a traveler, the idea of being able to speak to 40 percent of the world's population in their native tongue wasn't just appealing, it was intoxicating.

Under each language I wrote the major hurdles. The Foreign Service Institute, the branch of the U.S. government that trains diplomats in many things, including foreign languages, rates Arabic as a level 5 language on a scale of 1 to 5—in other words, one of the hardest for a native English speaker to learn.

Arabic uses a different script than English, and it is written right to left. So I'd have to learn how to write it from right to left, in a cursive script that at first blush looked elegant and complicated. Arabic also has spoken versions of the language that are completely different from official Modern Standard Arabic, which is relegated to newspapers and the speeches of politicians. There is also a third version of the language, classical Arabic, which is nearly identical to the Arabic of the Qur'an and is understood by Muslims around the world but is essentially a third version of Arabic and would be something entirely separate for me to master.

What's more, not only would I have to learn a new alphabet plus master writing in the opposite direction, but spoken Arabic itself was splintered by dialects that were very different from one another. And that's not to mention the challenging grammar and pronunciation that pops up in most every Arabic dialect.

That should have been enough to stop me in my tracks, but it didn't. Perhaps it was just my ego, but I figured: People learn Arabic every day. Of course it sounded daunting, but it was ultimately just a series of individual steps. On day one I had to learn the first letter of the alphabet. On day X I would be fluent.

Mastering a language would be like any other long-term project, I reasoned with myself. After all, Drew and I had filmed and edited an hour-long documentary. We didn't wake up one day knowing how to do that. We started at the beginning: We had an idea. We researched. We learned. We bought some camera gear. We raised funds. Sometimes it felt like I was getting my own personal MFA in documentary filmmaking: how much it costs, how to record sound properly, the correct way to set up shots for interviews, and a rapid immersion in the world of editing, color correction, and more. Now I felt like I could tackle a film with ease. And the experience taught me something else: The cool and interesting things that other people are doing or have done, the big daunting projects, are really just composed of a series of small steps. From the outset, they didn't necessarily know what would happen in step fifty-seven or how many steps it would take total. They just made the decision. They took the first step, then the next. And soon, wonderful things happened.

So that was what I was going to do.

I moved on to Spanish. It was a level 1 on the Foreign Service Institute scale: easy. I had studied Spanish on several occasions—first in school, then via audiotapes, then in a short but amazing immersion program in Guatemala, where I'd lived with a host family and spoken no English for a full month. At that point, my Spanish had gotten pretty good, but I'd since forgotten what felt like all my vocabulary. I had lost my Spanish from a lack of use. It would be interesting to see if I could retrieve it.

The real challenge with Spanish would be picking where to learn it. The language is largely the same everywhere, but accents and word usage change by region. Someone from Spain speaks Castilian Spanish. People from Mexico, Central America, and South America all speak Latin American Spanish, but there's a big difference in the way Spanish sounds coming from the mouth of a Cuban versus a Guatemalan (I tested this theory by visiting Cuba after studying Spanish in Guatemala and spending most of my time asking people to repeat themselves "un poco más despacio"—*a little more slowly*).

I wrote in big letters, *Latin America or Spain?*

Finally: Mandarin. Mandarin is considered by many to be the hardest language in the world for an English native speaker to learn (others say Japanese). Mainland China itself is still undergoing a transition to Mandarin from the many different Chinese languages and dialects spoken in provinces around the country, like Shanghainese, Cantonese, and more. The official Mandarin originates from Beijing, so pretty much everyone in Beijing speaks it, but for many Chinese people elsewhere in the country it's a second language. And for people outside the capital who do speak Mandarin, the accent changes quickly as you leave Beijing. The Beijinger accent, spoken quickly with an extra *r* sound added to many words, is considered desirable.

For writing, Mandarin uses Chinese characters that are reportedly very difficult to learn and memorize, even for native children—and there are two sets of characters, "traditional" and "simplified," which are basically what they sound like. Finally, Mandarin is a tonal language, which means that the way you say (or really, almost sing) the words can drastically change their meaning. We do this in English to communicate sentence structure sometimes—like the way you lift your tone to ask a question. Just imagine four distinctly different ways of doing that tone alteration for every single word you say, with the meaning of your words changing from something like horse (mǎ) to mother (mā) depending on how you pronounce it. I underlined *tonal language* three times for effect.

Mandarin was going to be tough, that was for sure. It was by far the most daunting to me, not least because I knew so little about Chinese culture. I had never been to China, and I had no sense of what it was really like. Was the pollution that bad? Was the whole country really crowded? What did people do for fun? Were there lots of old temples or just skyscrapers? How did people live? In tiny apartments? Shared homes? Did they eat rice for breakfast?

All these details had no effect on learning the language, but not knowing the answers meant landing in a country where I had no idea what to expect. I didn't even know what real Chinese food looked like. I had to imagine they weren't actually eating sesame chicken and fortune cookies—a hunch I had because in every country I visited, "Chinese food" seemed to be interpreted differently. There were some consistent themes— soy sauce, rice, noodles—but other than that, the phrase seemed to be a cultural shorthand for anything exotic. In Serbia, "Chinese food" incorporated a lot of oregano. In Colombia it was salty and sweet.

I stepped back from my Wall of Languages. It was beginning to look a little like *A Beautiful Mind* meets *The Beach*: From this angle I could see the swimming pool below and the Lanna-style pool house just beyond my whiteboard brain dump.

It was a big project—that was for sure. Now the only question was this: How does one even begin to learn three languages to fluency?

Three

Being the obsessive reader that I am, I downloaded as many books on learning languages as I could find, searching for some clue as to how to proceed.

Bilinguals are exceedingly common. All it takes is two cultures to bump up next to each other, whether that's through colonialism, occupation, or geography. Sometimes they are created through the process of trying to consolidate languages. In India, Hindi is the official government language, but regionally, there are hundreds of individual languages. Those languages are spoken in the home; Hindi is taught in the schools and used in movies and television. Voilà, you have a nation of bilinguals.

There's a common misconception that being bilingual is a sign of intelligence or advanced education. Sometimes it is. But it doesn't take any special education to learn a second language. You just have to be exposed to it and have a need to use it, and then your brain does the rest of the work. In theory you can artificially create this kind of situation. The Department of Defense has an intense language immersion program where they forbid English and just drill the target language until it takes effect. For the rest of us, there are second-language education programs that try to teach the language through a variety of methods, all of them imperfect when compared to growing up in a language-rich environment, but that could, in theory, work. I just had to pick the right technique.

I read the graduate textbook *Language and Bilingual Cognition* by Vivian Cook cover to cover and sent him an e-mail. Would he talk to me? He quickly got back to me with a yes and in fact, he wouldn't mind doing a video chat. I sat down with the professor, who peered out at me from my computer screen from his office in the United Kingdom, a line of books visible behind him, his hair a shock of white. Professor Cook was one of the foremost respected second-language acquisition academics in the world, was the 2014 EUROSLA Distinguished Scholar, and has written dozens of textbooks. Plus he was charming. His eyes lit up when he talked about languages. I wanted to talk to Professor Cook about how to best learn a language and the concept of immersion.

The idea of learning a language by immersion was popularized by Stephen Krashen, a linguist and second-language acquisition expert who wrote several papers on the topic in the 1980s, most notably his 1982 paper, "Second Language Acquisition." Krashen no longer gives interviews on the topic, so I wasn't able to speak with him directly. Still, when it comes to second-language learning, Krashen's theories dominate the field.

When I asked Cook about Krashen, he said, "The first thing that Krashen did was capture teachers' imaginations. He said things that reflected their experience, of the classroom and second-language learning."

Before Krashen, the conventional understanding of second-language learning was that it relied on four stages—speaking, listening, reading, and writing. Krashen made waves by contesting that assumption. He suggested that there are only two stages: acquisition and learning. Acquisition is the subconscious absorption of a language, which is how babies gain their first language. It's often said that children are like sponges for new languages, and for Krashen, acquisition is just soaking in the language. For children, learning comes later, in the form of classroom education, and in second-language schools that's the method they prefer. It's studying the grammar, memorizing vocabulary lists, and learning to translate. Krashen's theories were groundbreaking because he dismissed the speaking, listening, reading, and writing framework and instead broke it down into two major categories. We absorb, and we learn. That's it. Often not at the same time. In fact, Krashen thought traditional rote memorization and grammar studies, long a basic staple of second-language learners, could actually *hinder* second-language learning. He argued that real understanding of grammar was intuitive and gained only through use and exposure (in other words, Krashen's "acquisition").

Krashen's theory is a sexy one, to be sure. It deemphasizes traditional classroom education in favor of more immersive situations: listening to a native speaker, having conversations or interactions in the target language, watching movies. I wanted it to be true. I didn't want to spend hours upon hours studying tedious grammar and drilling vocabulary by myself. I'd love to focus instead on making local friends and talking to them. But how could I know for sure which way was better? I asked Cook about it and he confirmed my fears:

"The problem is that there is no way to test it. It's impossible to break down language learning into those two areas in a way that we can test. I worked on it with a group of graduate students and we couldn't figure out a solution. That's been the main criticism of Krashen in general. There's no empirical evidence to support his claims, and Krashen has stopped defending them. Still, they are very popular."

Over the years, I had seen countless ads for "immersive foreign language programs" in various countries. It's a popular experience for tourists, and that's the kind of program I did when I was in Guatemala a few years earlier, living with a Guatemalan family who spoke no English. My host mother would make me breakfast every morning and we'd talk about politics in Spanish. I'd go to the school and spend four hours a day one-on-one with my language tutor, and she would teach me some grammar, but completely in Spanish. We'd also walk around the town, go to the market, pick up lunch, and we'd chat the entire time in Spanish. By the end of the day my head would be throbbing and I'd collapse in my bed, exhausted, to meekly highlight words in my dictionary that I needed to practice for the next day. I wrote essays about my life in Spanish. I translated the newspaper. I talked to other students only in Spanish.

And it worked. After just one month of immersion, and no classroom drilling or homework, I was conversational, I could get by. Was that the power of immersion or just a lot of work on my behalf?

I explained my plan to Cook, and finally asked the question I had wanted to ask all along. "Professor Cook, if you were in my position, how would you learn these languages?"

He sat back. "If I were doing it seriously myself, I would do a combination of trying to find an environment where I had to use the language and at the same time studying the academic knowledge of the language."

Okay. So the expert on second-language acquisition would do immersion plus instruction. That was good to know.

AFTER SPEAKING TO COOK, I reached out to a number of so-called polyglots, people who speak three or more languages. One in particular, a thirty-year-old German woman named Judith Meyer, had studied twenty languages and speaks twelve of them at an intermediate or advanced level, including my target languages of Arabic, Mandarin, and Spanish. I asked her about her habits, the way she learns languages, via e-mail and I also read a few articles she had put together about her language learning history.

The first thing I noticed was that she was always studying—although not all the languages at once. She had been working on second languages since learning English in school, then Latin, French, Italian, and Mandarin all before turning eighteen. Once

I started to unpack her language learning history, twenty languages came into perspective. She had been doing this for twenty years. At eighteen she won a scholarship to study Mandarin in China, and later she stayed with a family in Quebec who spoke French. She majored in computational linguistics and made it a large part of her life. She now organizes the largest meeting of polyglots in the world, the Polyglot Gathering. At any given time she was studying one new language, then reinforcing the others by talking with friends in that language, reading books, listening to radio, or watching movies.

Even within that context it surprised me that she would fit in between one and five hours of language study on average per day, with more on the weekends. The catch was that she wouldn't study all the languages all the time—instead, she'd pick one to focus intensely on, and a few others to do maintenance work on.

When I asked her for advice for my project, the first thing she suggested was to get out of the beginner stage as quickly as possible. She told me, "It's easy to forget a language completely if you pause while you're at the beginner stage, but if you take a break from it while you're at the intermediate or advanced stage, you won't forget as easily. Real life has a way of interfering sooner or later, forcing you to pause your studies, so aim to be beyond the beginner stage by then. Work intensively at the beginning, using any opportunity to do another few minutes of your target language, and then you can relax once you've hit the intermediate stage."

At the same time that I was speaking to polyglots about how they learned their languages, I was reading up on the second-language acquisition literature available. There were generally just three types: textbooks with a focus on learning one language, usually in a classroom; commercial products that promised fast results (like Rosetta Stone); and anecdotal writings by polyglots, the only ones who seemed to address how to combine multiple languages at the same time. Despite their lack of empirical research, I tended to trust the polyglots' methods, because, to be blunt, they weren't trying to sell anything.

Only 20 percent of Americans are bilingual, and many of those people inherited their second language from their parents. In the United States, there doesn't seem to be a ton of interest in learning one new language, never mind three. The materials available even at the university level for multiple orders of languages were scant—historically, linguists focused on monolinguals and only recently (in the last twenty years) have bilingual studies become the norm. There simply wasn't any work being done on speakers of higher multiples of languages. Even Noam Chomsky once said that in order to study the mind and cognition, you don't want to muddy up the water with additional languages.

So it was with rapt attention that I read through Meyer's polyglot guides and jotted down notes on how she approached her own language studies. She wrote that she didn't take classes but would hire a tutor for occasional assistance, maybe once a week or every other week. I chuckled when she wrote this: "I hate Rosetta Stone. They are ineffective and are way overpriced, tricking people who don't know any better."

When Meyer is studying, she tackles the language from multiple directions: She reads each lesson from a textbook, reviews the grammar, does the exercises, memorizes the vocabulary, studies the dialogues, listens to the dialogue audio several times, and sometimes repeats it aloud. But she doesn't get too hung up on any one step, and that's only what she does at home alone. Then she goes out and finds as many supplemental materials as possible and talks to as many people as possible.

This did sound pretty different from Krashner's total-immersion, no-textbooks method. But it had clearly worked for her. It was apparent to me that there wasn't going to be a cookie-cutter approach to learning three languages that I could just apply. I was going to have to *learn how to learn*.

OUR THAI APARTMENT was getting crowded. My white-boards competed for space with the notes and printouts I'd taped to the wall. I had purchased some Thai alphabet wall hangings—*why not*, I thought, *maybe I'll learn a little Thai while we're here*—but in the end, I was so distracted with my research that I barely looked at them. I had picked up some Mandarin language-learning books at the used bookstore, I had index cards outlining the history and timeline of modern linguistics starting at Benjamin Lee Whorf and Edward Sapir and ending somewhere with researchers like Ellen Bialystok and

Patricia Kuhl, who were looking at the effect of bilingualism on the brain (in the elderly and babies, respectively). These wouldn't help me as I went about day-to-day language study, but it was interesting to read about their ideas and theories nonetheless.

Drew watched my tunnel vision with learned patience. After a few months of planning, reading, making lists, and crossing things off, I came up for air.

"Are you ready to go to Beijing?" I asked Drew. Cole was watching Thai cartoons whose characters sang about colors and the letters of the alphabet in cheery Thai that was unintelligible to me.

"Yes!" Drew grinned. "I can't wait for winter."

That week I had purchased our first winter jackets since leaving Boston, from a used clothing market in Thailand. My L.L.Bean coat cost $4 and no doubt had been discarded by a tourist traveling through, since Chiang Mai never dropped below fifty degrees.

"Okay, I think we're ready. I have a plan," I said, looking over my whiteboards for the millionth time.

"You always do."

BEFORE WE LEFT, I pulled up Marco Polo's book and biography. At seventeen, the son of an Italian merchant, Polo left home to see the world. He traveled overland to China, lived there for seven years, and then returned home at age twenty-nine. He didn't have a guidebook, a plane ticket, or any idea what lay ahead. He later wrote about his journey in a book called *Il Milione* (*The Million*), or as it's been adapted to English, *The Travels of Marco Polo*. That was seven hundred years ago.

Polo's adventure was so epic that it inspired generations of explorers. Two hundred years later, Christopher Columbus would take a copy of Polo's book across the Atlantic. It also generated its fair share of doubters, who in Polo's lifetime nicknamed the book "The Million Lies," as the content seemed so improbable. Consider this: A story we take for granted now, as cultural canon, seemed so far-fetched, so unlike anything Europeans had known before, that they doubted any of it was true.

Fast-forward to today and it's still not easy to get to Beijing from Venice. There are no direct flights. But if you're willing to have a layover in Germany or Belgium, you can get there in about seventeen hours. Not grueling enough? You can travel overland following the old Silk Road, although instead of merchant caravans, you'll be on highways. You'll cross from Italy into the Netherlands, to Germany, then into Turkey. You'll officially cross from Europe into Asia in Istanbul, a city straddling both continents, cut down the middle by the Bosphorus strait. From there you'll travel across Syria, Iraq, Iran, central Asia, and finally China.

Such a trip today would be choked with logistical issues that simply didn't exist in Polo's day. Crossing international borders, getting the correct visas, importing a car if you're driving, or arranging ground transportation, all require a level of skill, but one that is mostly bureaucratic. It speaks to our modern lives that today, replicating the most daring adventure in the last

thousand years would start with reams of paperwork and waiting in line at various consulates. The world has not only been
discovered, it's been regulated; borders have been constructed,
both legal and physical, and the travel industry has sprung up
in every corner of the world, ready to take your credit card and
give you a room and breakfast.

So what did intrepid travelers of yore do differently? They
traveled slowly. They relied on locals. They adapted to the customs and ate the food. They left themselves at home and let
the new place change them. If the travel bubble was the framework that held up my notions of self that allowed me to travel
untouched as "Christine from America," then to be successful,
to learn these languages, I was going to have to step outside
that comfortable framework.

I made one last call to Dr. Dan Everett, an American linguist
and the dean of arts and sciences at Bentley College, to ask him
about the line between culture and language. Everett wrote the
book *Don't Sleep, There Are Snakes*, an account of his many
years spent traveling and living in Brazil with his family to study
an Amazonian tribe of people known as the Pirahã. Everett
was the first person to fully document the tribe's language,
learning the language the way travelers must have long before
bilingual pocket dictionaries. He painstakingly noted every new
word, the pronunciation and meaning as best he could cobble
together from gestures and miming until he gained fluency in
the language. It's an incredibly rare thing, to learn a language
blindly in this way, as an adult. As a linguist, he also had the
academic understanding of how languages worked. I wondered

if my ideas about learning a language would match Everett's experience.

I had e-mailed Everett earlier in the week and we planned a time to talk. I didn't have a phone in my apartment, so I used my computer to call his office—while Cole slept on the bed in the same room. It was morning on the East Coast, evening in Thailand.

"Thank you so much for talking to me this morning." I told him about my ambitious plan, learning three languages in three different countries, and asked him about the best way to learn.

He explained, "Language is not a mathematical system and it can't be completely taught in books. My view is that people are born with the need to communicate. We don't learn languages as well unless we need them. We must depend on them for our survival."

Everett literally put himself in a life-or-death situation when he moved his wife and small children to a hut in the Amazon. When his wife came down with dysentery, she almost died before they were able to travel upriver several hours to get medical care. Poisonous snakes and plants were everywhere; without learning the necessary language, Everett and his family might not have made it at all. This reinforced what I'd been thinking about our project; we had to put ourselves in a place where we'd be forced to use the language just to get by. Only then would we really learn well.

We talked more about his experiences, and he touched a bit on how he learned the Pirahã language. He said that living in the Pirahã culture was incredibly necessary for learning the Pirahã language. "I think that one reason that adults have a harder time learning a language is that they have already acquired one culture and they want to live within that culture while they learn the other language."

I interjected. "Like, living your regular American life while studying Rosetta Stone Japanese in your spare time? But not going to Japan?"

"Exactly. And that's not going to work. When children learn their first language, they learn the language and the culture together, so if you don't replicate that, you are going to have less success."

Everett's children also learned the Pirahã language as well as Portuguese. Their family fell into habits with language, using Portuguese while in the Brazilian towns, Pirahã with the tribespeople, and English when they ate lunch together. Sometimes they'd forget to use English until someone said a certain word and then they'd all naturally switch back to English again.

I processed this, then asked, "So do you think you have to let the culture change you?"

"If you learn another culture, it changes you. I mean, it'll start with trivial things like words for new concepts that you didn't have before. I don't think that you start off wanting to change, you start off wanting to learn, and the learning itself changes you," Everett explained. It made sense to me.

These days, Everett's children are grown and raising their own families. His intention was never specifically to raise bilingual kids—it just happened as part of his research and career choices. I asked him how the kids did when they returned to the United States. He said it was actually pretty challenging.

"We had a very traumatic experience for them in 1984—they had only been back to the States a few times in the last seven years, and we came up to Cambridge, Massachusetts. They started school and the U.S. culture was the foreign culture to them, and they learned from that, I think they grew strength from that. But it was hard, initially, for them."

I thanked him for his time. I looked at my sleeping boy, his bare legs stretched out and his arms raised over his head, taking up as much of the bed as possible, a sleepy conquistador of mattress real estate, and let Dr. Everett's last words settle over me. It was hard. For them. Whatever happened next, I had to be very careful. I didn't even know how to protect Cole, but as we packed up our bags and I took down my whiteboards, I kept watching my son. Children were their own instruction manuals, I decided. If I listened and watched carefully, he would tell me what he needed. He'd let me know if it was too much, too fast, or too hard. I hoped that would be enough.

Four

I watched the cityscape through my misty window, searching for some clue about our new home. Cole slept on my chest, his face nestled below my collarbone, warm and soft. Drew sat next to me, cradling our backpack like a second child, our third suitcase wedged awkwardly between us. I leaned my forehead against the cool window, absorbed the details of each skyscraper, the hue of the glass, the shapes of the high-rises, the empty spaces between them, wondering if it looked more Chinese here, if there was some fundamental Chinese quality to this city, any particular sensibility that I could identify. So far, nothing I could pick up on—just large glass-and-steel buildings, silver cubes towering in clusters, dotted with cranes and the skeletons of new construction along the way.

I turned to watch Drew experience the new city for the first time. He looked out the window with keen interest, silently absorbing the result of my latest plan, giving away nothing.

We passed the Bird's Nest, an eighty-thousand-seat arena that was created for the 2008 Olympics. The interior lights of the stadium illuminated each band of steel, radiating colored light that mirrored prettily on its large reflecting pool. The scale and beauty of the architecture was impressive, a monument to what Beijing could be, but as of yet was not. I could tell the city was huge, with unmitigated urban sprawl—a "megacity" they called it. From the back of a taxicab it just looked like an hour of traffic between densely packed skyscrapers, gray and solemn.

The daylight had started to fade, but the millions of individually lit homes illuminated the sky. A thick haze had settled on the horizon, diffusing the light into a yellow glow. It was our first encounter with the infamous pollution: a thick, slightly brown blanket of smog that covered the city.

We were in Beijing.

Our friends had thrown us a good-bye party at the only Mexican restaurant in Chiang Mai with decent margaritas, and Cole crawled around under the table while we ate, the sound of motorbikes zooming by not diminishing the enjoyment of some decent guac. At the end of the night, I teared up a little when we were saying our good-byes. Drew and I had lived away from our families since college, but somehow leaving behind the small community we had cobbled together in Thailand stung more than missing our relatives back home.

Over the months of planning, as the word slowly got out to our extended network, I had been flooded with stories about China, which ranged wildly from "It's the worst" to "It's the best" with plenty of "meh" in between. One friend who'd visited had broken down after four days, emotionally exhausted from the attention her ample bosom garnered her—an elderly Chinese woman even reached out and cupped her breasts, unable to resist the novelty, mortifying my friend. Another friend, a corporate road warrior who lived in Singapore, raved about Beijing's food and shopping. Friends who lived in Shanghai and Kunming told me of the challenges of Chinese culture. As we drove through the city for the first time, I tried to hold back judgment. I knew it would take time to get a sense of the place.

Drew's parents were reluctantly happy for us. Yet I could sense his mother's unease when she asked, "Are you ever going to come home to the States, or is this forever?"

No, not forever, Drew assured her. We encouraged them to get passports, and we'd fly them out to see us. His mother discouraged the pipe dream, responding in one e-mail exchange, "I have no desire to see any country anywhere in the world." There's a Vermont stubborn streak in that sentence, one that Drew had inherited. His parents were retired, living in rural North Carolina, and while they didn't expect us to live near them, or even on the same coast, our habit of leaving the country seemed to be pushing it a bit too far.

I took some comfort from our friends Alison and Shawn, who had spent many weeks and months in Beijing as they waited to adopt each of their two children. They told us, "You will love Beijing. We miss it even now."

At the Beijing airport, I had given the taxi driver a slip of paper with our hotel address written in Chinese characters painstakingly copied from the hotel's website. An hour later, the driver stopped in front of a building with an intricately designed golden façade and a red-tiled roof. It wasn't until the driver took off that I truly felt the enormity of what we had done.

We moved to Beijing without any Mandarin—to learn the language, yes, but we had immediate needs to attend to and no language with which to do so: checking into our hotel, finding and purchasing food, and trying to find an apartment. Yes, there was a travel bubble, a network of websites, hotels, tour guides, and expat relocation companies, all ready and willing to usher us into an expat version of Beijing, where life was lived in English, for nothing more than a fee. But I had other plans. I wanted to discover Beijing myself, to learn the language as we went, to experience the city and culture in a way that wasn't filtered through the travel industrial complex.

It was the end of December, and our breaths billowed out in white clouds. Red and yellow neon signs with Chinese characters crowded the sides of each building, and barren trees lined the street. The city was quiet. Drew and I stood with our nearly two-year-old, plus three suitcases and a backpack, alone on Donghuamen street in the Wangfujing neighborhood of Beijing—just us and a line of red lanterns strung down the street, swaying in the cold night air.

Drew and I looked at each other and laughed.

LET'S SEE WHAT I'VE GOTTEN US INTO, I thought to myself as I bundled up Cole the next day. We'd successfully checked into our hotel the night before with the help of some miming.

Afterward, I'd given Cole a bath and put him to bed while Drew went out to get dinner. He came back with instant ramen buckets the size of movie theater popcorn and with a slew of seasoning packets that included pickled vegetables. We ate our enormous ramen, flipped through the TV channels, and went to bed. We still hadn't seen the city in daylight.

We set out with Cole in a comically large winter jacket (all we could find in Thailand, where winter weather gear wasn't needed or stocked) and we wrapped him and the entire stroller in a travel blanket that also doubled as a pillow if you folded it right. We were only a few blocks from the front entrance of the Forbidden City, so we headed there first, noting the empty streets except for the three-wheeled electronic rickshaws only manned by their drivers, the windows fogged up from his or her breath. We passed shops with beautiful gift boxes of teas and candies; souvenir stands selling panda bear hats for kids; hawkers with half-frozen, out-of-season strawberries; and convenience shops selling everything from bottled water to skin-whitening cream.

It was New Year's Eve day, so when we reached the Forbidden City it was completely devoid of other Westerners. A few intrepid local families milled around. I prepared myself for my first test: I had to order tickets in Mandarin. I couldn't help but think of Marco Polo, who worked so hard to get to China. All I had to do was buy a ticket. I had practiced a little before we came, using online lessons to memorize a few phrases. I walked up to the ticket office and said, "Èr" for two, and held up two fingers. A long beat passed, I could feel my cheeks warming up, flushed with embarrassment, and then the ticket seller responded in perfect English, "Do you want a map?"

"Yes, please," I said, sliding my Chinese yuan across the counter.

The majesty of the Forbidden City was impressive from afar. Up close the rows of chairs in the main plaza were covered in a thin layer of soot, the red paint on the grand center building was chipped in places, and the endless steps and handrails were dusty and gray. Cole kept kicking off his shoes. A Chinese woman came over and pulled down the hem of his pants leg, which had crept up to expose an inch of his ankle. I said, "Xie xie!" (*thank you*), and she said something in Mandarin. I tilted my head and bobbed it a few different ways, trying to convey *Great idea*, *I'm not sure*, and *We'll try that!* all in one movement. She nodded and walked away.

I passed. It was a tiny victory, but I took it. I had interacted with someone in Mandarin and held up my end, even if that just meant saying "thanks."

We holed up in the little café inside the Forbidden City and I cleaned up the soot Cole had gotten all over his hands while Drew ordered us some drinks. My face was frozen from the wind, but I was happy, sipping my steaming cup of tea with my family, in China, in the Forbidden City. I pressed the details into my memory like the imprint of a flower in a closed book, mental notes to save everything: the large ancient stones in the garden, the buzz of Mandarin, the heat coming from the kitchen, and the cramped little tables with families bundled up in full winter coats around us. Even the little kids were drinking tea. Eventually, Cole wriggled off my lap and bolted for the door, laughing the whole way—he was making his escape. His toddler threshold for sitting still had been reached.

As we walked out of the rear entrance of the palace, the air seemed worse, and a fog moved in thick and gray with flakes of what looked like ash. It reminded me of the book *The Road* by Cormac McCarthy. If there was anything more postapocalyptic than ash slowly falling from a gray sky, I couldn't think of it. I had just given up on trying to get Cole back into the stroller, pulling him up on my hip, when a hush fell over the city and the streets emptied around us.

"Mama," Cole cried, and arched his back, the warning sign of a dangerously jet-lagged and sleepy boy who could easily skew into tantrum territory.

"Drew, we have to get him home," I said, wrapping Cole's stroller blanket around him as he wriggled on my hip. "He's done."

"Okay."

Outside the palace, there was a line of taxicabs parked with their engines running on a day when almost no one was looking for a ride. Drew had a business card from the hotel with our address on it and a small map on the back showing its location in relation to the Forbidden Palace. It was only a few blocks. This should be very straightforward.

Drew knocked on the window of the first one and handed him the card. The driver shook his head, said something in Mandarin, then handed back the card and rolled up his window. *What?*

Drew tried the next one. No.

"It's really close!" Drew protested, but the driver coolly rolled up his window and stared straight ahead.

Oh, come on! I thought. The weight of Cole was making my hip and lower back ache, and he had started to whimper a little. We moved down the line of cabs.

At the last cab, Drew tried his best Mandarin. He said the name of the hotel slowly and pointed down the street, miming, "Not far, not far, just down this street" and with Cole about a moment away from a meltdown, the driver looked at my husband and tilted his head, then flicked his hand at us like he was flicking away a bug.

So we walked. It wasn't far, but Cole was done with life. He started to wail. I was singing songs to him, jog-walking down the street, bouncing him with every step. I zipped him up into my coat, saying, "shhh, shhh, shhh, shhh," but now people were coming out from the *hutong* courtyard homes, coming to the street to see this crying baby. One woman even stopped me to try to calm my child for me. She put her face inches from his (and mine) and cooed at him. He was not amused. Before long a small crowd formed around us. I said, "Xie xie," over and over, impatient to get through the crowd, and finally started just forcing my way past everyone, Drew following behind with the empty stroller. Meanwhile the day kept darkening as more and more smog rolled in.

Finally we burst into the hotel room. Cole stopped crying and fell asleep immediately. The cold melted off me, but I couldn't shake a sense of foreboding.

I looked up the pollution levels on the U.S. Embassy website. The hourly reading was at 300—extremely hazardous (to put that into perspective, Los Angeles on its worst days is a 30). We shouldn't have even been outside.

I felt a scratchy tickle at the back of my throat, the telltale sign of oncoming sickness. *This couldn't be good.*

Five

The sun woke me as it streamed in through the glass, which had become covered in condensation from our nighttime breathing. I gently eased myself out of bed to make tea. I had quickly discovered that tea in China was not just superlatively good, it was also varied: from ultralight white teas to refined jasmine green teas to the strong oolong and black teas, with endless variations that I never would have thought possible, rows and rows of it in the markets and grocery stores. For a coffee drinker like me, it was a revelation. One day I drank a translucent tea that tasted almost like blueberries. Another day, I created my own chamomile–green tea blend with fresh dried flowers and leaves I chose at the market. I couldn't read the labels, and even my dictionary was useless because it didn't let me look up Chinese characters, so I'd buy tea at random, surprised each time I brewed a new batch, wondering what I would be drinking next. It became my little ritual to sit in the quiet of that single room and to warm my hands with my hot mug, with my husband and child still sleeping, and prepare myself for the day.

I was still trying to find us an apartment, sorting through the different neighborhoods to get a handle on a city the size of the state of Connecticut. The lay of the land was simple enough. The Forbidden City marked the center of town, and everything radiated out from there. Highways ran in rings around the downtown area, slicing out broad cross sections that contained hundreds of microcommunities, places with names like Chongwenmen, Dongsi, Dongzhimennei, Dongzhimenwai, Fangzhuang, Lido, Lishui Qiao, Nanluoguxiang, Shanyuanqiao, Shangdi, and Xizhimen. The names blurred together for me as I read through online apartment listings—*Was it Fuchengmen or Fuxingmen that we didn't like*, I'd wonder, flipping through my notes, trying to remember what areas we had visited and which ones we had eliminated from our search.

I was anxious to get started on my studies. I had hired a tutor immediately upon landing in Beijing, an out-of-work engineer named Lido. We spent a full week together, but I made almost no progress. I couldn't even count from one to ten without him correcting my pronunciation at least once. At the end of the week he sent me a text: "There was a death in my family. I need to return to my village." I hadn't even paid him. Was I that terrible a student?

Learning Chinese felt like hitting my head against a brick wall. They say it's difficult, but I never once considered that I could spend forty hours studying with a tutor, one-on-one, and come out of it without even a single useful phrase I could utter correctly.

I needed a proper tutor, one with experience teaching English natives who found tones difficult. I figured once we found an apartment and put down some roots, it would be easier to devote my full attention to learning the language. Also, it was important that we pick a tutor who lived in whatever city neighborhood we landed in. Considering it could take two hours to drive from one side to the other, this was key. The days ticked by and I doggedly searched for houses, dragging Drew and Cole all over the city to look at apartments.

BEAUTIFUL PICTURES OF ICE CASTLES be damned, we had yet to see even one snowflake. In fact, I soon learned that winter is the worst time of year to come to Beijing. Beyond the cold, the pollution is higher because there's no rain to wash it away. There were no kids outside. On bad days, you couldn't see more than a foot in front of you, and the sickly smell of burned cabbage was undeniable. I checked the pollution levels posted by the U.S. Embassy, and the PM2.5, a pollution level measurement published daily by the Air Quality Index, was 502. The index only goes up to 500. It was literally off the charts.

For me, the pollution and the cold had joined forces and that back-of-the-throat tickle exploded into a massive head cold. And Cole was sick. He stayed up most of the night. Drew started coughing, too. We were miserable. Drew had taken on a large new client, so he was overwhelmed with work, but he seemed overwhelmed by China as well. The majestic snowcapped winter wonderland that I had shown him in photos had failed to materialize. Instead, he was in a city that felt too large to navigate, where it was winter without snow, and that had pollution that kept us housebound.

Finally I found something: a two-bedroom in Beijing's Koreatown, about an hour's drive from the university area. The price made Drew suck in air between his teeth, but it was either this place or getting on the next flight home. Plus it had an indoor heated pool.

"Cole would love that," I said.

We packed up, and an hour later we arrived in Wangjing, where I soon realized, as the driver circled up and down the main strip of road, that we were lost. I gave the driver my phone again, and he studied it, pinching with his fingers on the screen to zoom in and out of the Google Map.

I had tried for a few days to use Mandarin with taxi drivers, but after being literally kicked out of several cabs by surly drivers who did not want to deal with me, I'd resorted to always traveling with my home and destination addresses handwritten on a slip of paper I kept in my wallet. Plus I loaded Google Maps in *hanzi* (Chinese characters) on my phone with the start and end locations mapped. When I got into a cab, I would just hand the piece of paper to the driver. Then I'd gauge his reaction. He would never just take off and start driving. Never, not once. No one ever knew where we were going, except one glorious day when we got into a cab and announced in Mandarin,

"The Summer Palace." Normally, when I gave the driver the piece of paper, he'd shake his head no. Then I'd show him my phone, he'd sit there studying it for a long time, and then reluctantly, if we were lucky, he'd hand the phone back to me and start driving.

Finally we spotted it—the lonely entrance to our new highrise condo. There were Chinese New Year posters hung in the lobby windows and a lone red tassel blowing in the wind. It looked just like every other building on the block. Home, identical home.

Still, the apartment was quite nice, with a full bathtub, central heating (rare in Beijing, I'd learned), and a bow-shaped office overlooking the city on the north side. As I unpacked, I told Cole about the pool and how he would get to go swimming every day. He got so excited that we soon went to the front desk to ask about pool access. Between my dictionary and our broken exchange of English and Mandarin, the receptionist gave me the hours.

"Xie xie!" I said, happy that finally, at last, we were getting somewhere.

At the fifteenth floor, I put Cole down and tried to open the pool room door. I could feel the warm humid air, smell the chlorine, and hear the sound of someone swimming laps. But the door was locked. When I pushed on it, it gave just enough to let me see a sliver of blue. Cole gave the door a shove, too, then looked up at me. I sighed. We went back downstairs.

Key. Key. What's the word for key? Yaoshi? I tried "yaoshi" and she shook her head no. She called her manager and handed me the phone.

I put the phone to my ear and asked, "Is there a key?"

"Yes. There is a key," said the manager slowly.

"Great!" I gave Cole a thumbs-up. "Can we get the key?"

"Yes, you buy a membership."

"Uh, wait, it's not included?"

"Yes, you buy a membership," repeated the manager.

"Okay." We'd play his game. "I want to buy a membership. How much?"

"Uh . . . It's for one-year residents."

I paused. "So . . . not us."

"Yes," said the manager.

"So we can't buy a membership?"

"No."

We took the elevator back up to the apartment, defeated. I put Cole on the bed and collapsed next to him. The cool sheets felt good. Drew sat on the edge of the bed.

"Oh, who cares, Drew," I said, not really addressing anything.

"I like it here," Drew said tentatively, as if he were willing himself to believe it.

I put on a smile. "I know, this place is nice. And now I can finally get started on the language."

Drew rubbed my back. "Let's see what's on TV," he said, and pointed the remote at the flat screen bolted to the wall.

"Oh, look, Cole! It's Xi Yang Yang," I sang. *Xi Yang Yang*

was a cartoon about a wolf who is trying to eat a family of sheep but is forever thwarted. He's starving, the sheep are right there, but no matter what he does, no matter what scheme he comes up with, in the end, the sheep win.

I felt like I was the wolf. China was my sheep. It had seemed so simple, really. Move to China, learn the language, have a grand adventure and learn something new. But everything seemed so difficult.

I lay back again, closed my eyes, and listened to *Xi Yang Yang* playing in the background, the shrill voice of the main character distinguishable to me now. I wanted the Mandarin to get into my brain already, to take root. I listened to each sound with careful attention, trying to understand. It still didn't mean anything. Total nonsense. But I hoped that would change.

WITH THE POLLUTION, child-friendly activities like going for walks, playing at the park, or just playing outside had all been eliminated, so swimming seemed like at least one thing we could do beyond watching Mandarin cartoons nonstop while locked up in our twenty-fifth-floor apartment (which so far had mostly been what we'd done). We found a pool down the road from us, on the first floor of a brand-new mall with shiny floors, designer boutiques, and almost no customers. It was a private gym for the adjacent hotel, the kind of place that has high-end art and diamond necklaces for sale in the lobby, but they offered a day pass, so we gave it a go.

After paying an outrageous-for-China $10 each, we took our

mandatory swimming caps to the locker room. A half-dozen older Chinese women were standing there already, all completely naked, unselfconsciously bending over or lifting a leg to dry themselves. When Cole and I found our locker and started to change into our swimwear, they turned to watch me undress. I took off my top and my pants, and then, standing in my bra and panties, I turned to scan the room. They were still watching me. The friendly chatter had stopped and now, I was sure, I was giving these women their first glimpse into what an American woman's postchild body looks like. Off came the panties, up came the bathing suit, and remembering something from my high school locker room days, I managed to slip my bra off without revealing too much.

Cole was running around completely naked, and they pointed and laughed. I called after him in English and wished I had enough Mandarin—any, really—to make conversation with these women. I said, "Ni hao" (*hello*) to the women as I scooped Cole up, and when they responded, I had no way of guessing what they said. I felt like a mute without language, resorting to smiling too much and racking my brain for something I could say.

The pool was freezing. There were no kids—just one man swimming laps like he was trying not to disturb the water with each stroke. After five minutes, Cole's lips were blue and I sheepishly returned to the locker room, where the women were still naked and chatting with one another. This time I didn't bother to be modest; I stripped down and dressed as quickly as possible.

. . .

A FEW DAYS LATER, I interviewed an *ayi* (pronounced *ahh-yee*), which is the Mandarin word for "aunt" but is used to refer to a nanny or housekeeper—a woman who cleans, cooks, and looks after the children. In my case, she would provide some much-needed practice in Mandarin.

When I'd spent those months researching Krashner and Cook while in Thailand, I'd decided that my plan of attack for learning Mandarin would be all immersion, all the time. I'd get a tutor who only spoke with me in Chinese. I'd force myself to speak Chinese all day with shopkeepers, passersby, apartment staff, and anyone else I could snag for a few minutes. This was my grand plan. But two months into our language experiment, it was a nonstarter. Because of my lack of consideration of cold and pollution, plus just how big a megacity like Beijing really was, we had landed in the opposite of an immersion situation: completely cut off from the world. We spent each day totally isolated in our apartment, talking only to one another, breathing filtered air, and huddling under blankets. Our toddler didn't want to go out, and even when he did, we constantly worried what the air would do to his tender lungs.

So I wasn't living an immersive experience, to say the least. Since I couldn't spend my days outside, Marco Poloing through Beijing and striking up conversations with strangers all day, the only solution seemed to be to hire people to come to us. My tutors at first, and now an *ayi*, even though Drew and I both worked from home. It had to be better than nothing.

Yang Mei Hong arrived promptly, having no problem finding our apartment. I was cognizant that Beijing is extremely difficult, but only for new arrivals. The drama we constantly experienced navigating the city just didn't exist in the same way for locals. I sent Mei Hong the address and she took the right bus at the right time to our neighborhood and found our building among the row of identical ones without even breaking a sweat.

Meanwhile, I had been preparing for this moment with my Mandarin. I hired another tutor and asked him to translate a set of useful phrases for me, and recorded him saying each one. Then, I spent the entire weekend drilling and memorizing, exactly how Krashner said *not* to learn a language. It felt like preparing for a play.

When the front desk called to announce Mei Hong's arrival, I quickly checked my notes, running through them out loud and emphasizing the tones I had marked next to each word. The agency had warned me that she didn't speak any English, so I had to make this work.

According to the profile the agency provided, Mei Hong was born in Anhui Province, which is south of Beijing, close to Nanjing. In her picture she had side-swept bangs and a pleasant face that looked a little tired. She was just three years older than me, had never had children, didn't smoke, and lived with her husband. The recommendation letter came from an American family, and the mother raved about Mei Hong. "Yang Mei Hong has worked for our family for six years . . . She has lots of initiative . . . always clever . . . never taken a single day off . . . never asked for an increase in her salary."

The part that caught my attention was this: "She has been the most wonderful Chinese teacher we had. None of us spoke a word of Mandarin when we arrived here, and now, thanks to her, we are quite fluent. Especially the children! Amazing the way they learned with her not only the language but also some traditional Chinese music!"

She sounded perfect: like a Chinese Mary Poppins. I had visions of her cheerfully singing "A Spoonful of Sugar" in Mandarin. Cole would eat Chinese noodles and steamed dumplings while holding his chopsticks the right way (not like he did now, which looked like he was going to stab someone) and babbling away in Mandarin.

I pounced on the door before she could even pull her finger off the buzzer.

"Ni hao," I said excitedly.

"Ni hao," she responded.

"Huanying!" I said, making a sweeping gesture into the apartment. *Welcome!*

She stood there for a moment and then stepped two paces into the apartment and stopped.

"Leng bu leng?" *Cold out?*

"Leng." *Cold.*

Next came a tricky one. It had a swallowed syllable, something of the Beijing accent that I hadn't mastered, even when practicing with my tutor.

"Ni xiang he dian'er shenme?" *Would you like something to drink?*

She opened her eyes wide, not understanding. I tried it again, this time more slowly. I made a gesture of drinking. She declined. *Oh no*, I thought sadly, *now I can't use my little "presenting her with a beverage" prepared remarks.*

"Zuo ba," I said, and she turned and took a seat. *Please sit.*

"Wo shi Christine," but I didn't say Christine. I said my name in Chinese, Ke Lis Ting Na. Beijingers add a little *r* sound to the Ke, making it sound a little closer to Kristina. In fact, celebrities with crossover appeal in China all have Chinese names. Avril Lavigne, who is huge in China, is known as Ai Wei Er (it sounds like Avril if you say it quickly).

Drew was sitting in the living room, watching this play out with bemusement.

I continued:

"Ta shi An Der Lu," I said, pointing at Drew (sounds like "Andrew"). "Ta shi Cole." I gestured at Cole. "Ta liang sui le." *He is two years old.* "Ni xi bu xi huan xiao hai?" *Do you like children?*

I was talking slowly, with exaggerated pauses between each word, probably confusing this poor woman, and I just asked her a question—as if I could possibly understand what she said in reply.

Despite my lack of confidence, she understood. She started talking in Mandarin at a rapid clip, and I assume she told me how much she loved children and how her whole life she just wanted to play with a little kid as cute as my son. She was probably certified in first aid and had experience teaching children's swim lessons and once saved a child's life by accurately diagnosing her peanut allergy. Who knows? I let the syllables roll over me like a wave, smiling fixedly and nodding.

She stopped talking, and I assumed she had asked me a question. *Um . . .* I jumped up and gestured for her to follow me. To express this, I used the overly complicated phrase "Wo geng ne shou yi xia ne de gong zou," which I butchered, but it's okay, she got the point: I was going to show her what I needed done around the apartment. There was cleaning the bathroom, doing laundry, washing the floor, tidying up (a very easy "shou shi" and she responded "dui, dui," *yes, yes*), and making the beds. It was a short list because it had been so difficult to memorize.

She started going into my closet, pulling out buckets and mops, and I realized that she was going to start cleaning *right now*. Midinterview, as if I wanted her to demonstrate her cleaning skills to get the job. Her hair was pulled up in a ponytail that swung side to side and she bounced around the house, preparing to clean.

"Um . . ." I had not memorized any phrases for this, so I was left to comically mime, *Not now, later*, and ushered her back to the living room.

"Duo he ta shou hua," I said, pointing to my son. *Speak to him a lot.* For a moment I feared she'd think that that, too, was something she should do right now, but Mei Hong wisely chose to not take me literally this time and remained silent. At a loss for other words, I pulled out my laptop and opened up Google Translate, so we could type to each other. It was slow going, because the translation wasn't quite right; I had to unravel the mash-up of bad grammar and random nonsense words, but eventually I understood that she wanted Chinese New Year off the next year. I typed back that we wouldn't be here in a year, which only disappointed her more. She agreed to start today, and that was it. I had just hired a Chinese *ayi* to watch my child, talk to him in Chinese, and clean the house.

"Hen hao," I announced—*very good*—and went to my office while she cleaned my already clean apartment. To be honest, I basically ran and hid, because I was somewhat mortified. I tried to imagine the situation reversed: Mei Hong coming to the United States and hiring me to clean her house, using just the English she could pick up over the weekend. What could I have sounded like?

Later, Drew poked his head in and said, "That went great! I was so proud of you! But I have no idea what you said!"

I wanted to burst out laughing. Apparently, I was fantastic at Mandarin; it just depended who you asked.

Six

I started making progress. Finally. In my forty-hour-a-week study schedule, with the collection of books I bought at the Beijing Language and Culture University bookstore, plus my weekly tutoring and time spent chatting with Mei Hong, I was learning Mandarin. I still felt stuck in a pit of despair over the fact that this wasn't Krashner's kind of immersion. Because we were trapped inside all day, our lives seemed like some kind of dreary cross between what happens after the zombie apocalypse (you wait it out in your apartment) and one of those feverish nightmares you'd have in college about not having studied for the exam and madly trying to cram a semester's worth of knowledge into your brain in the five minutes you have until the test.

"Why do you want to learn these languages, anyway?" Drew asked me.

I didn't answer him.

I wondered if Marco Polo complained the entire way to Asia. Maybe if he had a head cold. I had been sick since the first week. I'm allergic to dust and dust mites—was I simply allergic to China, too?

I did want to learn these languages. My project so far seemed impossibly hard and not at all fun. But there was only one thing to do: try harder.

I swapped out all of my websites for Chinese ones. I would read the news in Mandarin, even if that meant translating the entire thing with an online translator. I started using some of the Chinese social media sites, too. I scrolled through endless Mandarin blog posts and memes. I signed up for an online Mandarin course, produced out of Shanghai, and downloaded Mandarin podcasts to my phone. I watched only Chinese television and movies.

I started working on my characters, signing up for another online course, this one focusing only on *hanzi*, or characters. It allowed me to start with ten characters, and as I memorized them, it would slowly add in more.

Five days a week, I spent eight hours working on my Mandarin: four hours with my tutor and at least as many studying. In my studies, I rotated through all of the core disciplines: I read chapters on grammar, I completed exercises, I listened to music or watched movies, I practiced my characters, I memorized vocabulary, I practiced saying the tones, I tried to write basic sentences in Mandarin, I did a little translation, and I read to

Cole from the children's books I had acquired, which was surprisingly helpful because I could actually understand the basic grammar and vocab used in books for little kids.

During my lessons we mostly spoke. My tutor Xue was college-aged, with long glossy hair, shy even by Chinese standards and seemed wholly uncomfortable sitting on my couch, based on the way she sat erect next to me, perched on the edge of the cushion. I spent most of the time reading lessons aloud to my tutor, completing verbal exercises, and having my pronunciation corrected. I even struggled with her name, which starts with a sound that doesn't exist in English, something between *sh* and a hard *j*, that required placing your tongue just behind your teeth.

The hours I was putting in meant I was quickly ramping up on vocabulary and grammar rules, and after six weeks my tutor said she thought I could pass the infamous HSK 4 test of Mandarin profiency in a few months. The HSK exam doesn't test speaking skills, only listening, reading, and writing. I was well on my way to learning Mandarin, purely through brute force. I was spending almost all my time studying, but if I continued at this rate, I would be looking at six months to reach proficiency instead of two years.

There was just one tiny little detail. I couldn't communicate.

In my lessons with my tutor, I could understand her perfectly, as long as she was reading from the workbook and I was following along. If she said one of the twenty-five vocabulary words we were working on for that chapter, I could understand that, too. But if she went off script? Called back to a word from a few chapters back without warning? It went straight over my head.

There were two major obstacles to my Mandarin studies. The first I had been warned about: the tones. Mandarin has four different ways of pronouncing each word, and it changes the meaning completely. I was prepared for that. It was daunting for sure. The word *cao* said one way means "grass" and said another means the F-word. Tricky.

The second obstacle only became clear to me once I got deeper into my studies and continued to struggle. The homophones. The damn, damn homophones. Single-syllable words that sound exactly alike and have the same tone. In English we have them, too, like *bear* and *bare*. In Mandarin it's worse. Every word, every single word, without fail, is a homophone. It's stunning. It's maddening. It's the one thing no one talks about.

I finally clued into how vast the problem was when I came across a soundboard from my online Chinese course (Chinese Pod). The soundboard was a downloadable file with a large grid. Down one side were all the individual morphemes, the smallest root words in the language. Words like *ting*, *dong*, *bu*, and so on were listed in alphabetical order on the left. Across the right were four columns, one for each tone. *Ting*, for example, was said four ways, with a level, rising, departing, or entering stress on the syllable. I counted the list. There were only 400 sounds. Total. For the entire language. Even when you multiplied this against the four tones, that just gave you 1,600 possible sounds to create the entire Chinese language. Compare that to the average English speaker's vocabulary of 20,000 words, most of which are not homophones, and you'll begin to realize just how many sounds have to repeat in Chinese in order to let people say whatever they want to say.

If you pick up a Chinese-to-English dictionary, you can see how complicated this gets. If I look up the word *star* on the English-to-Chinese side, it points me to *xīng*, with a flat, sung first tone. If I look up *xīng* on the Chinese-to-English side, it shows me three meanings for that one word, all with the same tone: star, prosper, or having a fishy smell. Same exact word, same pronunciation. Only the Chinese character (*hanzi*) is different for each. This means that while written Chinese is precise, the spoken language is dependent *entirely* on context—you can figure out what *xīng* means only by what words are around it. On top of this there are compound words, dozens of variations, like *xīngzuò* (constellation) or *xīngjiàn* (to build). So if I hear *xīng*, I can guess it means star, maybe prosper, or less likely a fishy smell, but I also have to be careful about what the next word is because from my rough count in my pocket dictionary, depending on the second syllable there are twenty-four possible meanings. That is, of course, if I'm correct in detecting that the word *xīng* was said with a high, flat tone, not one of the other tones, which could point me toward *xíng* (punishment), *xìng* (apricot), *xǐng* (wake up), or any of the dozens of variations for each one of those, giving me over a hundred potential matches.

Someone might say to me at the checkout line, "Zhǐ huò sùliào?" (*Paper or plastic?*) (although no one ever asked me this—China hadn't caught on to protecting the environment) and the feeling I would get would be as though they had said, "254, 345, 123, 998." The sounds in Mandarin are so similar and used so frequently that it became like memorizing numerical placeholders. I had no hook. I couldn't create a mnemonic like I might in Spanish (for example, to remember the Spanish word for king (*el rey*), I might picture a king with *rays* of light shooting out from his crown, which works because *ray* and *rey* sound the same, so I could connect the two and cement the memorization). How can you do this in a language where individual spoken words are not unique? It's hard to describe how this is different from English or even Spanish, but I couldn't get my brain to latch on to them as words. I would feel myself collecting the sounds—*Zhǐ-huò-sù-liào*—and then racing to hold them in my brain like a phone number while also trying to quickly translate them. What's *zhǐ*? What's *huò*? Are they separate words or together? Frequently, I had no idea.

Other times, I did pick up a word, like the sound *zhōng*, which is one of the first characters you learn because it's how you say China: Zhōngguó or, literally, *middle country*. (The United States is Měiguó, or *beautiful country*—you can see that the grammar itself is quite simple). The morpheme *zhōng* means "middle" and is represented by the Chinese character 中, which is easy to remember, since it looks like a line drawn through the middle of a box. I became an expert at hearing the sound *zhōng* and I noticed it all the time when I was reading the Chinese character subtitles scrolling along the bottom of the TV.

Recognizing 中 was a thrill. It felt like progress, but it bought me nothing in comprehension, since I couldn't understand any of the words around it. *Zhōng* 中 written could mean "middle," or it could refer to the Chinese language, Chinese people, or China if it's part of a larger word. As just the sound, it can mean "among" or "in." It could mean "heart" or "bell" or "clock." It can mean "death," "termination," "all night," or "wine cup." It could be part of a larger word like *Kōngzhōng fúwùyuán*, which means "flight attendant," or *línzhōng*, which means "on the verge of death." If you look at the word for "flight attendant" and you do the most literal translation possible, this is what *Kōngzhōng fúwùyuán* really means: "air middle clothes service person." Each syllable represents an opportunity for a language learner to go astray.

Here, finally, was the beautiful irony of spoken Mandarin: It requires context to understand the meaning, which requires understanding to get the context. I was a snake eating my own tail.

THOUGH I WAS PROGRESSING QUICKLY on reading and writing, despite my hard work, my daily attempts to understand what was being said to me continued to fail. When Mei Hong came over to me each day around noontime and asked me, I assumed because of the context, "What would you like for lunch?" I had no idea what she said. I might pick out three or four individual sounds that I recognized, but it was like fishing with a spear. My reflexes were too slow and by the time I started stabbing at the water, the fish had disappeared.

In immersion situations, this was okay, I decided. I called it "fake it until you make it," and because I could reasonably assume that she wanted to know my preferences for lunch, I could just pretend like I understood. At first, I'd start out with something translated, a little phrase to impress her, like "Why don't you make some traditional Chinese food?" and then when she didn't understand that, I'd move into caveman-speak, just listing ingredients: "Miàntiáo, shūcài, jī" (*noodles, vegetables, chicken*). More often than not, she'd look at me blankly. Too ambitious. Finally, we had to decide between *miàntiáo* and *fàn* (noodles or rice) until I realized that *fàn* was synonymous with "food." Rice is so essential that it is a placeholder word for food itself. *Wo yao chi fan* literally means "I want to eat rice" but more generally means "I am hungry" (with a hint of impatience). In fact, "Chi fan le mei you?" (*Have you eaten rice?*) is a way of saying "hello." After some practice, I had two words down to the point where she could understand me: *miàntiáo*, noodles, and *bāozi*, a steamed dumpling my husband especially loved.

After a few weeks, it became clear: She had not understood my Mandarin in our original interview, and she constantly needed to correct my pronunciation for simple words.

This wasn't immersion so much as oil and vinegar.

In my research on Krashen, he'd been quite clear with his theory that grammar study can negatively impact the student's ability to learn. Around now was when I started seriously questioning that. In my case, it was a distinct lack of extended education that seemed to be hurting me most. While it might be easy to pick up a Romance language like Spanish by hanging out with a family and taking some lessons, it was impossible to simply "immerse" in China without some serious education behind you. Even with my six weeks of intensive study, it wasn't enough. I started to look at pronunciation as the real gateway to speaking the language.

With my Chinese soundboard, I could look at the totality of Mandarin pronunciation within discrete units. For each morpheme, the four tones were recorded and I could click the button to hear the sound. I began to visualize how each tone sounded, like an action I had to perform. The level sound was flat, but I thought of a bell ringing out, clear and straight. The rising tone was like pushing the word up to the top of a roller coaster, slow and steady. The departing sound felt like dipping below the water level and then rising above it, back into the sky. The entering tone was like pushing a box off the top of a building.

I used these visualizations to help me re-create the sounds because when I listened to them enough on my soundboard I heard certain intonations that I hadn't noticed before. It wasn't enough for me to remember "rising tone = goes up" because that interpretation, by my English-speaking mouth, wasn't quite right. There was something else, a subtle way that it was spoken that wasn't so simple. It seemed to change the word and where it landed in my mouth.

I spent the better part of a Saturday, at least four hours, repeating the sounds one by one. I wore headphones and stayed with each one until I could reasonably reproduce it. Sometimes I'd say it two dozen times. I did this with all 1,600 sounds. By the end, my throat was a little raspy, but I was starting to get better. When my tutor came for my next lesson, my pronunciation had vastly improved.

I began to think of Chinese as being like singing. It's one thing to hear the note C played on the piano and to sing it back. It's another thing to hear that note, walk out of the room and return the next day, and then sing it back. Even if you get one note perfectly memorized, try taking a string of notes like C/B flat/D sharp and sing that in tune. The musicality of the language might have been the piece that I was missing. While Krashen was focused on pure input, if my native language didn't recognize the music of the language, then I couldn't hear it. If I couldn't hear it, if I was literally indifferent to those sounds, then the first thing I needed to do was to learn how to *hear*.

Seven

W̲ake up, Christine."

"Mm-hmm, in a minute," I said, snuggling Cole a little tighter.

"No, come on, come look," Drew said, like it was Christmas morning.

"What?" I slipped out of bed, trying not to wake my sleeping son, and followed Drew into the living room.

Snow.

The industrial vista stretching out in all directions from our apartment building was covered in the lightest dusting of white powder. There was the fine veneer of soot from the never-ending waves of pollution that still, even in this moment, hung over the city, like a low-lying, brown-tinted rain cloud. But through the haze, I could faintly make out the tiniest of snow-flakes making their way toward the earth.

"Snow!" I croaked, and then coughed.

"Snow!"

"It's a winter wonderland!"

I started to laugh, but it tickled my throat and sent me into a coughing fit instead. Drew ran over to the kitchen and grabbed the pills, a series of vitamins and cold medicine in foil wrappers, with Chinese characters written across each one. I dutifully swallowed them one by one, hoping that they were indeed the medicine I needed. I was dubious, though; I had spent an entire week using a moisturizer that I later discovered was just whitening cream. I knew my skin felt tighter after using it, but I didn't research it until I saw a photo of myself with skin so white it looked like I was a French mime with tiny wrinkles around my eyes when I smiled from the tightening (I don't think you're supposed to leave it on).

I looked at the snow again. "Let's go out today. I can't stay in this apartment anymore."

"Er . . ." Drew hedged.

"Come on! We need a jailbreak! This is not healthy!"

"Yeah, but Cole hates the cold, and there's nowhere to go, and he'll just start coughing again."

But I'd been locked in this apartment, hiding from the cold and the pollution, for too many weeks. Nothing could dissuade me. "Drew! You are the one who wanted us to come to Beijing in winter."

Cole started crying in the other room. I ran over and slid into bed next to him, lifting my shirt to breastfeed in a single motion. Drew followed me and watched us from the doorway.

"We need to get out," I whispered again to Drew.

"Well, okay, why don't you go out?" he replied in a whisper.

"And leave Cole?"

"Sure. Mei Hong and I can watch him. He loves her."

I mulled it over. "And then if he cries, then what?"

"Mei Hong knows how to handle him, and I'll still be here, too. It'll be fine."

I pictured wandering the snow-covered city alone. It was a lonely image. "Why don't you come with me? We can ... um ... go ice skating! And we'll bring Cole. I don't think I'm ready to leave him alone with Mei Hong just yet."

"Er ..."

"Drew!"

He relented. "Okay, fine, let's go!"

There's a moment in every marriage when you know exactly how your partner feels about a thing and you both agree not to talk about it. We had been dancing around the issue of staying in Beijing since we arrived. Neither of us was having a good time here, but was it worth leaving what version of home we had made here, just to run away from the pollution? I looked into other cities in China, but it turned out Beijing wasn't even among the top ten most polluted cities in China. I researched Harbin, in the north—the place where the ice castles were. To my dismay, I found an article from a few years earlier about a 2005 chemical plant explosion in Jilin that infected the water, including that in Harbin. Another article, this one from *New Scientist*, warned that the chemicals in the leak, benzene and nitrobenzene, could cause cancer or bone marrow problems. Was the water safe now? If we left Beijing for the ice castles of

Harbin, would I be bathing my child in only slightly cancer-causing water or *definitely* cancer-causing water?

Even as I researched other cities, I found similar levels of pollution to that of Beijing. In fact, even leaving China completely wouldn't be enough to avoid the smog: The U.S. Environmental Protection Agency issued a report stating that on some days as much as 25 percent of the pollution in Los Angeles comes from China. It was unlikely that moving to another city in China was going to improve our lot drastically if the smog could make its way across the Pacific.

I finished feeding Cole and got dressed. I pulled on black pants and a black shirt. I lined my top eyelid in black eyeliner, the same way all the other women in Beijing did their makeup. I slipped into the black shoes I bought at Walmart—a place that looks exactly like Walmart back home but is filled with completely different things, from Peking duck to illegal copies of DVDs—because I quickly noticed that almost no one wore white running shoes like the ones I had arrived with. I still had my bulky L.L.Bean jacket, but only because I couldn't find one of those puffy jackets with the belt cinching in your waist that all the women seemed to be wearing—at least not one that would fit my taller-than-average frame. I didn't blend in completely, but it seemed like people stared at me a little less.

Mei Hong arrived, and Cole greeted her in Mandarin. "Ni hao!"

She crouched down and talked to him in Mandarin. He talked back to her excitedly. Mei Hong stood back up and told me he wanted milk. I hadn't heard him saying "niúnǎi" (sounds like "new-nigh"), but she had caught it. It seemed more and more like his babyish babble contained fragments of Mandarin that I didn't notice—or maybe it was easy to interpret baby talk however you wanted. I went to go get Cole some milk, but Mei Hong skirted around me and reached the refrigerator first. I was still adjusting to having another pair of hands in the house.

We headed out after that, Drew in his gray jacket, Cole in his oversized yellow one with a scarf and knitted cap. My shoes clicked down the tile hallway to the elevator, and by the time we reached the lobby I could see my breath. Outside we walked a block to the main highway, Cole on my hip, as he had suddenly decided that he was incapable of walking anywhere. We hailed a cab; I pulled out my phone and handed it to the driver, with both the Chinese characters for where we were going and a map. I was sticking with what worked. Hou Hai Lake was a popular destination, so he ushered us in—had it been a more obscure spot it might take four or five tries to find someone willing to take the fare. When I set Cole down on the seat, the driver turned around and yelled at me because his shoes were touching the seat. I put him on my lap. Drew gave me a look. I shrugged.

It wasn't snowing anymore and miraculously the sky had cleared. There was a hint of blue. The smog had lifted. The driver dropped us off at the entrance. Though we were still in the middle of the city, the skyscrapers had dropped away. The lake was lined with trees in the distance, and little *hutong*-style buildings dotted the edges. It was bigger than I expected, certainly bigger than what I'd imagined would be in the middle of an industrial city like Beijing. Overhead, large speakers pumped out Chinese pop music. It sounded like REO Speedwagon and Arcade Fire had a Chinese baby. It was sort of sappy, a little catchy, and completely in Mandarin.

Drew's eyes lit up as he gazed over my shoulder at the frozen lake. "Oh, we are so doing that!" he said, and broke into a big smile.

Ice chairs. His inner Vermonter was completely delighted. The concept behind the ice chair is so brilliant it's crazy that it hasn't caught on in the States. It's a metal chair with a wicker seat, and the whole thing is set on two blades, like a skinny set of skis. You can hold on to the back of the chair and ice skate while pushing the chair to keep your balance. If you don't have skates, you just have to push the chair around in your sneakers without slipping and sliding. Or if you have a wife and a two-year-old, you put them in the chair and push them around as fast as you can go, laughing uproariously the whole way.

We rented one, and Drew pushed Cole and me around the lake while Beijing's answer to Damien Rice echoed across the frozen emptiness. I looked over my shoulder at Drew, and his cheeks were red, his lips chapped. He had a big smile across his face. Maybe I should have brought him to Harbin after all, where there is reliable snowfall and endless cold and ice.

Just then, Cole started crying. He was cold and a wet trail of tears clung to his cheeks. I picked him up and we scurried across the ice to the closest restaurant, pushing through the plastic flap hanging over the doorway into a steamy room packed with people. Everyone was eating with their jackets on, a habit we had quickly picked up, as central heating was not common. There was a menu with pictures on it. We pointed at a few items to order. Sweet and sour soup. Some kind of chicken with rice. Dumplings.

The food came out quickly, with steaming bowls of rice served on the side.

"Oh my God, so good," Drew said, stuffing dumplings into his mouth.

"I know!" I took a huge mouthful and spoke around it. "See, you like Beijing, don't you?"

"I like Beijing *food*," Drew clarified, reaching for another.

"Well, fair enough." I swallowed. "Your language lesson last night was brutal."

Drew had been taking a few lessons a week with a tutor from the same agency I used. While he had said originally that he wouldn't attempt to learn the language, he had reluctantly agreed that he'd need at least some Mandarin to maneuver his way around Beijing—and to be honest, I essentially compelled him to take the lessons. But he never studied in between. When I asked him why, he told me he had trouble focusing on rote memorization because of his ADHD.

The night before, his tutor, Wang (it's her family name and it means "king," she confided in us on the first day), came over to work with Drew, and she reintroduced the vocabulary from their last session. To test him, she ran down the list, giving Drew a pop quiz in Mandarin.

"Zuijin?"

"Uh . . ."

"It means 'recently.'"

"Okay."

"*Shenti?*"

"Um . . ."

"It means 'health' or 'body.'"

"Okay."

She didn't just let him get them wrong; she switched to English and had him guess the Mandarin word. She made him repeat all the words down the list. She then paused and gave him ten minutes to memorize them as she played on her cell phone. Drew shot me a miserable look as he hunched over the vocabulary list, with Wang's phone music playing tinnily in the background. Ten minutes later:

"*Zuijin.*"

"Uh . . ."

It was really hard to not laugh. I knew what he was going through all too well. They spent two hours together, and by the end Drew was only able to tentatively memorize his list of words: *zuijin, shenti, bijiao, chengji, nuli, fenchang, tai, li, you, mei, kongtiao, tongwu, li, yuan, jin, xuexiao, duo, ting, zenmeyang, bucuo, toufa, chang, yanjing, gezi, gao, dianshi,* and *mamahuhu.*

The next day Drew seemed in a better mood than he was the night before, and was even able to laugh about the terrible lesson. "Yeah, now I can't even remember the different words for 'please' and 'you're welcome.'"

"I noticed that," I said, laughing, too. "You said *bú kèqì* to the waiter just now."

"I did? Crap, what's the right one?"

"For 'please' it's *qǐng. Bú kèqì* means 'you're welcome.' So you basically asked for the chicken and said, 'You're welcome.'"

Drew burst out laughing. "Ha! Oh God. 'I want this, see that chicken there, yeah that. You're welcome.'"

"You are welcome, sir. I will eat your chicken."

"Hey, get me some more tea—YOU. ARE. WELCOME."

"They should be so thankful to serve you."

"I know, right?"

I took another bite and fed Cole half a dumpling. "Hey, look at us, we left the apartment!"

"We are in the city even. Out and about." Drew put his hand out for a high five, and I slapped it.

Then Drew became serious for a moment and looked at me over his steaming rice. "Christine, China is the worst."

He didn't have to list the reasons why. We were all sick, we spent every day locked inside, and when we did go outside the world seemed overwhelming and foreign and dirty. I sighed. "I know. But what can I do?"

The question hung over us and we continued eating in silence. We had a lovely day, but the reality was that living in Beijing was taking its toll on the whole family. When I envisioned this Big Life Project, I only thought of the positives. I didn't consider that it would be hard on everyone, and I especially didn't consider that I'd be caught in the middle of it all, trying to make everyone happy, to maintain balance, to hold everything together. Maybe it was just the cold medicine affecting my judgment, but I didn't know what else to do except to keep going.

Eight

W hat's the word for 'pollution'?" I asked my tutor, Snow.
She gave me a word and I checked it in my dictionary: fog.

"No, this stuff," I said, pointing out the window that lined the length of our apartment in the sky.

Outside was indeed what looked like fog, tinged slightly yellow and so thick that the view was obscured except for the faint outline of the building next door.

"The pollution, from the factories, the bad air . . ." I said, sweeping my arm to indicate *all of this*.

"Oh that, we don't talk about that. It's not polite."

I wasn't about to argue. Snow, real name Xue, who like many young people in Beijing had adopted an English nickname, was the best tutor I had found so far, but we often failed to connect on cultural issues. She would pause thoughtfully at times, or burst into giggles at my questions. She was exceedingly polite;

she wouldn't even take a seat until I did. If I forgot to offer her a beverage, she might ask, timidly, if it was okay for her to get herself some hot water.

At one point, frustrated at the lack of baking supplies available in any of the grocery stores, I asked her, "What's the point of an oven? Just to dry your socks?"

She laughed. "Dui." *Yes*. And that was it; she wasn't exactly forthcoming. If I was hoping for a cultural guide to life in China, I was looking in the wrong place.

So I started doing my own research.

The idea of learning Chinese by treating it more like musical studies had set me down a path of trying to delve into the beast that is otherwise known as Chinese Internet. It should be a tourist attraction all its own. Take a handful of intrepid foreign tourists, sit them down in front of a computer, and walk them through the amazing and glorious network of websites that you can only access from within mainland China.

A lot has been written about the Golden Shield Project, often called "the Great Firewall of China"—a program that was started in 1998 and began heavily blocking certain websites and keywords in 2003 under the philosophy of protecting the Chinese public from unsavory content. Deng Xiaoping, the former general secretary of the Communist party in China during the 1980s, was quoted as saying, "If you open the window for fresh air, you have to expect some flies to blow in," which became the underpinning of the Golden Shield Project: an online flyswatter. Since then, China has blocked popular social media sites like Facebook; search engines like Google; file-sharing programs like Dropbox; blogging software like Wordpress; keywords like *dictator*, *genocide*, and *oppression*; certain news outlets that have been critical of China like the BBC; events like the Tiananmen Square massacre; dissidents like Nobel Peace Prize winner Liu Xiaobo; any news or blogs from Taiwan; and pornography.

It's not so much that typing in one of these phrases will bring up a big red warning screen: *Caution, this page has been blocked by the People's Republic of China, you know, for your own good*. Instead, if you type "Facebook" into Baidu, the most-used search engine in China, you just won't see facebook.com as a result. The top result instead takes you to a page called "lianpula," which says *facebook* at the top of it but is clearly not the social media site that the rest of the world knows and loves. If you type in "Tiananmen Square massacre," it brings you to dozens of pages that have titles such as "Tiananmen Square Massacre: The Myth" and feature convincing news articles that have, finally, figured out why this myth has persisted for so long.

The unintended consequence of this firewall is that China has created its own version of the most popular websites. Instead of Facebook, there's Sina Weibo, a sort of Facebook-Twitter fusion that focuses on microblogging. Instead of Google, there's Baidu, a popular Mandarin-language search engine. Instead of YouTube, there's Youku, which, because of China's lack of copyright laws, allows users to upload absolutely anything. It's like YouTube and Netflix on steroids. There's no studio control, no Hulu-style selection criteria, and certainly no copyright protection like there is on YouTube. Missed an episode of your favorite TV show? Go to Youku and stream it without guilt.

Of course if you go to Youku.com from outside mainland China, you can search for anything. If you type in "喜羊羊与灰太狼," it will give you a list of the latest episodes of the adorable *Xi Yang Yang* cartoon, but try to play one and you receive a message: *This video is only available in mainland China.* While the Great Firewall keeps Chinese citizens away from foreign websites, they also have access to a vast array of content only available from within China. You can download endless movies, television shows, and music—all for free.

China isn't the only country to block certain web content. When we traveled in Thailand, we would sometimes stumble upon a website that was blocked, replaced with a message in Thai from the government. However, China is the only place I know of where they've re-created all the most popular web destinations and services, plus given users unlimited, free, streaming access to almost anything. When I asked my tutors about the firewall, they didn't seem too concerned—after all, they can even access Hollywood films that are still in theaters but are already live on Youku, dubbed and subtitled in Mandarin. Perhaps they feigned ignorance out of fear, or maybe they really didn't notice, since the available options are so robust. Foreigners in China routinely use virtual private networks, or VPNs, to circumvent the firewall, but when I asked my tutors, they didn't even know what a VPN was.

It took me some time to get comfortable using Youku and not worrying that the Internet police were going to come arrest me for copyright violation. But then I realized that I had access to a virtually unlimited supply of native Mandarin-language content. If I wanted to train my ear, this had to be a good place to start.

As soon as I'd started thinking of speaking in tones as something similar to music, something shifted in how I approached my vocabulary drills, and I started to get them much more easily. My realization that music and language might be connected in ways that have a practical application for second-language acquisition had started when I came across Diana Deutsch's work on absolute pitch. She's a researcher at the University of California, San Diego, in the psychology department and is the editor of a seven-hundred-page textbook on the subject, *The Psychology of Music*. Deutsch herself has perfect pitch, which occurs in about 1 in 10,000 people in the United States. She has been researching the intersection of memory, music, and tones for over forty years.

I first became acquainted with Deutsch when researching how to best learn Mandarin. In 2009, she performed an experiment that tested two groups of music students—one group from the United States and another from East Asia—to determine how many of them had perfect pitch (the ability to accurately identify a musical note from a sound). The test was simple. She took the students into a room and played a series of individual notes for them, then asked them to identify each note and write down their answers. What she found was astounding. While both groups had a larger-than-average number of students with perfect pitch—after all, they were music students—she found that the students from East Asia had perfect pitch nine times more often than their American counterparts. Deutsch's hypothesis was that their early exposure to a tone language, such as Mandarin, did something to their brains and conditioned them to be able to hear music more effectively.

Perfect pitch is still rare, but in 2004, Deutsch did a study of speakers of Mandarin and Vietnamese (both tone languages) and recorded them saying the same word over several days. They might come in on a Monday, say the word *ma* with a flat tone, which is Mandarin for "mother," then come in a week later and repeat the same word. She did this several times for each participant, recording the results. What they found was that more than half of the speakers repeated the word with the same tone and pitch, within less than half a semitone (a semitone is the difference between, say, C and C sharp). Even outside the phenomenon of perfect pitch, these tone language speakers were producing sounds with stunning accuracy.

Until the middle of the twentieth century, researchers believed that music lay on one side of the brain and language on the other. However, in the 1990s, Seiji Ogawa and Ken Kwong created a new way of looking at the brain called fMRI (functional magnetic resonance imaging). The fMRI was noninvasive and didn't emit any radiation. It used powerful magnets to map the brain, specifically the brain's blood flow. Using it, researchers were able to see which areas of the brain were activated in an image that looks like a heat map. Because the technology was so safe, they could use it in ways that they couldn't with older brain scan methods (it would be unethical to expose people to radiation just to figure out which part of the brain fires up when they think in French versus English).

The fMRI was the springboard from which all the current research into bilingualism arose. For the first time, researchers could ethically peek into our brains whenever they wanted and start figuring out what exactly was going on in there. I looked at PubMed, the online repository for all research studies, and searched for topics related to bilingualism. In 1973, there were just 3 studies. In 2013, there were 278.

I e-mailed Professor Deutsch about her work and asked her a few questions. One interesting thing she said, almost as an aside, caught my attention: "On the whole, it seems to be very difficult for non-tone language speakers to learn, say, Mandarin tones, *with the exception of those with perfect pitch*" (emphasis added).

If you are one of those rare people born with perfect pitch in the United States, you could potentially learn Mandarin very easily. The only thing—well, maybe not the *only* thing, but a big thing—holding me back from hearing the sounds in Mandarin accurately was my lack of perfect pitch. As someone who does have perfect pitch, Deutsch described it as being the same as seeing colors. I don't need to see the color red next to the color blue to recognize red by the contrast—I just see red and know it's red. It's the same for her, with sound. For the rest of us, we can be trained in relative pitch—if we know we are hearing a C then we hear a second note, we can learn to detect the second note based on the first (the underlying principle of tuning forks). For Deutsch, it's like she has a built-in tuning fork. Her perception of the note is accurate, consistent, and effortless—so much so that she could tell you the note a dripping faucet was producing.

From her research it seemed that even when perfect pitch was not flipped on, tone language speakers still had some kind of neurological advantage that seemed directly tied to music.

So how would I get there? Perhaps in another twenty years, the research will have continued and linguists and psychologists will have hammered out how to effectively learn languages by tapping into the natural ways music and language overlap. Until then, I had the practical matter of how to put this knowledge to work in my studies.

As a child, I took clarinet lessons and later oboe, so I had some music background. I could take music lessons again, perhaps train myself on relative pitch, the second-best option when you're not blessed with perfect pitch. There were ear-training CDs I could buy that expose your brain to music and train your ear to hear the differences between notes, but that seemed to me to be a very specific kind of hearing and I wasn't convinced that being able to hear notes was necessarily the fastest way to hear Mandarin. While people with perfect pitch might be natural Mandarin learners, there's no evidence that music education in general prepares English speakers for the task. I didn't need to learn relative pitch; I needed to train my brain to recognize the musicality of Mandarin, to hear the differences in tones. What if I listened to Mandarin music, as a way to develop my ear for the language? That would require source material and lots of it.

The search engine Baidu had a music portal, so I started

downloading artists at random from the front page. Music played while sleeping has been shown to aid everything from insomnia to mild depression to schizophrenia. Researchers from Northwestern University published a study in *Nature Neuroscience* in 2012 that showed that hearing a piece of music while you sleep can improve your performance of that same piece of music when you're awake.

I wasn't sure what music would be best for this exercise, so I started with the most popular songs. Every night before going to bed, I would start my Mandarin music playlist, pop in my earbuds, and lie down in bed. After a few nights, though, I began to wonder if this was the right approach. After all, pop music sung in Mandarin (or Cantonese for that matter) favors the melody over the tones. It's impossible to do both—you can't pronounce the up and down tones of each word while also harmonizing with the music. So they drop it or deemphasize it. I could listen to C-pop (or Mando-pop as it was sometimes called) all day long, but without the tones, would it be any different than listening to any other kind of music?

I had hoped to combine the awesome power of music and language, but like so many things in China, I felt thwarted before I even began.

I changed directions. I downloaded advanced Mandarin lessons because they don't use any English, unlike the beginner or intermediate lessons, but they also speak slowly and clearly when compared to native speech. I loaded up my iPhone again; I started listening to the soothing sounds of gently spoken Chinese each night as I slept. Perhaps this would be similar to the effect the researchers at Northwestern found when they studied the effect of listening to music on your ability to play that music. Maybe listening to spoken Mandarin at night would help me speak it better the next day. Of course, I still had to use the language during the day and continue my studies, just as the students had to be actively trying to learn the piece of music they were listening to at night. So far there wasn't any *Matrix*-like ability to download a language into your brain.

"What are you listening to?" Drew asked me in the dark.

"It's a podcast on nanotechnology in Mandarin," I answered.

"You're weird."

Every morning I woke and put my earbuds on the pillow next to me, the muffled sounds of looped lesson plans still audible. Would this work? Could my brain be forced to adjust to Mandarin while I slept, the neurons firing with each word heard, eventually forming new synapses? It was worth a try.

Nine

Life with Mei Hong was helping one person learn Mandarin: Cole. I was thrilled. Mei Hong came to us five days a week, from eight a.m. until five p.m., and she chased Cole around, saying things to him that only the two of them seemed to understand. She called him Ke Ai, which means "cutie." She made us lunch—usually noodles and some kind of vegetable dish—and while we ate she followed Cole around some more, trying to feed him mashed-up peas.

Then again, Mei Hong's sense of boundaries was, let's just say, *unusual*. For example, my naptime ritual with Cole became a bizarre situation where I would breastfeed my baby to sleep as he played with my necklace, looking into my eyes—the calm, peaceful look of drowsiness washing over him—and next to us, Mei Hong would rub his back and watch me, too. I would just think: *Dear Mei Hong, please stop looking at my breasts.*

Here I was, unable to say anything because of a tangle of

problems beginning with the fact that I didn't know the word for *boobs* in Mandarin and complicated by a social face-saving system that I was still figuring out. The bedroom was darkened, the door was closed, the soft hush of pumped-in heated air lulling Cole and me to sleep, and she'd walk in and lie on the bed next to us, forming a mommy-nanny sandwich around my twenty-two-month-old.

Um, hi, Mei Hong. How are you?

For Cole's part, though he loved Mei Hong, his apparent dislike of Beijing was becoming more obvious. One day I was carrying him the four blocks home from the store, because he still wouldn't walk in the cold. I had him plus two bags of groceries on my hips when he arched his back and started to throw a fit. I tossed the groceries on the ground, unzipped my jacket, and unceremoniously shoved him in. It didn't entirely quiet him down, but it helped a little. I trudged back toward the house, fussing toddler inside my coat, heavy plastic bags cutting into my hands, the biting cold stinging my cheeks. Beijing was so crowded, at any time of day, throngs of people, dressed in dark, somber colors and striding with purpose—yet none of them with cranky toddlers shoved into their jacket.

We're all still sick. I'm always tired. Burned out. Mandarin is hard. Everything is difficult. The city is too big.

My stubborn resolve to stay and make it work—to force Beijing to fit—had exhausted me.

The day after Cole's meltdown, I enlisted Drew to come with me to search for baking supplies for Cole's second birthday cake. Our giant grocery superstore didn't have any baking pans, save for a few casserole dishes, and while I could get flour and sugar, I couldn't seem to find baking soda, or even boxed cake mixes because Beijingers don't seem to bake at home. We got an apartment with an oven (or, as I joked with Snow, the sock warmer), but my victory was short-lived because I couldn't find the pans to put in it. We had spent the last two years eating out of hostel kitchens and staying in kitchenless guest houses, so I was desperate to cook again, to do all the baking and household nesting I had been putting on hold—and that counted double for a birthday cake.

We hadn't left Cole alone with Mei Hong—or anyone—before, at least not completely; even when I went out, Drew was always there in case Cole needed him. But Cole loved Mei Hong, and we'd only be gone for a short time, we reasoned. It was practically sunny as we headed out, and I told Mei Hong that she could text me if there were any problems. Cole was sleeping. I figured he'd be okay for at least two, if not three, hours.

We didn't find the baking supplies I wanted, but we soon ended up at a café working on our laptops and had a surprisingly nice time. I enjoyed a huge latte, writing about our experiences in China with Cole, and sorting through some photographs I had taken at my last cooking class (I was making an effort to get out more, even if it took me an hour to get anywhere). I started to worry about Cole, so we headed back early—just two hours after we had left.

As I walked in the door, I heard crying. Cole tottered out of the darkened bedroom. He hadn't slept through his nap at all— the tears streaking his face showed that he was completely cried out. He looked exhausted and defeated like I had never seen before.

How long has he been crying?

I scooped him up and pressed my face into his neck. He softened into me. I motioned to Drew to come to me, and I whispered to him to ask Mei Hong to leave. I took Cole into the bedroom and lay down with him. After he fell asleep, I sobbed into my pillow. Everything that had been building for the past two months—the fatigue, the challenges, the constant sickness, the cold and frustration and the unrelenting pollution—it all came spilling out of me.

I couldn't do this to my child.

My mother removed me from our home when I was twelve. The day before, her hockey-player boyfriend had been fighting with me, yelling at me about something—I couldn't even remember what now, but it was usually because I didn't make my bed or he was drunk, or both—and I yelled back. *You're not my father*, I'd say. The vast injustice of this awful man coming into our home, still married to his wife, making my mother cry when he stood us up on holidays, and determined to break my willfulness, set me on a stubborn path of no return. I knew he would hit me, I knew it would hurt, but I didn't care, he was *wrong*. So I yelled back at him when he yelled at me. This time, he grabbed me by the throat and lifted my ninety-six-pound body off the ground, his face red and his eyes dark with hate. He wanted to kill me. I thought, *Good. Do it*.

My mother was standing in the room, arms folded over her chest, watching. It was my little sister, two years younger than me, who ran over, screaming and crying, "Stop it! Stop! You're killing her! You're going to kill her!" She tried to pry his hands off my neck. For a long moment, he refused to stop. I couldn't breathe. He stood there, lips curled into a snarl, until he finally dropped me to the ground. I ran to my room and slammed the door.

I heard him yell at my mother, "That's it, Karen. It's either her or me."

The next day, my mother took me for a drive and didn't tell me where we were going. We arrived at my aunt's house and inside, I sat on the edge of her sofa while they explained to me in neutral tones that I would live there now. The raw wave of emotion that rose up from my gut cut through all my defenses. My mother had chosen *him*. She was giving me away.

Twenty years later, I became a mother who never lets her child cry—ever. My mother had told me stories of me crying it out for hours. She told me these stories as proof of my innate angry disposition, inherited from my no-show father. I heard them as stories of an unloved baby who was left to cry alone.

So when Cole cried, I picked him up. I comforted him. I would hold him in my arms until he fell asleep; then, afraid to wake him, I would sit for hours with him sleeping on my chest. I wasn't just mothering my baby; I was trying to heal myself. To convince myself with every sacrifice, with every kiss and embrace, with all the softness and love I could conjure, that I was not like either of my parents.

I had hit my breaking point. To see Cole crying, to walk into that scene was triggering for me. I saw myself, the sad little girl, walking out of that room. No one had scooped me up. No one had saved me.

The ground felt like it shifted.

I had been operating under the premise that I could do this hard thing, I could figure out China and the language, while also protecting my son from the effects of change. I would be his constant. I would shield him from the stress of living in an unfamiliar place, emotionally creating a bubble to protect him, where his days were largely the same: time with Mama, playing with toys, a nightly bath, and snuggles in the bed. But I had been distracted. I was always studying. In the last few weeks, Cole had started biting—hard: Mei Hong, mostly, but sometimes he would run into my office while I was working and go straight for my arm. It was like he was trying to escape her and send me a message with his teeth.

This wasn't working, especially not for him. The idea that I could make the same mistakes as my mother, even accidentally, was unthinkable.

I took a shower and pulled my hair into a still-wet bun. I curled up with the laptop on the couch, blanket over my legs, and started planning. It was two days before the end of the month. Everything from the apartment to my tutors to Mei Hong was on a monthly payment schedule, and our fees for the next full month's rent, lessons, cleaning, everything was due in just forty-eight hours. If we left now, like *right now*, we could potentially exit China with the least amount of financial damage.

With my credit card in hand, I bought flights to Thailand. I found a guesthouse along the river in Chiang Mai and booked it. I sent Drew downstairs to tell the front desk we were vacating. I had prepaid for Mandarin lessons, cooking classes, and a photography workshop, but I could not bear another moment in Beijing.

I took all my Mandarin books and threw them in the trash. Drew took all my Mandarin books *out of the trash* and poured me a glass of wine. We packed up what we could and left behind our kitchen supplies, a few toys, some books, and a bunch of CDs.

I texted Mei Hong and told her we were leaving. She never wrote back.

Drew seemed relieved but worried that I'd regret the decision. I wanted to reassure him, but I didn't know what to say. I was just done. That was the only thing I knew for sure. No more cold, no more Mandarin, no more pollution, no more Beijing. I fell asleep in Drew's arms that night, my cheek against his warm chest.

Ten

On the flight out of Beijing, I sat in the window seat, with Cole on my lap. As we flew higher and higher through the ashen clouds, I scowled out my window. Then it happened. We broke through the cloud cover and the sky was filled with light. Above the smog, the gray miserable day, was a cloudless blue sky and blazing sun.

"Look, Cole," I said, and pointed out the window.

It was a beautiful day out; it just depended on your perspective.

We touched down in Thailand during the burning season. The farmers in the north were lighting their spent fields on fire, an environmentally treacherous yet effective way to renew the soil for the next year. The haze that hung over the city was cause enough for local residents to flee to the south, if they could afford it, to wait out the annual burning of the fields. Coming from Beijing, we took a deep, long inhale of that smoky air and sighed in relief.

"Wow, what a difference," Drew said.

"I know," I said, smiling. "I feel like I can breathe again."

It only took a few days of sun and watermelon smoothies for the persistent throbbing in my forehead to go away. My sinuses cleared. The eight-hundred-pound gorilla that had been sitting on my chest for the last few months was gone. We took long walks along the Ping River, wearing flip-flops and T-shirts. Cole jumped at the opportunity to play with other kids, making friends with the guesthouse owner's toddler and playing happily in the dirt together with sticks.

At first we didn't talk about Beijing. We remained in a state of shock, making the motions of living—eating Thai food, reading books, and playing with Cole—but an endless horizon of the unknown stretched out before us. *Now what?*

Childhood trauma is a wound that never heals. It scabs over, forms a scar. It fades to just a slivery thin line on your skin, a story you tell, the time *that thing* happened to you. But unlike physical wounds, it can break open again. I had packed away my childhood for a decade before having Cole. It was my origin story, but it didn't define me. I never used it as a crutch. In fact, I prided myself on most people never suspecting that I went through high school as a ward of the state, living in foster care. I got a little thrill if someone assumed I had an idyllic childhood. All I had ever wanted was to fit in, *to pass*. I was normal, damn it! Even in my graduating class, people didn't know that when I turned eighteen, not only could I vote and buy cigarettes, but I officially aged out of the foster system. My social worker left me a voice mail. I never heard from the Department of Social Services again.

So it had surprised me when having a child brought old, buried memories forward. Even the pregnancy had kindled emotions I hadn't felt, memories I hadn't thought about in years. When I was six weeks pregnant with Cole, I officially cut off ties with my mother, formally and for good, struck suddenly by the clarity that no, I do not want this woman in my child's life or mine anymore. I mourned the loss of that relationship over those nine months as my belly swelled, but when Cole was born, all of that changed. I had a child now. Whatever reasons my mother had used to justify her actions over the years paled against the glowing love I had for my own child. I could never, ever do to him what she had done to me. It was beyond belief.

Drew gave me space to sort through those feelings, but then he gently pulled me back.

"So how are you?" he asked late one afternoon as we sat reading our books. Cole was napping next to us on the bed. The sky was all reds and oranges, a final flare for the passing day.

I stretched my legs out from beneath me.

"I'm better. I think."

Drew moved over closer to me and put his book down. "I am so sorry I made you go to China in the winter," he said.

"Ha! Please. I volunteered. Besides, it wasn't just the winter. It wasn't just China." I tried to figure out what I was trying to say.

"Well," Drew ventured tentatively, "it was pretty bad."

I tossed my book on the bed and faced him. "Yeah, but we also totally isolated ourselves. I mean, there's a huge expat population in China. We could have made friends with Americans, we could have had some support, a friendly ear, anything."

"Right," Drew said.

"I just really underestimated how big an adjustment it would be, both in terms of language and in actual culture, and I took it all on. It wasn't just, 'Oh, hey, let's take some Mandarin lessons.' I literally tried to Marco Polo my way into China without any guides, just land and figure it out from scratch." I laughed a little.

"Yeah, and Marco Polo didn't even learn the language."

"Right, Marco Polo didn't learn the freaking language. Details like that seem sort of hilarious in hindsight."

There was a long pause, and I rested my head on him. Life was so relaxed here. I could just sit in Thailand forever, moving between the hammock and the market, the ruins and *wats*, the serene hidden gardens and tucked-away spirit houses.

"So should we go back?" Drew asked, breaking the silence first. I took stock of my feelings for a second, waiting for my gut to tell me.

"No. I need more time. We could go back somewhere in the south of the country sometime, or maybe go to Taiwan. But later; I can't return yet. It's too fresh."

"Oh, thank God." Drew exhaled, and we both laughed. I stood up and pulled him up with me. It was going to get dark soon. One of us had to go pick up some food before Cole woke up demanding dragon fruit.

"What about you? Are you done with me yet?"

"Never." He kissed me on the forehead. "Home is wherever you are." I squeezed his hand, and he grabbed his motorbike helmet and headed out the door.

HOME IS WHEREVER YOU ARE. That phrase stuck with me as I thought about what would come next. I had put myself under so much pressure in China, isolating our family from any hint of expat culture, soldiering through cultural clashes without any community to fall back on, drilling vocabulary for hours and hours. What did I have to prove? And the situation with the nanny could have been handled so many other ways other than, you know, fleeing the country. I alternated between mortified and humbled and had frequent pangs of regret, both about starting the project and about giving up on Chinese. The part that haunted me most about our time in China was that Drew deserved better, too. This crazy bastard was on board with whatever I wanted to do, even after Beijing, even after I failed, even after I crumbled and called it quits. I owed him something great.

The next day was the Sunday Walking Market, the best part of the week in Chiang Mai, if you liked food. Cole marveled at the twinkling lights strung around the *wat* and the live music played on the street, while Drew and I strode from stall to stall buying anything from five-baht sushi to samosas to chicken satay served with little plastic pouches of peanut sauce. We settled at our table, under the enormous knotted and twisted tree that acted as a makeshift umbrella over the *wat*'s central garden.

"What about Beirut?" I asked Drew, as he cut up Cole's pork shoulder, rice, and pickled vegetables.

"Okay," he said, pouring the broth that came with Cole's meal over his meat.

"It'll be summer. Warm, beautiful. It's on the Mediterranean. We can go to the beach. Rent a house. I'll take Arabic lessons; you guys will just play."

"I have never really considered Beirut," Drew said, pushing Cole's plate toward him. Cole grabbed a handful of rice and shoved it eagerly into his mouth. "I mean, isn't it dangerous?"

"Well, the civil war ended years ago. There have been some issues, but as far as the Middle East goes, it's probably one of the safest places to travel." I swallowed my bite of chicken. "Plus it had the French rule for so long, it has that beautiful French look. They call it the 'Paris of the Middle East.' Plus it's on the water."

"Sounds good."

"It will be totally different this time. Everything. No nanny. No seclusion. No avoiding the expat scene. It's warm weather, right on the sea, it'll be great. I'm thinking French cafés and speaking Arabic. Lebanese food and beaches. You'll love it." And I meant every word—I wouldn't isolate our family again like I had in Beijing.

Drew looked at me. "I'm not learning Arabic, though; you know that, right?" he said, opening up his curry and shoving a big bite into his mouth. He gave an appreciative groan. "So good. How is yours?"

"Spicy! My face is on fire. But it's good."

We ate in silence for a while, huffing and puffing through bites toward the end, as if breathing over the food in our mouth would somehow cool the intense heat of the Thai chiles. I ate around the red and green sliced chiles; each one represented a world of pain, but the entire dish was still infused with a deep, sinus-clearing heat. It hurt, but it was oh-so-good.

Finally Drew put down his fork and looked at me. "So Beirut, then."

I nodded.

"You're ready? You're not going to try to Marco Polo your way in there and make yourself crazy, are you?"

"I am going to work on that. This will be better." I paused for a moment, then added reasonably, "Even if I *do* go insane again and think I am some kind of superwoman who can do everything at once, we'll still be living on the ocean. It's still warm. It's still a hell of a lot easier than China," I said just as the loudspeaker crackled to life. It was the Thai national anthem, which is played everywhere in Thailand at eight a.m. and six p.m. We stood respectfully, along with everyone else, and stopped Cole from fidgeting. After it was done, we sat back down.

"Let's go," Drew said.

"Back to the house?"

"Yes, and to Beirut. Let's do this."

"Okay!" I leaned over and kissed him. "I'm so happy. You will love this. I promise."

PART 2

LEBANON

Eleven

The Mount Lebanon mountain range runs parallel with the sea, encircling Beirut in a natural barrier from the rest of the Mediterranean basin; its neighbors Syria, Jordan, and Israel; the Arabian Peninsula; and farther afield, Iraq and Iran. The snowcapped mountains found their way into the Old Testament with the name Lebanon mentioned seventy-one times, but the country, the lines we see on the map today, didn't exist until after World War II, when it was carved away from greater Syria with the stroke of a pen as the League of Nations drew new maps for the region.

They didn't choose the country lines at random. The French had occupied Lebanon since 1923 and when the League of Nations ended the French mandate in 1943, they drew the country lines to create the only Christian-majority country in the Middle East. Historically, there has always been a large population of Maronite Christians in the Mount Lebanon range, so they simply chopped Syria into two countries, the fully Muslim Syria and the largely Christian Lebanon. Voilà! (As the French would say.) A nation was born.

It was a fateful decision. The Muslim population continued to grow, quickly outpacing the Christians. Soon the majority-Muslim country was ruled by a minority, the Maronite Christians, with the inequity built into their constitution. It tore the country apart. After the establishment of Israel, thousands of Palestinian refugees flooded into the country, skewing the scales even further. In 1975, the tension reached a tipping point and the Lebanese civil war began, pitting Muslims against Christians and turning Lebanon into an unmitigated war zone for over fifteen years. More than 120,000 men, women, and children were killed, and more than one million Lebanese fled the country. There are now more Lebanese living outside Lebanon than within it. And these numbers can barely give a hint of the toll the war took on the country. An entire generation grew up with daily mortar blasts, sniping, and rockets fired into residential areas.

However, since 2005, Syria, which stepped in after the civil war, has stopped being an occupying force. It has been largely peaceful, with a few notable exceptions: conflicts with Israel in 1996, during the Grapes of Wrath War, as Israel named it, when Israel fired over 1,100 rockets into Lebanon, and again in 2006, when further rockets were launched into Beirut. Granted, a few years was not a long respite from such a tortured history, but around the time I was looking to learn Arabic, Beirut in particular was coming back. Oil-rich gulf tourists were already frequenting its posh resorts. The entire downtown area had been rebuilt and stuffed full of luxury-brand retailers. The *New York Times* named Beirut the number one place to visit on its 44 Places to Go in 2009.

And to put it bluntly, the other options weren't great either. We had been in Cairo earlier in the year, but now there were second waves of protests breaking out there. The effects of the Arab Spring were still being felt. We couldn't return, at least not yet, not with so much uncertainty. Syria was in the middle of its own civil war. But in Beirut, unlike much of the Middle East, the war-weary Lebanese had forgone the Arab Spring. It seemed unlikely, but between Beirut's location on the Mediterranean, its reputation for hospitality and great food, and its lack of current major conflicts, the city had shaped up to be the best place to learn Arabic.

Beyond that, the major draw was the bonus languages. Lebanon is caught between three worlds: the long-lasting effects of French occupation, its Arabic roots, and the influence of international English-speaking tourists. Happenstance and history had created a city that was effectively trilingual. It brought out the anthropologist in me, curious to see what life with three languages would look like. How do they manage that with their children, with their friends, and in their marriages? I wondered. In a way, Beirut was a blueprint for how Drew and I could expect life with multiple tongues to unfold.

Still, Arabic was the official language. Beirut would be a great place to learn to speak the language of 295 million native speakers, the fifth most spoken language in the world. Arabic has its own alphabet, with twenty-eight letters and a curvy script with dots and accent markers that looks like pure calligraphy. It is also the language of the Qur'an, in the form of classical Arabic, which has stayed consistent over the 1,400 years since Muhammad walked the earth. That's a critical fact because in Islam, the faithful read the Qur'an in the original language, which is something that's not possible with the Old or New Testament for the majority of Christians (unless they can read classical Hebrew, ancient Greek, or Aramaic).

However, "Arabic" is really an umbrella term for many splintered dialects, which makes learning the language challenging, because speaking one dialect did not guarantee that you could speak Arabic with just anyone. Someone in Dubai might not be able to understand me at all. In Lebanon I'd be studying Levantine Arabic, which has about 21 million native speakers— roughly equivalent to the number of Dutch or Kurdish speakers. But, I reasoned, even if you learn the more popular Egyptian Arabic, that's still got only 55 million native speakers (comparable with Thai or Italian speakers).

So, learning Levantine Arabic wouldn't be exactly the passport to the Middle East I had once assumed. At best it was perfect for a small region and ranged from merely helpful to outright useless in the rest, which was saying something, since the Middle East spans three times the length of the United States and there are dozens of Arabic variations. Yet I still wanted to learn.

I had zero experience with Arabic. I didn't even know the

word for "hello"—I'd later learn that it's *marhaba*. I spoke to my friend Dan, who is French-Armenian and grew up in Abu Dhabi. Dan had a thick dark beard and long hair pulled back in a ponytail. He was a photographer, which you'd know instantly because he always had his dSLR around his neck. He speaks English, French, Spanish, Arabic, and a smattering of Thai. His family had a home in Lebanon, up in the mountains overlooking the city. We ran into each other in Chiang Mai and he further confounded my Arabic concerns.

"Well, there's the spoken language, but there's also a totally different written language," he explained over *kao soi*, a Burmese-influenced curry dish with crispy noodles. We were at the Free Bird Café, our local spot for Friday lunches.

"Really?" I asked, trying to wrap my brain around that.

"The written language is Modern Standard Arabic. Occasionally it's spoken aloud, but usually only when politicians are giving a very formal speech or something like that. And then there's the street Arabic, the local dialect of wherever you are."

"So what would happen if you learned only Modern Standard Arabic; could anyone understand you?" I asked between bites. We were sitting on cushions on the floor. The table was only a foot off the ground. The space converted into a community center for Burmese refugees, and some of our friends taught free English classes there at night.

"It's possible." He pushed an errant strand of hair behind his ear and looked thoughtful. "It depends on how much education they have—the more educated, the more likely they'll know Modern Standard Arabic. But generally, no one speaks it. They'd probably just laugh if you tried it with them. Everyone learns the dialect at home. You don't learn MSA until school. But in Beirut a lot of schools are French. So in some parts, they speak French first, before they learn MSA. Like Ashrafieh. You should live there. It's really nice."

"Ashrafieh? Cool. I'll look into it." I leaned back. "So what should I learn first? MSA or street Arabic?"

"Oh, Lebanese. Learn Lebanese street Arabic first, then MSA. It'll be better."

BEFORE LEAVING THAILAND I tried to find Lebanese/Levantine Arabic study materials but came up short. There were plenty of materials there to learn MSA but not the Levantine dialect. I turned to the Internet and looked at the Rosetta Stone page for Arabic. Bad idea—they didn't even mention that the course would teach MSA (and therefore be useless in daily life) before sending you off to the shopping cart. In fact, they wrote about their Level 1 course, "Ideal for beginners, you gain the confidence to master basic conversational skills, including greetings and introductions, basic questions and answers, shopping, and more." Why would anyone want to start with basic conversational skills, greetings, and introductions for a version of the language that is only written and rarely if ever spoken?

As a native English speaker, I found it strange that the written and spoken languages were essentially two separate beasts.

I read that this split between written and spoken language is known as *diglossia*. Researchers at the University of Haifa found in 2009 that MSA was stored in the brain as a second language. If you take into account the local dialect and MSA, native Arabic speakers were actually diglossic. By default, Arabic created one-language bilinguals, at least neurologically, with the language centers organized more like a bilingual's than a monolingual's.

So how does one go about learning a language that is actually two languages in one? Here again I took a page from Krashen. The acquisition-learning distinction, the idea of thinking about absorbing the language from the environment (acquisition) versus learning it in a classroom, is the underpinning of the entire foreign-language-by-immersion movement, and it's the principle by which I organized our lives in Beijing: I lived in an environment where the language was used constantly, I created situations where I was forced to use the language, and magically (or so it seemed), I planned to become fluent. Except it didn't quite work, did it? Beyond being overwhelmed, what I found was that I couldn't use the language well enough to be understood on the fly in Mandarin. Sure, I got really proficient at saying "Ni hao" and "Xie xie" (*hello* and *thank you*), but it was only near the end that I could make myself understood well enough to communicate with a taxi driver—and then only in a very limited manner ("No not that building, *that one*," aided with lots of gesturing). By the end I was dubious about my brain's subconscious ability to absorb a language. However, I could never get over the "comprehensible input" hump to truly test his theory; listening to Mandarin I didn't understand, even within context, even with physical cues, wasn't enough to bridge the gap of understanding.

Yet I knew this method worked, at least for some languages. I had experienced firsthand the miracle of immersion while living in Guatemala, when a single month of Spanish deep diving produced better results than years of intermittent studying. I was the most fluent I had ever been in the language. But for a tonal language? Or a language that's drastically more difficult for an English speaker to learn? It didn't seem possible to me now, at least from my efforts in China, to pick up Mandarin or any tough language without months and months of formal grammar and vocabulary study, well in advance of stepping into the country. Krashen had always stated that learning is less important than acquisition, but I seriously doubt he ever tried to learn Mandarin.

So for Arabic, I decided to modify my approach. Arabic is not a tonal language and it has a different alphabet, something I'd have to learn, but the alphabet is certainly a heck of a lot easier than picking up the Chinese character system with its word-specific symbols. If I could combine what I knew worked—the immersion and acquisition that Krashen wrote about and that I experienced in Guatemala—with the academic and learning aspect that I was sorely missing in Beijing, maybe this would work out.

That meant taking my friend Dan's advice and learning the spoken language first. I'd take an academic approach to get me past that "comprehensible input" phase as quickly as possible so that acquisition and absorption of the language can occur, by enrolling in a school and taking formal classes. Once I learned the rudimentary vocabulary well enough to follow a conversation and deduce new vocabulary through context, I'd slip into the immersion mode that Krashen wrote about, and I'd be able to speak the language in my daily life. Then from there I could start studying Modern Standard Arabic, which would let me read the newspaper and communicate in writing.

First things first: I was going back to school.

Twelve

It's easy to imagine Beirut before the civil war: a port city with French-style architecture, large beachside hotels nestled along the Mediterranean, the American University of Beirut brimming with smartly dressed students, and Mount Lebanon in the distance. Now, the pockmarked buildings and crumbling sidewalks are gnarled into a knot of alleys, stairways, and gardens, with overgrown vines climbing the sides of the occasional abandoned home. Eager to see our new city, we spent our first day walking around the charming old homes in the French-dominant neighborhood of Ashrafieh. Overripe oranges fell off the trees as we sauntered underneath. It was as if everyone had agreed to turn their tiny courtyards, alleyways, and rooftops into botanical gardens—and the temperate Mediterranean weather had conspired to let that happen. Beirut seemed like everything that Beijing was not: alive, growing, green, and scented with oranges and flowers. We loved it immediately.

In neighboring Gemmyze we found a French-style bistro that served chilled rosé at sidewalk tables. The sun was setting and the street had a pink glow. In a few hours this would become the nightclub section of town. A mix of Arabic and French floated above the postwork crowd at the café. I ordered Cole olives to keep him occupied so Drew and I could enjoy our wine. Our waiter switched to English, with only a light accent, after he heard me try to pronounce the French from the menu.

At first it's hard to grasp how this trilingual city works. On the street you'll see French street names, Arabic building numbers and license plates, and English signs. There seem to be no clear distinctions as to why they use what language when. The language mishmash feels like the way bilingual couples talk to each other—it doesn't matter if they say, "Do you want *une café*?" or "*Voulez-vous* something to eat?" Except, here its trilingual, so it's more like, "Hello, *habibi, ça va?*" (Hello [English], *love* [Arabic], *how are you* [French]?). Linguists call this *code switching*, a fluidity between languages that people slip into when they are around other bilinguals.

A group of twentysomethings swirling their glasses of wine behind us were chatting in French and then reverting to Arabic when the waiter came to refresh their drinks. Eventually one of them leaned over and said to me in English, "So where are you from?"

"The U.S., but we've been traveling for a while," I said. "We're here to learn Arabic. This is actually our first night in Beirut."

"Oh, fantastic!" she said, seeming genuinely excited. "We

are coming from Jordan for the weekend. We are studying Arabic, too. How long are you staying?"

"Six months."

"Oh, you will be very fluent by then—"

Her friend cut in to agree. "I've been studying for two months in Jordan and I can get by pretty well," he said.

I smiled, and they soon faded back into their conversation as Cole polished off his olives. Since China he'd become a fearless eater. The setting sun reflected off our wineglasses while we ordered more food, cheese, cured meats, and a small quiche. The Muslim evening call to prayer rang out from the large mosque downtown. Drew and I made a deal: We would live in Ashrafieh with the cute French cafés and overripe oranges. We would enjoy the summer in this land of beautiful people, where glamorous hotels lined every inch of the shore, where instead of sandy beaches there were endless infinity pools, with bar service, techno music, and the sweet aroma of fruit tobacco being smoked out of *argileh* water pipes, poolside. It was the beginning of the summer on the Mediterranean and I imagined this was like living in the French Riviera, except in Arabic.

We paid our check and returned to the hotel, walking through a cool stone archway to a private garden, where the hotel owner smoked cigarettes all day while his too-thin wife argued with potential customers about their reservation dates. "I'm sorry, I don't see you in the system," she'd say on the phone, a common refrain she'd stick to, as various hotel-booking websites sent her faxes and e-mails with reservation information, which ended up on her desk in a large overlooked pile. Her system on a guest's arrival was to sort through all of the papers, often while lighting another cigarette, and then, exasperated, give up and hand you the key to whatever room was open.

Our room had marble floors, white painted moldings, and French-style windows. The next morning, the owner brought us a plate of Lebanese bread, *labneh*, marmalade, and a good salted butter. They said something to Cole in Arabic as they scooped him up, then asked, "Français?"

"No, English."

"Ah," he said, and then waved Cole's hand at us, "Say bye-bye to Mama!" and I waved as he took Cole outside. I watched them through the window for a minute, then went back to our breakfast. Drew and I silently conversed with a few meaningful looks:

This is okay, right?

Right?

I hope!

We had relaxed a bit since China. In Thailand it was common for the waiters to take our son while we ate, and play with him in the back of the restaurant. It seemed like some cultures viewed small children as community property. If the locals knew you well enough, they even stopped asking permission—after a while, the woman who ran the smoothie stand in Chiang Mai began to wave frantically at us when we arrived. She would run over, abandoning her customers and blender, to take Cole without a word and bring him back to her stand, holding him on her hip and feeding him strawberries while continuing to blend smoothies.

Still, I walked over to the window and looked down at the street below. The owner was holding Cole and waving Cole's little hand at the guy who ran the *shawarma* shop across the street. A half an hour later Cole was returned, happy and clutching a lollipop.

WE NEEDED TO FIND a place to live, and this time, I looked for a local agent who spoke English to help us. The agent we ended up hiring spoke three languages: French, Arabic, and English. His English had only the slightest accent. He picked us up at the hotel to drive around Ashrafieh and look at houses, making small talk with Drew while Cole and I sat in the back. He talked about *the conflict* as he drove through the intense traffic, going down one-ways in the wrong direction, swerving around cars, gesturing like *eh, I'll give you the back of my hand* and then shouting Arabic out his window. Arabic when spoken is beautiful, like a very guttural poetry. But yelled, it sounds intense. The hard *kh* and throat-scraping *gh* sound violent.

I tried to make conversation. "So, people really love to party here, huh?" I asked. We had heard the clubs going until daylight, and this was on a weeknight. People streaming out of the clubs in the morning went home as everyone else headed to work, the new day's sun not shaming them at all.

"Yeah, of course," he said. He kept checking his hair in his mirror. He wore a lavender button-down shirt that had been freshly pressed—in fact, he looked like he could have come from the clubs himself. The entire car smelled of his cologne, like musky sandalwood. "When the Israeli air raids came, people just moved from the clubs on one side of the city to the other side, then kept partying."

Drew and I looked at each other in disbelief and sang out in unison, "Really?"

He shrugged as if to underline how not-a-big-deal this was.

The agent was talking about the thirty-four-day conflict in 2006 between Israel and Beirut-based Hezbollah. It was hard for us to imagine incoming rockets being an insignificant enough occurrence that you'd just go to a different nightclub instead of running to shelter. Then again, by that time, Beirut citizens had already lived through the Lebanese civil war, so anyone in their twenties or thirties had most likely grown up with the sound of incoming artillery.

"Do you know what the main business is here in Beirut?" our real estate agent asked us.

"Ah, tourism?" Drew offered.

"No. Money laundering. Look at these." He waved at the businesses we were passing, little shops full of odds and ends.

"They don't make any money. It's all fronts. If you need money laundered, you send it to Beirut."

"Ha!" Drew said, but I was dubious. Sometimes it's fun to impress the tourists with half truths. I suspected he was putting us on. This guy couldn't have been more than twenty-one, but I could taste the hustle on him. After all, his whole business was based on trying to put something together from only his contacts and his English skills: connecting tourists and incoming students with apartments, raising the price to take a monthly cut, or negotiating a finder's fee with the largely Arabic-speaking older generation. I wondered if he told the same stories to all of his clients. Probably.

Despite my skepticism, when he pulled into a side road and led us down a cracked set of steps to the back of an old church, I inhaled sharply.

"Wow."

The house was perfect. It was shaded by a canopy of flowering trees, set far from the street, half forgotten, with a towering church and apartment buildings obscuring it from the street, a relic from a much smaller Beirut. It seemed to be the best of all worlds, a country house plopped unexpectedly in the middle of a busy city, a little oasis waiting for us.

From the roof we could stretch our arms out and touch the tops of banana and orange trees with the tips of our fingers. There were deep red blossoms spilling over into the stairwell. The small courtyard below was a small jungle of a garden with broad-leafed plants, cream-colored roses, and the beginning of some kind of vegetable patch.

"We want it," I said. The agent played it cool, but I knew he'd just made a big commission. He called the owner, a lawyer whose office turned out to be only a block away. The owner of the house came home to negotiate the deal. We all shook hands and then he and the agent turned to Drew and said, "Okay, let's talk."

The men were going to negotiate, apparently. They left me outside with Cole while they ironed out the details inside for what seemed like hours. Normally I would handle this kind of thing. Drew was ill equipped for negotiating in general, let alone a rental contract with a lawyer in another language; he's too nice, too accommodating, and too American. When he returned sheepishly with a handwritten Arabic contract, I laughed.

"I love this house, but we just got screwed," I said.

"I know. He was funny; he was very intense and wanted all of the rent at once."

"Did you say no?"

"Yeah, of course. I was like, 'I have had bad experiences in the past,' and he was like, 'Why are you so serious? Look at you, you look at me like you will eat me.' It was weird."

"But the house is ours, right?"

"Yup!"

"Okay, good, because I don't think Cole will ever want to leave."

Cole looked up at us from his current work of filling a flowerpot with dirt and then dumping it out again. He looked quite pleased to be absolutely covered in potting soil. After being cooped up in a Beijing high-rise condo, I was happy to see him being a kid, outside again, in the dirt.

That was it. Beirut was our new home.

Thirteen

Two men were yelling in my kitchen. The first was an old man in denim, who moved with the steady pace of someone walking underwater. The second was our perfumed and crisply dressed landlord, Pierre the lawyer. The day before, the old man had installed a new washing machine, something we had requested when we moved in. An ancient gas stove hulked in the corner, next to a faded refrigerator and dusty countertops. But the washing machine was shiny and new, the stickers from the store still affixed to its face.

To get the washing machine to work, the old man had snaked a crimped tube down from the roof, where the water cistern was located. We visited the water cistern every morning to turn on the city water, to fill up the cistern, before the city turned the water off for the day. Sometimes we forgot, and on those days we'd have no water. More often, Drew would turn it on, we'd forget to turn it off, and two hours later we'd hear the telltale drip, drip, drip of an overflowed cistern spilling excess water into the street.

The old man had drilled a hole in the ceiling and pushed the crimped tube through, then used duct tape to attach it to the washing machine. It worked marvelously at first. The washing machine hummed ever so slightly and we left our clothing to a well-deserved scrub.

Then, yesterday: Drip. Drip. Drip.

"Drewwww! Is that the water?" I yelled from the bedroom.

He rushed upstairs to the cistern and I could hear his loud walking above. He returned a moment later.

"Nope, it's still filling up. Not overflowed."

"What is that, then?"

We walked into the living room and the dripping soon became a splashing sound. The kitchen. We rushed in to see the crimped tube, torn duct tape and all, dangling loose from the ceiling and flooding the kitchen at an incredible clip.

"Turn off the water, Drew!"

He ran outside and cranked the water faucet shut. The stream lessened, then abated.

"Duct tape. Oh, God. What was he thinking?"

"I'll call Pierre."

Now, here we were, and Pierre was in our kitchen yelling at the old man. What could he be saying? Rationally, I suspected it was something like this:

"Okay, so you're going to fix this?"

"Yes, no problem, I will fix it."

"Great! I am glad to hear it. Thanks so much."

The thing is, that Arabic when spoken loudly could sound harsh. It was impossible for me to tell if what he was really saying was something more like: "What the sweet baby Jesus is the matter with you, you doddering old fool? I will ruin you! Don't you know who I am? Well, do you?"

I had no idea. They smiled at the end, and it seemed amicable. The entire interaction was so far removed from the reserved culture in China—I couldn't imagine what my tutor would have done if I started shouting at her. The woman wouldn't even take her coat off until I instructed her. Another previous tutor had skipped out on collecting his last paycheck just to avoid confrontation with me.

The washing machine issue resolved, it was time for me to go to class, and Pierre addressed me in silky English, "Do you want me to walk you to the stairs?"

I sighed internally, but said, "Thank you."

"It's on the way to my office, no problem, no problem."

Ashrafieh was perched on a hill overlooking downtown. To leave our neighborhood we would go down one of the many staircases that are found at intervals between the center and us. That was where we were headed, but it always took forever. Pierre insisted on accompanying me to the staircase as an act of chivalry but knew everyone in our little neighborhood, so he greeted almost every person we passed. When he spotted one gentleman, he said, "Here, take this . . ." and dropped his phone and keys into my hands.

The men embraced and kissed each cheek, then talked in Arabic for minutes while I stood there holding Pierre's stuff, feeling diminished. The conversation wrapped up, and he took his things back. We walked in silence to the stairs that he knew I'd been on many times before, and he told me, "Okay, the stairs are right here."

I *know, Pierre.* I smiled at him and thanked him.

"Be careful!" he said. I nodded.

I WAS THE WORST STUDENT in my Arabic class. I had found the school online, my other options being another private school or the American University of Beirut. My school was the cheapest one, closest to my house, and it let me enroll online, so I signed up for classes before ever seeing the place.

When I arrived, I found hand-painted murals on the outside of a bustling restaurant filled with students smoking pipes, eating hummus, and listening to club music. Upstairs was a hostel. Students studying here for the summer could pay a little extra to stay at the hostel, so there were several rooms of dorm beds. My classroom was in the adjacent building, a simple white room with a U-shaped formation of desks. Our teacher, Majed, stood at the whiteboard, writing Arabic letters with a dry-erase marker.

On the first day, Majed asked, "So does anyone know the first letter of the Arabic alphabet?"

One student's hand shot up. "Aleph."

"That's right, and here's how you write aleph in Arabic," Majed said, turning his back to us to write on the whiteboard. *Wait, some of the students already know some Arabic?* I thought with a panic. I scribbled notes furiously on my notepad to keep up.

Majed started on the right side of the board and moved left (Arabic is written from right to left). As he wrote, he spoke the entire time, explaining that the letters in Arabic have four different forms, depending on where they fall in the word. In English, that would be like using a different letter *T* for:

table—beginning, or initial

castle—middle, or medial

hat—end, or final

t—by itself, or separate

In Arabic it looks like this:

Position in word:	Initial	Medial	Final	Separate
Glyph form:	ﺘ	ﻨ	ﺖ	ﺕ

"Who knows the second letter?"

Same student. "Ba'?"

"That's right." And he proceeded to draw a bracket like a stretched-out *U* with a dot under it. "Alone," he announced. Then a backward *L* with a dot under it. "Beginning." Then, the same backward *L* but with an underline on both sides, and a dot. "Middle." Then, the same one as alone but with a leading line. "End."

Position in word:	Isolated	Initial	Medial	Final
Glyph form:	ب	بـ	ـبـ	ـب

My classroom time was straight rote memorization for four long hours each day, but doing it alongside other classmates in a community felt completely different from memorizing vocabulary solo in Beijing. After class, we all headed down to the restaurant together and ordered food and drinks. We told stories about ourselves and how we ended up in Beirut. I was daunted that I was so much further behind than almost everyone in the class, but having some kind of connection, to be able to gripe about how hard Arabic was and then laugh about it took the pressure off.

After class, I would walk home through Gemmyze, where the school was located, up the big hill to Ashrafieh. For reasons I had trouble naming, living in this city felt easier. There was no lost-in-translation feeling, even though I didn't understand the language. I still didn't have a good dictionary, which was an issue I'd had in Beijing, since you can't really look up Chinese characters in a dictionary. In Beirut the problem was that they simply didn't have a decent dictionary for the spoken Levantine dialect. When I inquired at the school, they shrugged. "Ah, we are working on creating one."

Nonetheless, I didn't have that head-swimming sensation of not knowing what was up and what was down, like I did when I was in China. In Beijing I would walk down the street squinting at stores, trying to guess what they sold, the nearly identical red block Chinese characters on the front of each one giving no clue. Once I walked into what I thought was a restaurant only to find out it sold car stereos. In Beirut, on the other hand, a chicken joint looked like a chicken joint, not a pharmacy or a shoe store. They'd put a big cartoon chicken on the front of the store, just like they would back home. Even if you didn't speak a lick of the language, you could still find your way around. Culturally and visually, Beirut just made sense to me in a way that Beijing hadn't.

In class, I learned the phrase *inshallah*, which means "God willing" (or more accurately, "Allah willing," but I soon learned that *Allah* was just Arabic for "God"). It sums up a certain fatalism that exists in the city. Majed reviewed the syllabus with us and announced our first test would be in two weeks. *Inshallah*. Nothing was certain.

I soon learned that in Beirut, while there were Muslim and Christian parts of the city, there wasn't a hard line. Even for the observant, everything seemed more lax than other places in the Middle East. There was a large Muslim population in the city, but you could still order alcohol at many establishments. Many people were Muslim, but women weren't forced to cover up—it was summer and there were plenty of tank tops and sundresses being worn on the street. You can't really say that about much of the Middle East, and had I been in nearby Jordan, I would have certainly worn a headscarf. As the historic crossroads between the East and the West, Beirut had developed into a cultural melting pot.

The French occupation had also indelibly left its mark on the culture. Beyond hearing French on the street, there were other artifacts. Beirut was a city full of cafés, with a twist—the Arab influence meant you could smoke a hookah (*argileh* as it's called in Arabic) in any of those cafés, or almost anywhere else you went. For lunch and dinner, you'd have the *mezze*, a collection of dishes from tabbouleh to hummus to stuffed grape leaves. Pita bread was served with everything. Or you could get a fantastic *salade niçoise* with a glass of white wine. The city was bicultural.

Food I could recognize, people who reacted in ways I expected, taxi drivers who would always take my fare, students from the United States, and so on, made me realize how devastating a complete and utter disconnect from your home culture could be. This tiny foothold into life in Beirut made such a huge difference in our day-to-day experience of the city. When we were in Beijing, I didn't know what was off—I kept blaming it on the winter weather—but as I practically skipped to class each day in Beirut, the difference was obvious. Living in a bicultural city meant I had a bridge, a path, and a way to connect. I wasn't constantly trying to figure out what things meant—why did people stare at me in China, why did my tutor quit without even collecting his pay, why did my other tutor giggle when I asked certain questions? In Beirut, everything was different, yes, absolutely, but this I could handle. These were my people.

My enthusiasm impacted my studies as well. Before long, I slowly started passing the other students by, although that may have been thanks to Beirut's endless nightlife, which left the partiers in our class wandering into class with epic hangovers that no doubt didn't help their studies. Sometimes there are advantages to being a little older, wiser, and hopelessly over the entire club scene (having a two-year-old settled that once and for all).

LIVING IN BEIRUT, I started thinking about one myth that persists about bilinguals—that they are *all bicultural*. But that's actually rarely the case. If you look at Beijing, my tutors were all bilingual but none were bicultural. They spoke English but had never lived outside China, and they had no understanding of the differences between Chinese and American culture except through TV and film.

In Beirut, my teacher Majed became my unofficial cultural liaison. After class each day, I'd pepper him with questions: What was polite, what was not, what did certain expressions mean, how did local people really feel about certain topics. Because he grew up in bicultural Beirut, he lived in two worlds. He was Arab, but he also spoke French. He was Muslim but also had a deep understanding of Christianity. He spoke English and got to know many of his foreign students from the United States, Canada, and parts of Europe. It wasn't until I came to Beirut that I understood how rare this was.

Before embarking on this project, I had read everything I

could find by François Grosjean, perhaps the most prominent bilingual researcher of the realities of living in multiple languages. Grosjean said that most bilinguals are not, in fact, bicultural, writing that "there is the misconception that all bilinguals are bicultural (they are not) and that they have double personalities (as a bilingual myself, and with a sigh of relief, I can tell you that this is not the case)." He used Europe as an example: So many Europeans speak English, but that doesn't mean they automatically understand American or British or Australian culture (or any other culture in which English is spoken). By that same token, my native English doesn't make me bicultural either. I can't speak to, say, British culture with any kind of authority. A big part of what I was missing in China was that cultural piece. By going it alone, trying to work only with Chinese tutors, by not participating in the existing English-speaking community *or* learning about Chinese culture, I had completely hamstrung my efforts.

In fact, it was worse than that. Because I didn't understand Chinese culture, I began to resent it on some level. I was deeply frustrated by what seemed like meaningless difficulties I continued to face, just because I didn't understand the cultural context. Now, here I was in the Middle East, a challenging place to live by any standard, in a city that is bordered by Syria, which was in a civil war, and had Israel to the south, Lebanon's sworn enemies, with nightly news reports of violence and kidnappings on the outskirts of town. Yet it all felt so much easier.

While I didn't need to become bicultural to become bilingual, I did begin to wonder about my family's cultural identity.

Would we be changed by this experience? Would my child have a different cultural identity than me? And what is culture after all, except a set of values that you identify with—most likely because it was how you were raised or the environment you grew up in? Was I inadvertently also raising a bicultural kid? What would that mean?

Two-and-a-half-year-olds have a cunning way of putting these kinds of questions into perspective. When I returned home from class each day, Cole would run out to me with his arms outstretched. We'd have a snack and watch *Garfield* in French on TV. There was plenty of time to answer these questions later.

Fourteen

Drew loved Beirut. It was the little things, like going to a different shop for each item on our grocery list: picking up bread at the bakery; vegetables and fruit at the stand on the corner; milk and hummus at the corner store, where a young man named Gilbert worked with his father. Drew knew the guys at the phone store where he topped up his cell phone data, the lawyer who was renting us his house, the owner of the family-run kitchen supply shop (the father patted Drew hard on the back after we cleared them out of pots, pans, plates, cups, and silverware when we first arrived). There was a transgender hairdresser around the corner, a sign of the progressive times in Lebanon. Next door, the Armenian Orthodox church played music for four hours every Sunday. The sound of singing floated into our walled garden. And if you walked into town, you'd sometimes hear one man singing from his apartment, practicing for the next week's mass.

Outside Gilbert's corner store (a place known as "Smuggler's"), a small card table was set up. Every day, four old men would shuffle up to sit around this table for a few hours and play cards. Whenever Drew passed by with Cole, who was often dressed up in his latest favorite outfit, a Superman Halloween costume we'd picked up impulsively in Thailand, the men would cluck at Cole and say, "Ayyy Suupppperman!" in thick accents.

Each day when I returned from class, Drew would report the latest news from the neighborhood.

"I found a place that sells brooms," he told me one day.

"Really?"

"Yes, they don't sell anything else, just brooms. They have a son Cole's age. I am going to go back later and get a broom. The owner doesn't speak any English, so he just talks at me in French. I'm like, 'I have no idea what you are talking about,' and he keeps talking. He asks me questions about Cole, and I try to guess what he's asking, like, 'Oh, how old is he?,' so I say, 'Two.' He'll just nod and keep talking."

"That's funny. Did you find the locksmith?"

"Yes! But he wasn't in his shop. It was open, but there was no one in there. I went back an hour later and it was still empty. If I knew how to cut a key, I could have just done it myself." Drew grinned in delight.

WHAT LANGUAGES BEIRUT residents spoke seemed to depend on their age. When we first arrived, we assumed everyone spoke Arabic, French, and English in that order. But we discovered that actually, the older generation mostly speaks Arabic and French and the younger generation mostly speaks French and English. Our neighborhood in particular was heavy on French and light on Arabic, probably because we were on the Christian side of the city. Still, many people in the city spoke all three, and it was not uncommon for us to walk into an office and hear the receptionist answer the phone in one language, switch to another for the conversation, and then hang up and address us in a third. It made us wonder if someday we'd be like them, jumping between languages with total ease, having an intuition about which language to use by looking at someone, and never getting mixed up between the three.

Researcher Arturo E. Hernandez shared his experience of learning multiple languages in his book *The Bilingual Brain*. At age twenty, as a native Spanish speaker with English as a second language, he went to Brazil to study in Portuguese (his third language). He became so fluent in the language that after two years, people mistook him for a native, but his Spanish and English suffered. He struggled when he returned to read English textbooks, and his grandmother thought his native Spanish sounded "strange."

In the late twentieth century, people began thinking of the brain like a computer, and languages like individual software programs you can load up. It was clear from Hernandez's experience that language didn't exist in separate silos in the brain, but that there was overlap and individual languages could influence one another.

One interesting field of research is that of how language is processed in bilinguals who have a traumatic brain injury. In his book, Hernandez shares an interesting case he found in the journal *Brain and Language*. In this case, the patient, A.S., spoke Farsi as his mother tongue, and also spoke German and English. At age forty-nine, he was injured in an explosion that damaged his brain. As he recovered, he could only speak a few words of Farsi, his native language, but could speak fluidly in German, one of his acquired languages. After about three weeks, he was able to switch back to Farsi again, but he wasn't able to use his English, his third language, until he had fully recovered his Farsi and German. The languages were stored in different parts of the brain, but it wasn't pure silos; there must have been a bridge between his native language and English but not one between his native language and German. Perhaps it was because he spoke German longer that it had become a fully formed language in his brain, but his English was still being translated from his native Farsi. It wasn't just the languages you spoke but the order you learned them, the depth of mastery and a million other factors that informed how your brain organized itself. No doubt it would look different for everyone.

In his 1881 book *Les maladies de la mémoire*, the father of French psychology, Théodule-Armand Ribot, wrote of a forester living on the border of Poland who grew up speaking Polish and later in life moved to a German-speaking area. While in this town, he didn't hear or speak Polish for more than thirty years. During an operation, he was given anesthesia and spent the next two hours unconscious but speaking in Polish. His conscious mind was put to sleep, but his childhood memories of Polish came bubbling to the surface.

Over the last century there have been theories about how language is stored. Some people think that everyone has one dominant primary language that is stored first in certain parts of the brain. If you later learn second or third languages, depending on how old you are when you learn them and how often you use them, it can alter how your brain uses and retrieves all languages. But, as with studies on the musical brain, the recent development of fMRI has revolutionized the world of bilingualism research and called this theory into question.

Using fMRI, now we can actually see what happens in the brain, instead of trying to intuit what is going on by observing bilinguals or learning languages ourselves. In a study published in the journal *Nature*, researchers put bilingual subjects into fMRI scanners and asked them to think about something that had happened during their day, in either their first or second language. They found that for *early* bilinguals, those who learned two languages simultaneously when young, the areas of the brain that activated as they thought about their day greatly overlapped. In other words, the brain scans looked pretty similar no matter which language the subject was thinking in. However, in *late* bilinguals, those who learned their second language in adulthood, the scan showed comparable but *separate* areas of brain activity. The age of acquisition had more of an impact on the brain scan than the number of languages they spoke. So when I thought about multilinguals "switching" between languages, this couldn't be further from the truth. The dominant theory of language acquisition for the last hundred-plus years—that everyone has one dominant language and that other languages are stored separately—is true only if you learn your second language late in life, but even then, the complexity of the human brain allows for languages to live together, to influence each other, and to act independently. We have shifted from the brain-as-a-computer hypothesis and languages as individual pieces of software to a more nuanced view. There's not a single model; it's all interconnected, and for the multilingual individual, it doesn't feel like "switching" at all—it's all part of the same fabric.

When I spoke to Vivian Cook, the U.K. professor who studies second-language acquisition, this was one of his biggest points. As technology has improved we've gone from thinking of language ability as a few separate silos, stored and accessed individually in the brain, to an overlapping and organic instrument that is shaped by the number of languages, the frequency of use, the age at which each language was acquired, and other factors. Your bilingual brain might not look like my bilingual brain, but we could both speak the same languages.

One of the allures of learning a language, and perhaps the biggest myth about bilingualism, was that having more than one language somehow makes you smarter, that it's a special skill, the exception and not the norm. Linguists like Vivian Cook now argue the opposite: that bilingualism is not some superhuman feat but, instead, an ordinary part of human existence. The human brain is more than capable of handling more than one language, and it's only the exception, the scarcity of multiple languages in the environment during our formative years, that leads to monolingualism. Other researchers support this. Patricia Kuhl studied Catalan and Spanish bilingual infants and found that they could detect subtle differences between the two languages as early as age four months, even though they are both Romance languages and have shared word sounds and vocabulary and a similar cadence (linguists call this *prosody*). Being bilingual isn't a special skill; it's the way we are wired to develop.

So what is the bilingual advantage? Research shows two interesting things. For young bilinguals, there is an increased ability in the area of executive control. In a 2004 study, researcher M. Rosario Rueda tested bilingual children using a task-switching game that tested their ability to select correct answers based on mapped criteria while using executive control to dampen down "noise" or distractions (they played a game the researchers called "the hungry fish game," during which the kids were asked to feed the hungry fish by pointing to its mouth). They found that the bilingual kids performed better and more accurately at around two and a half years old than their monolingual peers. The difference between the bilingual group and the monolingual group became smaller at three and four years old. So while there was a "bilingual advantage," it was short lived.

For bilingual adults, there's no increase in IQ or other cognitive ability when measured against single-language adults. If you think of the brain as a muscle that only has to work in order to do something difficult, this makes sense. The children were better able to switch between tasks because being bilingual requires them to do this more than their monolingual counterparts. But when adult bilinguals were tested cognitively against other adults, measuring their ability to complete a puzzle, for example, there was no significant advantage. The brain was able to handle the two languages efficiently, so it didn't need to compensate by boosting brain power.

However, the difference in cognitive ability shows up again later in life. As gray matter begins to recede, bilingual seniors retain more of their cognitive abilities, such as memory and problem solving, for longer than their monolingual peers. More specifically: If you're like the rest of us, after your twenties you'll slowly start losing brain mass. That loss accelerates when you get into your fifties. By the time you hit your seventies, you will have lost 5 to 6 percent of your total brain mass compared to what you had at age thirty. By age eighty, you can lose as much as 25 percent. But the situation may be different for bilinguals. Bialystok's research showed that even in bilinguals with significant impairment from dementia, the rest of their brain seemed to compensate for the loss, allowing them to stave off the effects of dementia for much longer than their monolingual peers (four to five years before symptoms begin to show), even when their fMRI scans showed similar loss. This fact is what started me on this entire project. After my grandfather's struggle with dementia, I wanted to do anything I could to decrease the effects of the disease, if I was unlucky enough to get it, and set up Cole to have the best chance possible as well.

EVEN KNOWING THAT adult bilinguals don't have any magical cognitive abilities, it was hard to not feel that there was indeed something superhuman about bilinguals while observing life in Beirut. One day, armed with coupons for a beach club on the shores north of Beirut, we decided to spend the day lounging in the pool. At the pool, I saw children no older than my son switching between languages. It was fascinating the way they would read my face and guess my language. The adults were typically better at it—if I was waiting in line at the grocery store, the clerk always switched to English before I said anything. The children at this pool, though, would try Arabic sometimes, but mostly they mistook me for French.

One little boy swam over to me and said something in French and I tried to respond in kind, "Bonjour!"

His mother spoke to him in English: "She speaks English. Use your English."

He resisted. He continued with French.

"Tut tut, English," the mother corrected.

He reluctantly said in English, "Can I use that?" pointing to the water gun we had been playing with in the pool.

"Yes, of course."

Despite knowing that this was completely normal, and perhaps not that big of a deal, I was highly impressed. It was like watching small child prodigies sitting down to play Bach on the piano or reciting pi to the two hundredth digit.

I think part of that amazement that monolinguals feel toward bilinguals comes from our own experience learning languages. My son, who had never struggled over a vocabulary book for hours, was not at all impressed. In fact, the multiple languages didn't even give him pause. Kids didn't need words to play, and they ran around, shouting, laughing, and using whatever language they spoke or felt like speaking, whether or not it was understood.

Fifteen

W here's Cole?" Drew asked me as I worked on my Arabic homework in the living room.

"I thought he was outside with you."

"He was, did he come inside? I was cutting down bananas— look!" he said. He held up a broom with a knife taped to the end in one hand and a large stem of bananas, a bunch of twenty or so of the small, nearly ripe fruit, in the other.

"Holy crap, Drew!"

"I know, right? Rawrrr!" He lifted the bananas over his head as he roared. Then he dropped them to the floor. "Whoa, those are heavy."

"Wait, where is Cole, though?" I said, getting up. I looked outside and he wasn't in our small fenced yard. I ran around the house and he hadn't wandered into the junglelike vegetation that was growing wild in the back.

"Drew! Where is he?" I yelled.

I ran inside and Drew passed me and said, "Nope, he's not in here." We both hustled back outside together.

"*Cole!*" we screamed in unison.

Cole laughed.

We looked up. There was Cole, hanging on to the stairs leading to the roof above us.

"Oh my God, Drew!" Drew ran up to get him. Cole hadn't just climbed stairs for the first time; he had also climbed the outside of the stairs, hanging on to the handrail and slowly working his way up to the top until he couldn't go any farther. My two-year-old was dangling one story above the concrete. Drew took the stairs two at a time and pulled him up over the handrail and into his arms.

"Drew! You have to watch him!"

"I know, but he's never done that before." Now that we'd found Cole, Drew seemed embarrassed.

"Okay, so let's find a way to block off the stairs. And you really do have to watch him. No multitasking."

"I know, but the bananas—no, never mind, you're right. I am so sorry."

"It's okay. Whoa. I think I had a mini stroke there." I sat down hard on a chair and exhaled.

Drew sat beside me. "Yeah. Me too."

Before we had a child, it was so different. It was just the two of us, traveling, in love, and we were the best of friends. We got along famously. We only fought when we got lost ("Take a right!" and of course, Drew takes the left and says, "Why are you yelling?"). All of those things were still true, but the combined effects of little sleep, a crying baby, these new demands, and my reduced free time (due to studying) just exaggerated everything. I was crankier with Drew, more curt, less patient, and if I didn't watch myself, I could take out my frustrations on him.

This climbing-the-house phase of Cole's was completely new to us. The logistics of traveling just got more complicated. Instead of a baby we could pick up and carry around the world with us, we had a curious little monkey who apparently wasn't afraid of heights.

Drew and I gave each other a look. Eventually we'd have to settle down. This was really happening.

IN CLASS, WE WERE FIGHTING with Majed. Our textbook wasn't consistent on the spelling of words, and to us as native English speakers this seemed like an atrocity. Majed was in a tough spot. The language, after all, was written in a different set of letters than English. Also, since the dialect is only spoken, even the Arabic script was an approximation of how the Beirut dialect is pronounced, and there were little things that a native Beiruti knew that seem completely confusing to someone just learning.

On top of that, some words in Arabic are pronounced differently based on the first letter. Take the liaison. For example, the word for Monday is *el tanein*, which is how it's spelled in Arabic script. However, Majed kept spelling it as *et tanein*; because that's the way it sounds; the *el* borrows from the *t* in *tanein*, making it flow better. *El tanein* becomes *et tanein*.

Both are correct, and I'd argue that Majed's spelling is better because it emphasizes how it's pronounced. He brushed off the student's criticism and continued to drill the days of the week: "Sunday . . . *el ahad*, Monday . . . *et tanein*, Tuesday . . . *et talaataa* . . ."

"But the book says *el* 2a7ad, *el* tanein, *el* talaataa, and so on . . ." The book was using Arabic *chat*, a form of writing that's used when people text one another. Letters not in English, like 'ayn (ع) were represented by the best possible alternative, in this case, the number 3.

Majed ignored the student. "Please take out your homework." He wasn't going to entertain any more questions.

I pulled out my notebook and opened to the page of exercises I had carefully written out in Arabic script the night before. Majed checked each student's work and grew more and more agitated.

"Kate, where is your work?" he demanded of a girl in the second row.

"I didn't do it."

"Why?"

"Because I didn't."

Majed seemed flustered. "I gave you an assignment; why didn't you do it?"

Kate crossed her arms. "I don't feel like I have to explain myself to you."

Majed just stood there, wide-eyed.

"What?" Kate said defiantly. "I didn't do it. I am paying for this class, and if I don't do the work, that's up to me."

Majed let out a big sigh. He went to the next student. No work. The next, the same thing.

"Where is John?" Majed asked the room at large when he came to an empty seat.

"Uh, I think, I think he's going to be a little late."

Another sigh from Majed.

Most of the students were here on summer vacation from their college schedule, so while studying Arabic in Beirut may have sounded like a good idea to them initially, the class was quite intense, requiring four hours of classroom time five days a week and as many hours doing assignments at home (Majed loved worksheets). I can only imagine it wasn't what these kids had bargained for, for summer break.

Majed came to my desk. I meekly handed him my sheet of exercises, and he corrected my homework right there, writing over my script in parts where I didn't form the letters quite right, making a check mark next to the correct answers.

"Good." He moved on.

The next day, Jason, the student who knew the letter *aleph* on the first day and seemed the most experienced with Arabic, dropped out of the course. Natalie followed a few days later. Then it was Josh. Soon there were just four of us: a broke backpacker from the United States, a chemist from the Netherlands, Kate the British art curator who recently lost her job in Dubai and who refused to do her homework, and me.

"Maybe now that those three are gone we can learn something," the chemist said during our daily coffee break. "No more complaining."

"Yes, we waste too much time arguing with Majed," I said.

"That's because he's a horrible teacher," Kate interjected.

"Maybe we're just frustrated because Arabic is hard," the backpacker said.

We shuffled back to class and Majed announced, excitedly, that we would be drilling vocabulary. At this point, we sighed and opened our books.

AT FIRST I HAD BEEN frustrated by the rote memorization style of the class, but as I learned the Arabic script and began speaking the language, I didn't care how it was taught because Arabic enthralled me. The script itself is so beautiful it has me completely charmed. Here was the simple word for "house," *bayt*:

بيت

To read it, I just counted the dots and the positions from right to left. Once you know it, it's quite simple. Yet the script was so elegant that writing in it felt like I had mastered a kind of calligraphy. I wanted to write everything in Arabic. I would point out signs to Drew and tell him the letters. I often didn't know what they spelled, or even how to pronounce them, because written Arabic on the street almost always leaves out the vowel markers because fluent people know that *byt* is *bayt*. This seemed impossible to me at first, but if you think about it, a fluent English speaker could still read English if you dropped some vowels, such as the letters *i*, *e*, and *o*:

A flunt nglsh spaker culd stll rad nglsh f yu drppd sm vwls. . . .

So written Arabic on the street would skip the vowels similarly, for efficiency.

But it was the writing, not the reading, that amazed me, the way Majed drew lines from Arabic poetry into a knot of intertwined letters. I noticed that the logos of many businesses are just the Arabic letters written creatively. Like the news organization Al Jazeera: Their logo looks like an artful rendering of a flame, but it's also their name spelled in Arabic. I practiced my writing every day, trying to copy the little flourishes that Majed put in or the way they draw two dots as a single line, little handwriting tricks that make it flow even more easily.

Given the disparity in written versus spoken Arabic, it was not surprising then that unlike other languages, written Arabic isn't processed on the same side of the brain as when it's spoken; the left side of the brain handles the written language, while the right side handles the spoken. Researchers suggest this is because the right hemisphere processes letters in words in a global sense, but because you have to count dots and be concerned with specifics in Arabic, the task shifts to the left hemisphere, the same way it would if you were solving math problems. Most other languages like English or even Hebrew (which is also written right to left) are handled in the right hemisphere for both written and spoken.

. . .

ONE THING I DIDN'T EXPECT from learning Arabic (although in hindsight perhaps it should have been obvious) was how much it would be tied to Islam. Remember, Arabic is triglossic—there is the spoken dialect, the written language (Modern Standard Arabic), and then there's classical Arabic, the Arabic of the Qur'an. For Muslims, even those living in Asia or Africa, everything religious is done in Arabic, from reading the Qur'an to their daily prayers to the *Shahadah*, the acceptance of Islam:

لَا إِلَهَ إِلَّا اللهُ مُحَمَّدٌ لُ سُورَ اللهِ

Translation: "There is no God but Allah, and Muhammad is the Messenger of Allah."

Iraqi-born British theoretical physicist Jim Al-Khalili notes in his book *The House of Wisdom* that "classical Arabic, being the language of the Qur'an, has not changed at all in fourteen centuries, making the writings of the early Islamic scholars as accessible today as they were then." When you consider that *Beowulf* was written in Old English around that same time and is completely impenetrable to modern English speakers, that fact is kind of astonishing. Here's an excerpt, taken at random, from Beowulf: "Nalæs hi hine læssan lacum teodan, þeodgestreonum, þon þa dydon, þe hine æt frumsceafte forð onsendon ænne ofer yðe umborwesende." I put that into Google Translate and clicked "Detect language" and it chose Icelandic. It certainly wasn't modern English. Imagine reading the Bible in clear-as-day English from the original.

According to Pew Research, over 80 percent of Muslims are not Arab; in fact, 60 percent of them are in Asia—yet they use classical Arabic for religious purposes. Because of this link between Arabic and Islam, by 2050 Arabic is expected to become the second most spoken language in the world (Mandarin is expected to remain well in the lead).

Even in spoken Arabic dialect, there are constant references to Islam—like in English when we say "Bless you" after someone sneezes. At home I practiced greeting people with "As-salam alaykum" (*Peace be upon you*), but decided to stick with the secular "Marhaba" (*Hello*), feeling too unsure about using a Muslim greeting when I wasn't Muslim. However, even then the response to "Hello" is usually "Marhabtein" (*Two hellos*; literally *Two marhabas*)—or if you want to combine French and Arabic you can say "Bonjourtein" (*Two bonjours*). Why? Majed told us, "Never respond with just 'hello'; do something more." Later I'd learn this idea comes directly from the teachings in the Qur'an: "When you are greeted with a greeting, greet in return with that which is better than it, or (at least) return it equally" (Qur'an 4:86).

As I discovered these aspects of Arabic, I became more interested in the history of Islam, and bought the book *Destiny Disrupted* by Tamim Ansary, an American historian who grew up in Afghanistan and now lives in San Francisco. Ansary had been hired to write a Texas classroom history book earlier in his career, and was told to devote only one chapter of thirty to Islam and the Arab world (which stretches from North Africa across the Middle East and Arabian Peninsula all the way to Asia)—and that it should be in the "Ancient Civilizations" section. In *Destiny Disrupted*, Ansary takes a look at the "alternative world history of Islam." Because he was a secular Muslim, his quest wasn't as much about personal identity as it was about reconciling the Eurocentric Western world history that he covered as a textbook writer with the narrative that he grew up hearing in the Islamic world.

Some might be surprised to know that the prophet Muhammad came in A.D. 570, quite a long time after Jesus, and in a time with writing, so there is a written account of the things the prophet said, the revelations he spoke of, that forms the basis of the Qur'an. Believers consider it to be the verbatim word of God as spoken by Muhammad. There are also interviews with people who knew him, and even further interviews and character checks on those people. These documents form the basis of the *hadith*, which informs Muslim traditions. There are experts who spend their entire lives studying these documents and producing their own analysis. Of course, the same is true in Christianity and Judaism, and this is well known in the West. But when it came to Islam in the Western media, I had only ever heard a single view of Islam, which I now learned is much more complicated and varied, with a sea of voices over the centuries.

Even the scope of what is now the Middle East surprised me.

For example, when Shakespeare was writing *Othello*, the Moors he wrote about were in fact Muslims by another name, living in what is today modern Spain. The Middle East also played unwilling host to the likes of not just the Crusaders, but also the Mongols. Genghis Khan reached as far as the fabled city from *The Arabian Nights* (now known as Baghdad) and tossed its entire Persian library into the river. He would have continued to Greece, Rome, and onward, perhaps erasing all of Greek and Roman history with it, but he died and his empire fell apart. The simple luck of geography saved one civilization's legacy while erasing another.

And then there's Palestine. Ansary wrote that in 1883 it was 4 percent Jewish. By the end of World War I it was 11 percent Jewish, and by the end of World War II it was about 50 percent Jewish. By the end of World War II, after Jews fled mass executions in Europe and immigration rates were capped in the United States, they headed in large numbers to Palestine and started buying up land. The problem was that the landless Palestinian natives who had been working the land for hire now had nowhere to go. To put this in context: There are 320 million people living in the United States. What if 320 million immigrants came into the country within half a century and bought the majority of the land and houses? What would happen to the Americans who hadn't owned their houses and now could no longer rent? How would Americans feel? I started to get a sense of the origins of the Arab-Jewish animosity in the region.

Jerusalem, which straddles the border between Israel and the West Bank and is home to some of the holiest sites in both Judaism and Islam, was another hot point of contention. Of course, the right to live in Jerusalem has deep historical and religious roots for Jewish people, and on Passover they even say, "Next year in Jerusalem." However, it is possible to simultaneously feel for the plight of Jews, persecuted during the Holocaust and now settling in their holy land—and also to feel for the native Arab community who had their concerns brushed aside. After World War II, the League of Nations blithely cut and formed countries to benefit Western interests—nobody asked the people of Palestine for permission to have their land taken from them. World War II had driven the Jewish community into Jerusalem, but to the Arabs in the region, this didn't entitle them to take over the country. Tensions eventually boiled over after Israel formed a nation, and in 1967 the Arab world attacked. Israel won a decisive victory, claiming the Gaza Strip, the West Bank, and the Old City of Jerusalem, among other spoils. Syria, Egypt, and Jordan suffered heavy losses. It became known as the Six-Day War.

THERE WAS ONE PASSAGE in which Ansary described Islam in a way that I found really moving: "Yes, Islam prescribes a way to be good, and yes, every devoted Muslim hopes to get into heaven by following that way, but instead of focusing on isolated individual salvation, Islam presents a plan for building a righteous community. Individuals earn their place in heaven by participating as members of that community and engaging in the Islamic social project, which is to build a world in which orphans won't feel abandoned and in which widows won't ever be homeless, hungry, or afraid."

I wasn't raised with any particular religion except my mother's strong belief in crystals, astral projection, and the potential for meditation to help her win the lotto—and once you grow up without a religion I think it's difficult to add one later in life. However, I can still be moved by religious expression. I found that there was something beautiful about the call to prayer, the melody itself, and the mindfulness of the ritual involved.

I didn't think that learning Arabic would change how I felt about Islam, but I found myself having conversations about religion with Majed frequently after class. He'd explain a Muslim principle to me while chain-smoking cigarettes on the classroom balcony, and then he'd ask me how it was possible that the Holy Trinity was three people in one.

"No, seriously, how does God, who is the same as his son, send himself, as his son, to earth to die? I mean, how does that *work*?"

It was funny because as much as the Middle East represented *the others* to us, we were *the others* to them.

Sixteen

Gone were the little Mandarin words Cole had picked up. *Niúnǎi* was no longer milk; it was just a distant memory. He moved on from watching *Xi Yang Yang*, although from time to time we did play it for him—the sound of Mandarin in the house was oddly comforting. Something else had happened. I noticed it when we were talking with the two women who ran the shop where I got my paper supplies. That day, a little boy about Cole's age was playing behind the counter. I wanted to use my Arabic a little, so I tried to start a conversation. Toddlers are fantastic language partners because they almost never stump you with new vocabulary.

"Marhaba," I said, leaning over. He looked up at me. "Shou issmak?" *What's your name?*

"Henry," he said, with the French pronunciation "Ahn-ree."

"Cole, can you say hello?" I said to my son. He remained mute and wide-eyed.

In China, he was joyfully shouting "Míng tiān jiàn!" (*See you tomorrow!*) to our nanny, in addition to saying his regular English expressions. I wasn't sure when things changed, but when we returned to the house, I started noticing that he wasn't asking for things by name in *any* language anymore. He had regressed into grunting and pointing. It wasn't "juz!" for juice, it was "ehh!" with pointing. He stopped saying compound sentences like "op dis" (open this) or "go ou-side" (go outside), and when I played *Xi Yang Yang* as a test, he was silent as I sang the intro song to him.

I had read about some language confusion in the many books on bilingualism I had devoured before starting this experiment. The authors were careful to underline that confusion is likely, especially when you move around a lot, but it was always temporary (unless your child had a language impairment). I was confident that our rapid transition was the cause—after all, we did just move from China to Lebanon, switching from English to Mandarin to Arabic in less than a year. According to the experts, a language freeze like this represents a desire to not say the wrong thing. Cole was still learning, still processing and still building language skills, but was choosing not to express anything verbally because he wasn't sure yet which version was the right one. Sometimes this freeze was referred to as a "silent period."

The research has shown that for bilingual children the milestones are all the same. Babbling starts at the same age as the first word—at about eleven months. However, vocabulary in toddlerhood might not be equal in both languages. Linguists

Virginia Volterra and Traute Taeschner studied two Italian-German bilinguals and found that one girl had a vocabulary of eighty-seven words with just three words that matched in both languages (*water*, *yes*, and *there*). The other girl had six words with equivalents in both tongues and a total vocabulary of eighty-three words. If the child is hearing more than one language on a daily basis, then the opportunity cost is that the child is hearing *less* of each individual language than a monolingual would of their one language (for example, a 65 percent German/35 percent Italian-exposed child will hear 35 percent less German spoken in a day than a 100 percent German child will hear). So while their overall vocabulary across all languages would match that of a monolingual (or exceed it), it might be less than a monolingual in each individual language. In our case, Cole might have received 35 percent of his input in Mandarin for a few months. Certainly it was enough time for him to learn some words and to recognize Mandarin sounds, but since we left Beijing, his exposure had dropped to zero.

Did that Mandarin exposure help my son? Maybe. There are a number of studies on the residual languages of children who are adopted. It's a perfect test environment because it happens so often and it's a very clean break. One study examined Korean children who were adopted between ages one and three years and moved to the United States to join non-Korean-speaking families. Years later, the children were tested on their ability to "hear" sounds that were difficult for English speakers to distinguish but occurred naturally in Korean. The adopted children were able to hear the sounds, and the researchers suggested that they'd also be able to learn the language with a native accent if they later chose to pursue Korean. The hypothesis was that one never really loses a language, it just lies dormant, ready to be reactivated. So even if he didn't remember any of the Chinese he'd learned at age two, if Cole later chose to study Mandarin, he might have a leg up.

Because Cole was exposed to Mandarin after almost two years of English, he wasn't bilingual from birth; he would be a *successive* bilingual (or language learner). In François Grosjean's book *Bilingual: Life and Reality*, he tells the story of two brothers who were acquiring French. The ten-year-old was very outgoing, and the five-year-old was reserved and quiet. As you might expect, the outgoing child tried French and made errors but kept charging forward. The younger boy hardly said a word until three months later, when he started using the language with *fewer* errors than his older brother, even though his brother had been speaking the language the whole time.

So while I was studying and practicing my Arabic, Cole was silently taking it all in. There was no way to know exactly how much impact any of this would have, but it couldn't hurt.

As far as learning languages, while children absorb it naturally through exposure, as an adult, I do have a slight advantage—for the moment—over my son because I can learn and produce language much faster than he can. Part of that advantage comes from having a fully formed brain stocked with language centers that know how to produce at least one language: English. Cole, on the other hand, was still learning English, and now we were training him in Arabic and Mandarin—at this point building his understanding of how languages work across several tongues. This meant he was building his brain, too.

Whether I reached proficiency in these languages or not, I'd never reach native-like fluency—my brain had already formed. If an fMRI scan were done of me speaking Mandarin or Arabic compared to speaking my native English, it would show activity in different areas, not the same areas that it would show if I were natively bilingual. And I'd probably never have that "ear" for the language. I can hear something in English and know if it's right or not, sometimes without knowing why—but I'd never get to that point with Arabic or Mandarin. I would also most likely always have an accent. On the other hand, if Cole learned his second languages to fluency before he was seven, he wouldn't have an accent, he would have native understanding of what "sounds" right or not in the language, and his brain would look just like a from-birth bilingual.

By the way, this brain development is so important that if you don't learn *any* language by the time you're about thirteen years old, it's probably impossible for you to ever fully use any language correctly. Of course, who doesn't speak before they are thirteen? It's rare and usually occurs only in cases of severe neglect, so it's challenging to draw a hard line between the effects of abuse versus the lack of language input. However, in the 1970s, a young woman named Genie was found locked up in her parents' Los Angeles home, naked, strapped to a training toilet for most of the day, forbidden to speak and kept in severe isolation her entire life. She was thirteen.

Researchers followed her language development for a few years and found that she was able to learn, gaining about one year in mental age for each year that she was in treatment. Eventually, though, they concluded that her grammar and syntax were severely delayed because she had missed language input in her formative years. Her brain could not catch up. It had matured without a language and it was impossible to add one back in.

In another case, a six-and-a-half-year-old child named Isabelle was found having spent her life locked up in a darkened room with her deaf-mute mother. After they escaped, she was first tested at a mental age of nineteen months with no language skills at all. Within eighteen months she had rebounded, increasing her vocabulary to 1,500 words and speaking in more complex sentences than Genie had achieved. This led Stephen Pinker, a Harvard researcher, to propose that the difference between the two children was the age at which they first acquired language at all. Those early years of brain development are beyond critical.

However, if you've missed your childhood window for second-language learning, how do you overcome the challenges of learning it later in life? There was a study in 1989 of Koreans who moved to the United States between ages three and thirty-nine. In the long-term, they found that the three- to seven-year-old group grew up to be identical to native speakers. For the grown-ups, those who had moved to the United States after age eighteen, the results were mixed. Their age didn't matter, but other factors did: getting an advanced degree, where they worked, how hard they attempted to learn the language.

For kids, it's about biology; for adults, it's about desire and determination.

CURIOUSLY, AS COLE ENTERED this silent phase, his physical activity skyrocketed. He climbed everything, from the wrought-iron bars in our windows, to the entertainment center, to the top of the furniture. He became fearless about jumping off things, too, scaring Drew and me half to death as he would scamper up on our bed, climb the bars on the window, and then jump from ceiling height to the bed, laughing the entire time. We quickly learned to keep the French-style window closed at all times, so he couldn't get to the bars and perform his high-flying act. At the same time, Cole started taking off his diaper, insistent that he didn't need it, until we suspected that he might be ready to potty train. We bought a training toilet (with characters from *Cars* the movie and a stick-shift "flusher" that made the sound of an engine revving when you pressed it down). Drew showed him how to use it, and from that moment on he stopped wearing diapers and used his little toilet. I couldn't know, but I wondered if his development had put speech on hold for a moment while he focused on other skills.

Still, I couldn't help but be a little nervous for my temporarily nonverbal son. I wrote down a list of his current words and promised myself that if he hadn't improved in the next few months, I'd take him to the best speech therapist I could find in the States. Eventually my plan was to speak these languages with him, but for now, I would be happy when he started asking for "juz" again.

Seventeen

There was a civil war going on in Syria, an hour away from us by car. It wasn't a lack of concern that kept us from thinking about this as we walked across Beirut for lunch one Saturday morning. It wasn't that we didn't care or were the type of people who ignored world events. It was just that it didn't seem possible, as we sat in a restaurant overlooking the sea. The taste of salt in the air and a sweeping view of the Mediterranean and the coastline in the background conspired to keep our attention right here, right now. Syria was closer than Boston is to New York City, but it might as well have been on the other side of the world.

A group of Arab women sat at a table, all in black, having lunch together and talking in muted tones. The waiter brought our menus, the wind mussing up his hair. We ordered a spread of food and lounged on the cushions, enjoying the warmth of the sun. After lunch, I left Cole and Drew to use the bathroom. Inside, a flat-screen TV was playing the news. When I saw that there was a shooting, I stopped to watch for a moment, absorbing the footage of protesters and police barricades on loop.

I caught my breath. It was in Arabic, so I only caught every third word or so, but the video made it clear enough. The shooting had happened that morning in the area we had just crossed to get to the ocean. Apparently a Lebanese Shia clerk had been kidnapped in Syria (probably by the Free Syrian Army), and people had gathered in Beirut to protest, until a lone gunman started shooting AK-47s into nearby buildings. When we were there, we hadn't noticed anything at all awry and had heard no gunfire. It seemed Beirut had a way of absorbing these kinds of things.

I often walked past protests, sometimes violent, in Beirut, while just one block away people enjoyed lunches and cocktails al fresco. It had been happening all summer and usually had to do with the Syrian war. The stated goal of the Free Syrian Army was to stop anyone who killed civilians, but there were reports of other activities, too: kidnappings and executing soldiers. In May, the Free Syrian Army had kidnapped eleven Lebanese pilgrims, mostly Sunni Syrians who had defected from the Syrian military. In Beirut, the response to these activities in Syria was swift, and Syrians were targeted for harassment. One family, the Meqdad clan, had gone on a kidnapping spree in southern Beirut, taking twenty Syrians who they claimed were members of the Free Syrian Army. Hezbollah, who had been covertly supplying military support to the Syrian government, threw up their hands.

It was an incredibly complex situation, and if you started to untangle it, it became even murkier. Syria's government was Shia, governing a largely Sunni population (87 percent). A civil war broke out and Syria's neighbor, Lebanon, governed by Hezbollah, also Shia, couldn't come out and openly support the Syrian government because Lebanon was 54 percent Muslim and 40 percent Christian. Of the Lebanese Muslims, half were Sunni and half were Shia. So Hezbollah, despite being Shia, couldn't take sides without risking unrest. So instead they allegedly sent three thousand fighters to assist the Syrian government (which they denied, of course). On top of this, you had the problem of Beiruti militaristic family clans, like the Meqdad clan, which boasted ten thousand members. The clans often took justice into their own hands. Hezbollah looked the other way. So effectively you had a paramilitary group working within the boundaries of Lebanon, outside the law. What did this mean for us on a daily basis? There were protests all the time, and we tried to walk by them as quickly as possible.

I FELT NUMB TO THE NEWS of the shooting. I even started to try to rationalize it in my head, to do the mental calculus that justified walking around a place where people are getting kidnapped. The list went like this: We live in Ashrafieh, not the dangerous parts of town; we're tourists, we're not Syrians; we never go to southern Beirut; as long as we stay away from protests we will be fine. *Inshallah.*

When we asked locals about the protests and the violence, the general sentiment was "Welcome to Beirut." Was this what Beirut did to you? The shoulder shrug, the going about your day anyway, pushing a stroller through the mortar-blasted neighborhoods while blocks away they are burning tires and waving flags?

Perhaps I really was becoming more Beiruti, because the problem that I constantly thought about in Beirut was not the violence—it was the infrastructure. Basic repairs were throttled by bureaucratic infighting. The power grid couldn't handle the summertime power surges, so the city, unable to break the bureaucratic choke hold so they could repair and upgrade the system, had decided instead to impose three-hour rolling blackouts on a daily basis. On top of that, the Internet was slow, even by developing-nation standards, and while Drew was trying to upload a large video file for his work he ran through $100 worth of data charges to upload 5 GB worth of data. The water was always running out—we were constantly refilling our water cistern or forgetting to do so. And while it was a blessing that our stove was propane, the method of getting a replacement tank was to call "the guy" who called "the other guy" who showed up on his motorcycle with a tank strapped to it, to swap it out for you.

The electricity went out, the water was restricted, the Internet was slow and expensive, everything ran by propane, and it was *still* hugely expensive to live here. I had lived in countries with similar infrastructure problems but never paid so much for it. We were easily spending as much in Beirut as we would in Boston, but with less infrastructure than even rural Mexico.

AT SOME POINT, I stopped reading the papers, because the daily local news was too alarming. There was a strike at the electric company, which I knew because I walked past it each day and saw the signs and a handful of Beiruti soldiers standing guard. So we didn't receive a bill for the next four months.

Meanwhile, Hezbollah chief Hassan Nasrallah made a rare public appearance, and he urged the citizens to calm down, saying, in effect, "Listen, this is your city; it doesn't really do much good to burn tires and shoot things up in your city if you're mad about Syria, ya know?"

There was only one thing to do: adapt. We bought candles for the power outages. We made sure our laptops were always charged so we were prepared when the power went out. We downloaded the power outage app—and yes, this was the insanity of the situation, they made a *mobile application* for the blackout instead of just fixing the electricity shortage. We found cafés that had generators and Internet so we could upload work. I stopped reading the news, I pretended like everything was okay, and I tried to just enjoy the city.

. . .

I STARTED DOING BETTER in my Arabic classes. I had adopted a technique for improving my pronunciation that was working exceedingly well. After Beijing, where I did some nighttime listening to Mandarin, I had decided that passive listening probably wasn't doing me much good. After all, Patricia Kuhl's study with infants showed what a difference talking to a live person versus listening to a CD had on retaining language. The CD had zero effect.

Each day in class, I put my phone on my desk and when my teacher was speaking, usually going down a list of vocabulary words, I recorded him. Then, while walking home, I put in my earbuds and listened to the recording, repeating each phrase. This active listening and speaking, repeating over and over again the same phrases with a native speaker in my ear, vastly improved my accent and helped me memorize new words quicker. It had the added benefit of distracting me, because walking home, past the now-empty electric company building, with child-men in full army gear with machine guns and smoking cigarettes outside, made me nervous. I could see the baby fat on their faces. They were too young. Their weapons were so big. What if they got spooked by something and started shooting things?

Usually my imagination would get the best of me, and my heart would race as I walked by and imagined a thousand deadly scenarios. However, now, with my teacher Majed in my ear, I could just walk down the street, quietly saying Arabic words as he said them back to me, the sun warming my skin, the street traffic, honking horns, and dangerous military youth all fading behind me.

For the rest of my studies, I completed all of Majed's worksheets, the packets getting thicker every week. I loathed them. The exercises were excruciatingly boring: Here's a sentence, take the subject and change its gender! But I also did other things. I wrote essays in Arabic; I copied and recopied Arabic words into my notebook. I committed everything to memory. We watched *Spider-Man* and random kung fu movies dubbed in Lebanese Arabic.

On the weekends, I went to the local farmer's market and bought cherry jam or homemade tabbouleh. I made elaborate Lebanese spreads for the family with special pickled vegetables, cheeses, dips, and breads. Drew was so in love with the pita bread, it was so fresh and good, that we'd pick some up almost every day. The roses in our yard started to bloom, the bananas began to ripen, and Cole had slowly begun speaking again.

One day, I took the long steps to our house in Ashrafieh, and someone had spray-painted in huge block letters in both Arabic and English across three flights of stairs:

LET'S

THINK

POSITIVE

Eighteen

I studied for my final exam for Urban Arabic in the dark, sitting outside in my garden, the sound of my neighbors conversing on the street the only noise. It was another blackout, this one unscheduled, so we had no idea when it would end. I read by candlelight, flipping through my two notebooks, both completely filled with notes. Some of the pages were covered with new words I'd heard on the street, with or without English translation. Other sections had pages and pages of carefully copied vocabulary lists with my English translation and little notes about pronunciation.

The day of the exam, my hands were slick with sweat as we waited for Majed to hand out the materials. When he placed a thick packet in front of me, I quickly flipped through the contents. Sentences in Arabic to be translated into English. Questions in Arabic requiring Arabic answers. Grammar and vocabulary quizzes. Reading comprehension. All straightforward. I took my time, turned in my test and spent the next twenty-four hours playing the test over in my mind. Had I missed something? Would I pass? I felt like I had come so far, but who knew for sure?

The next day, Majed prepared to give us our exams and he stood in front of me. "I am so disappointed. Why didn't you study?"

My jaw dropped. "I did!"

He smiled. "I know!" He handed me my exam. Ninety-five percent—I had gotten an A and, I later found out, the highest mark in the class.

I was elated. After the brutal hit my confidence took in China, this was total vindication. Arabic was hard, but it *wasn't that hard.* I would now be moving on to the advanced class, and six weeks after that I would start MSA—the literary language of Arabic.

Back home, I showed Drew my results and did a happy dance. We poured a glass of wine and had a toast. "Cole, Mama can speak Arabic!"

Of course my joy was short lived, because soon after my exam, and all through the next two weeks, I felt extremely ill. I wasn't sure if it was the flu or what. One night I tried to drink a glass of wine in an effort to relax. I finished the glass, ran to the bathroom, and immediately threw up.

I tried to take it easy, but it was time for class again, and this time I enrolled in private lessons with Majed. I didn't want to go into the advanced course and run into the same rote memorization techniques. Plus, with the same students as my first class moving on to the second, my hope was that I'd avoid all the "why the teaching method sucks" arguments that seemed to take up so much of our class time. I also scheduled fewer classroom hours so I that could spend more time using the language outside my studies. I planned on using the rest of my tuition money to take nonlanguage classes in Arabic, maybe some cooking classes—or if I had to, hiring someone to hang out with me and chat in Arabic.

Even though I was sick, I still went to my private lessons with Majed. I had a plan. Much like the soundboard for Mandarin, in which each morpheme was recorded as spoken by a native, I wanted to get every piece of vocabulary we had ever covered into one recording. So I drew up a massive vocabulary list, taking all of my notes and textbooks, and for our first lesson, I asked Majed to be my vocal talent. It was a lot to record. But it would give me a complete audio guide to the language and I could really drill into correcting my pronunciation. (I never seemed to attack my *kh* and *gh* sounds well enough to satisfy Majed). Majed did it but hated the entire concept. It was like trying to get a cat to take a bath. On my recording, there's a lot of sighing between words, and by the end he was rushing through the words as fast as he could go.

I was working through the advanced textbook on my own, and Majed and I would meet to go over my work and talk about grammar and new vocabulary. By this point, everything was in Arabic. There were no more translations to get me by, so sometimes I wasn't clear on the pronunciation if there were no vowel markers on a certain word or if there was a certain Beirut twist that wasn't explained in the text.

I'd been excited to get away from the rest of the students and focus on learning instead of complaining, but I soon realized that it wasn't only the rest of the class that had frustrated me, but also the style of instruction. Majed had a set idea of how to teach, and even when I tried to push him hard toward a more conversational approach, he kept veering back to standing at the whiteboard and reciting grammar rules. I thought I would learn more from simply keeping up running dialogue in Arabic. Majed was growing frustrated with me, but can one really learn a language simply by being lectured to for ten hours a week about the grammar rules? It wasn't connecting for me. I was stubbornly insisting on the kind of instruction that I needed.

Meanwhile, I was feeling increasingly ill. I hadn't consumed any alcohol since the wine-vomiting incident—just the smell of it turned my stomach—but then again it seemed like everything I ate did that. I'd been sick for about 10 days, and every afternoon I was taking longer and longer naps. One day I came home and walked into the kitchen and was almost knocked back by the smell.

"Drew, come here!"

"What?" he said, rushing over.

"Do you smell that? What is that?"

"I don't smell anything." He sniffed the air like a hound.

"You don't? It smells like rotting fruit and vegetables. It's disgusting!" It was a sickly sweet odor, like rotting fruit.

"Nope."

Then, I remembered—I'd smelled this scent once before, almost exactly three years earlier. *Oh holy crap.* "Drew, I'm pregnant."

He looked floored. "No, you are not! *Come on!*"

I took a pregnancy test the next morning, while Drew paced outside the bathroom door. Two blue lines. Pregnant.

I laughed, a deep, body-shaking belly laugh, and Drew didn't even have to ask what it said. "Really?" he called out.

"I told you!" I yelled from the bathroom.

"I can't believe it! Wow, that's so crazy . . . and awesome!"

"Oh my God, we're having a baby!"

"A baby!"

We danced around and hugged each other. Then I had to go lie down.

I DIDN'T EVEN KNOW how far along I was, so when I went to the ob-gyn with Drew and Cole in tow and she asked, "When was your last menstrual period?" I had to count back. I finally realized I'd had my last one the day we arrived in Beirut.

"May," I said.

She looked at me and said, "Three months ago? And you're just coming in now?"

Gulp. I was saved by her phone, which she picked up and answered in French, then switched to Arabic. She had a thirty-second rapid-fire conversation, hung up, and without a beat turned to me and said in English, "Okay, let's go take a look."

I hopped up on her examination table. Using her ultrasound wand on my belly, she showed me what looked like a very large baby.

"Yes. Okay. Mm-hmm," she said.

"What?" I asked.

"You're thirteen weeks pregnant. Everything looks good. There's the heartbeat."

Drew picked Cole up and pointed at the screen. "Cole! You're going to be a big brother!" Drew said. We watched the baby wiggle.

I had some blood work done, stocked up on prenatal vitamins, and paid her in cash. Our travel insurance didn't cover pregnancy, so it was all out-of-pocket. The total was $72. I tried to remember my per-visit cost before insurance in the States, and it seemed like a deal in comparison.

There wasn't much time to consider the pregnancy and what it meant for our plans. I had just finished my sessions with Majed; I bought out the school's entire stock of Beirut films and their even more advanced *Cultures and Conversations* textbook and wished them adieu. From here on out, I would go it alone, studying Arabic at home, perhaps hiring someone to speak with me. My days of rote memorization were behind me. It was all good timing because as a little respite from the summer heat and the never-ending wave of blackouts, we had to do a visa run; our tourist visa was about to expire, so we had to leave Lebanon for at least one day, then return and get a new ninety-day tourist visa. We decided to make a holiday of it and took the short flight to Cyprus to hang out at a beachside resort for a bit.

We went from sitting in the dark for hours a day during the rolling blackouts to being spoiled by constant electricity, free and strong Internet, and even cable TV. I watched *16 and Pregnant* for the first time. We rented bikes and rode along the coast, swam in the clear waters, and ate ice cream after lunch. My morning sickness subsided almost completely. Drew constantly rubbed my belly and whispered "We're having a baby" in my ear. After our daily swims, Cole quickly became accustomed to the idea of having Mama join him for his naps, our sunburned faces next to each other on the pillow, the taste of salt on our lips.

Nineteen

We returned from Cyprus tanned and happy. Our return coincided with that day's rolling blackout, so the apartment was dark. We dropped the luggage in the bedroom, and I lay down on the bed with Cole for his nap. Drew made lunch in the kitchen. The sunlight lit half the room and gave him enough light to prepare chopped beef and hummus, with a heavy dose of olive oil and freshly cut yellow and orange bell peppers. Cole drifted off next to me, his freckles more pronounced across the bridge of his nose, a new development since Cyprus, hard-earned by spending entire days on the beach.

A few days later, while working on my computer, I got a message from a friend: "Have you heard? Are you leaving?"

Far away, across the Atlantic, on the other side of the United States, a man named Nakoula Basseley Nakoula had uploaded a video to YouTube. That film, *The Innocence of Muslims*, made its way to Egypt's media over the summer. The *New York*

Times described it: "The trailer opens with scenes of Egyptian security forces standing idle as Muslims pillage and burn the homes of Egyptian Christians. Then it cuts to cartoonish scenes depicting the Prophet Muhammad as a child of uncertain parentage, a buffoon, a womanizer, a homosexual, a child molester and a greedy, bloodthirsty thug."

Nakoula was an Egyptian-born filmmaker and radical anti-Islamist, out on probation for bank fraud charges. His amateur filmmaking shouldn't have been seen by anyone much less the whole world, but on September 8 it was broadcast on al-Nas, an Egyptian media channel with Arabic dubbing.

This would change everything.

On September 11, protests broke out across the Middle East, including at a U.S. consulate in Benghazi, Libya, where U.S. Ambassador Chris Stevens and three of his staff were killed. My friend's message reached me that day, before I had even heard the news.

I pulled up Al Jazeera, which had the best real-time English-language reporting for the Middle East. Drew and I sat glued to our computers, watching live updates from across the region. In Cairo, three thousand protesters demonstrated, tearing down the American flag. In Yemen, three protesters were killed during clashes with the police. Protests occurred in Iraq, Iran, and the Gaza Strip. Police teargassed ten thousand protesters in Sudan. In Tunis, four more people were killed. In Lebanon, in the northern city of Tripoli, protesters burned down a Kentucky Fried Chicken—because Tripoli didn't have a U.S. embassy to attack. One person was killed.

I e-mailed my friend Kayt, whose ex-husband was in the military, and asked how worried I should be. She said, "Not to alarm you, but nonessential personnel are being flown out of Beirut."

There was a part of me that didn't want to believe it. We waited. We watched.

The pope came to Beirut that weekend, speaking about the need for peace in the region. We didn't go to see him speak because it seemed like an opportune moment for something bad to happen, but we did catch a glimpse of the armed procession pass us by in Gemmyze: SUVs with mounted machine guns with men perched on the sunroofs. The crowd on the street watched in silence.

That same day, the United States publicly ordered nonessential diplomatic staff to leave Sudan and Tunisia. Hezbollah, headquartered in Beirut and part of the democratically elected government in Lebanon, called for a week of protests against Americans. The following Monday, tens of thousands of Beirutis took to the streets, and Hezbollah chief Hassan Nasrallah gave a rare speech, his first since 2008, saying, "The world does not understand the breadth of the humiliation. The world must understand the depth of our bond with our prophet."

The day of the Beirut protests, we stayed inside. Friends were sending us messages, wondering, "What's happening? Are you leaving?" We didn't know what to do. We watched it all unfold from within our house in Ashrafieh. The few times we did venture out for groceries, everything seemed exactly the same. The sun was shining, the birds were—no kidding—chirping in the trees, and the blossoming tree in our courtyard had shed so many of its flowers that we shuffled through a mound of fuchsia petals every time we walked out our gate. But we knew things could change very suddenly.

In 2006, during Hezbollah's conflict with Israel, the city shut down, the road to the airport was blocked, and all commercial flights were grounded. Travel host Anthony Bourdain was filming an episode of his show *No Reservations* in Beirut during this time and had to be airlifted out. There was no other way out: Syria to the north and behind you and ravaged by civil war, the sea in front of you, and a closed border with Israel to the south. We had watched this episode years before thinking of coming to Beirut, but as everything unfolded, I kept remembering it. If things did get shut down, we could be stuck in a city that could unravel into protests, fires, shootings, or worse.

It was a delicate balance, both traveling to the Middle East with a child, which in general is safe to do, and the reality that sometimes, for certain periods of time, areas of the Middle East aren't safe. It was a privilege to travel here, but even more so, it was a privilege to be able to leave, something our neighbors didn't have as an option, so we weighed it carefully. It would have been easy to overreact.

Drew and I tried to stay calm, and it mostly worked. Maybe that was part of living in Beirut. We'd gotten used to the blackouts and the water cistern and the duct tape, and we'd also gotten used to a low-level but constant threat of violence. We were becoming a little like our neighbors. But the difference was, they had earned that indifference through a traumatic fifteen-year civil war. They lost loved ones. Their homes. Their liveli-hoods. A study by the American University of Beirut in 1999 showed that at one point most twenty-somethings in Beirut were suffering from PTSD. The weight of what they had seen stayed with them for life. While the Beiruti indifference was easy to adopt, for us, it would always be superficial. When it came down to it, we weren't war-hardened and we hoped to keep it that way.

We became news junkies, not just following Al Jazeera any-more but seeking out writers and activists on Twitter, looking at all the major news sources plus the blogs and photos from people on the ground. It was desperation, a need to put some context on this. Was this the beginning of something larger or just a really bad week in the Middle East?

Then things started to wind down. Drew looked up from his computer and announced, "I think we'll be fine."

"We will?" I asked, fanning myself with a paper fan. The electricity was out again. Our ceiling fans hung useless over-head.

"I mean, we'll watch it," he said. "What do you think?" He was sitting on the couch across from me. Cole clambered up his shoulder, trying to navigate his way to a higher perch on the back of the couch.

"I don't know."

As PROTESTS AROUND US began to wind down, there was more violence in Tripoli. Tripoli was forty-five minutes north of

Beirut, just a quick drive up the highway. We tracked it online obsessively, checking Al Jazeera every few hours.

Then the power went out. At first we thought it was just an unscheduled blackout, like the others we had experienced over the summer. We packed up our laptops and headed to a café with a generator (you can tell which cafés have one—they are the ones with AC and lights on) and checked the news.

That night, we made dinner in the dark: I opted for apple slices and a small salad. It was too hot to eat. We sat outside in our garden, eating by candlelight, a slight breeze tickling our sweating bodies.

"Let's go to bed," I suggested to Drew, who had grown quiet over the last twenty-four hours.

"It's only eight o'clock," he said, and swatted away whatever was buzzing near his head.

"I know, but the electricity will be on tomorrow. Let's go to bed, rest, and start over in the morning."

"Okay."

The next morning, I woke to the sound of birds and the morning light falling on my pillow. Cole was still asleep next to me, and Drew was typing on his computer at the desk.

"Is there electricity?" I asked, squinting in the half light.

"Not yet," Drew said without turning around.

"What time is it?" I said as I sat up in bed.

"Ten a.m.," Drew said flatly.

That day the electricity stayed off all day long. Anxious that we'd gone more than twelve hours without checking the situation in Tripoli, we returned to the café to catch up on the news and to charge our computers. When we returned home, the house was still dark. After another backyard dinner eating the things that were slowly melting in the powerless fridge, we walked to Smuggler's, the corner shop up the road, to ask Gilbert about the electricity. "What do you think? When will it come back on?"

Gilbert was stocking jars of pickles and listening to Lebanese pop music on the tiny TV his father had installed right in the middle of the shelves. "No idea, a few more days?"

He was right. On the third day, the electricity returned, suddenly and without notice. The lights all turned on, and the fans; the TV roared to life playing an Islamic prayer, with handwritten Arabic over an illustration of a mosque at night. That afternoon, the electricity went out again without warning, and we were done. We packed up the laptops, headed to the café, and looked at the price of flying home. How could we stay safe if we didn't have access to news and couldn't keep track of what was going on in our area? The Middle East was dissolving into protests against Americans, and if it happened in our neighborhood, we wouldn't even know until they came for us.

I kept running through it with Drew over our laptops at the crowded café. It was packed with people who had come to charge their devices and check e-mail. I talked quietly.

"I mean, if something happens, the protesters will shut down the road to the airport. That's the first thing they do."

"Right," Drew said.

"And I'm pregnant."

"Right."

"And we have Cole."

"Christine, why are you trying to convince me? I am convinced. Let's go. Let's get the hell out of here."

I e-mailed our friends and Drew's parents about our decision, and they were relieved. It suddenly seemed cruel to have put them through so much concern.

We packed up and left. I said good-bye to everyone, and our friend Gilbert called a cab for us. He seemed so unfazed. When we climbed into the cab, I wanted to puke. I felt so sick about being able to leave when so many cannot. I remember when I lived in Seattle, just after 9/11, I heard someone say, "We should just bomb that whole region back into the Stone Age." Years later, driving out of Beirut, I was retroactively furious about the ignorance and hate in that statement.

About a month after we left Beirut, a car bomb went off in our neighborhood. I watched the footage on CNN and sobbed. It went off on a Friday afternoon during rush hour, one street over from the mall that we frequented. That mall was where we bought Cole his first bike, his little bouncy house, and the *Cars*-the-movie-themed training toilet. The façades on surrounding buildings fell from the blast. The entire area looked like a war zone. The beautiful French architecture in rubble, the kindly neighbors now with faces full of fear, soot-stained and bleeding, fleeing the scene. Eight people were killed, another eighty wounded. The target was intelligence chief Wissam al-Hassan, who was linked to the Syrian opposition. He was killed, but at what cost? The scene left behind was an angry twist of metal and fire and destruction, and for two days straight that scene played on every cable news station for audiences around the world, reducing an entire city full of charm and grace to its latest worst moment.

I checked in with everyone I could. All my friends were okay. Five days after the bombing, my school sent me an e-mail announcing the schedule for the winter term. Life in Beirut continued, without pause, because what else could they do? I finally understood what my teacher Majed meant when he said in that first week that we'd have an exam, *inshallah*. God willing. Nothing was certain, not even a test, not even the electricity, not even whether you're living in peace or war. But you move forward anyway. And you hope.

Twenty

For weeks, we lived with one foot in Beirut, even while we adjusted to life in Thailand. Slowly, as my belly continued to grow, we shifted our attention from all that had happened to what was about to happen. Eventually there was no avoiding it, the question we had put off asking.

Where should we have this baby?

I was sitting in the waiting room of the Chiang Mai Ramkhamhaeng hospital, starving. I had been fasting since midnight in preparation so I could down a big glass of syrupy sugar sludge and be tested for gestational diabetes. On the wall was a large display of perfectly airbrushed Thai models, with Chinawhite skin. They were selling skin-whitening products right in the middle of the hospital, a product that was so common in Thailand that I had to routinely check to make sure I didn't accidentally buy whitener in my face wash, lotion, or deodorant.

We could have the baby here, I thought.

My Thai doctor spoke English. He had trained in the United Kingdom. There were private hospitals here; I had the brochure from Bumrungrad in Bangkok, and beyond being internationally accredited, they had suites that looked like hotel rooms, nicer than the guesthouses we normally stayed in. And there was pricing to consider, because as a freelancer, living overseas, I didn't have U.S. health insurance. I had to figure out somewhere safe, peaceful, and affordable.

The sugar syrup made me gag, but I managed to keep it down. The doctor let me leave the hospital for the hour I needed to wait, so I took the motorbike to the grocery store to buy lunch for Drew and Cole. The Tops Market in the basement of the Kad Suan Kaew Mall had the best penang curry in Chiang Mai. It was so spicy that some days we couldn't even finish it, pushing it aside with tears in our eyes. It was delicious, though. They'd make it in huge batches for their mostly Thai customers, so by the time we ordered the curry, it had been prepared and sitting under the lights for half a day—and we'd learned by now that the longer curry sits, the better it tastes. When we ordered, they'd cover our bowls with wisps of kaffir lime leaves.

The women there didn't speak English, but they knew our order: two *penang moo* (pork—it had to be pork, forget chicken in your curry, it dries out too much), to go. For Cole I got the *khao kha moo*, pork leg on rice (no spice), served with pickled greens, a hard-boiled egg, and cilantro. I couldn't contemplate eating anything at the moment, but I had promised the boys before I left that I'd bring back lunch.

Back at the hospital, I was taken into a private room to have my blood drawn. I looked up and away from the needle as the nurse inserted it and saw a faint splatter of blood on the ceiling. I looked down toward the wall on my right and noticed that it was a little grimy, a faint gray smudge on the white paint. *It's not exactly clean here*, I thought. *Maybe I won't have this baby in Thailand. At least not in Chiang Mai.*

Two days later, my tests came back clear. I paid the bill in Thai baht, the equivalent of $30 for the test and a checkup with an obstetrician. The pregnancy was going well, the baby was healthy, and I had finally moved into that happy, rose-glow second trimester during which you're no longer sick and your bump is big enough that you look pregnant but not so big that it's hard to move around.

Drew, on the other hand, was exhausted. After we landed in Thailand, he collapsed emotionally. We had just lived in two challenging places back to back, learning languages that he had no interest in really learning. Drew's good-natured, easygoing attitude hid so much, but back in familiar, easy Thailand he seemed to unclench for real.

"Being stuck there was my worst nightmare," he finally confided in me. Our last days in Beirut had shaken him. "It's my job to protect you guys. But if the worst had happened, there would have been nothing I could do."

We watched the Beirut car bomb footage together, and he held me as I cried. I had a suitcase of Mandarin and Arabic books and while he never mentioned it, I knew he would never want to study those languages again.

We'd given up on China because of our own circumstances

and had to leave Beirut because of a situation out of our control. Spanish started to feel like the promised land. I had faith in this language project, but my husband's was shaken. I wanted to take him somewhere that would definitely, without fail, work. *It had to work.* If we found ourselves packing our bags at midnight again, I didn't know what Drew would do. I had painted this vision of our future together, learning these languages, traveling to exciting (but not too exciting!) locales, having the time of our lives. It was about time I delivered.

Drew left the decisions of where to have the baby and where to learn Spanish up to me, and dove into life in Thailand: hammocks, good spicy food, and cable TV. The electricity always worked, the showers were hot, there was fast and plentiful Internet, and while there were social and political problems, in this year at least, no one was burning American flags.

I kept a low profile in my research this time and skipped the whiteboards. No index cards. No Language Learning HQ. Just me, on my laptop, pretending to surf online, while I actually Googled "birth story [insert country name]." I found out that if you have a baby in Mexico, you can apply for dual citizenship for your child. In some countries, this dual citizenship also gives you a direct path as a family to obtain long-term residency visas.

"Hey, Drew, if we have the baby in Argentina, we could *at any point* live in Argentina long-term."

"That's cool," Drew responded without looking up from his computer screen.

"Do you want to live in Argentina?" I asked tentatively.

"I don't know."

"What about Peru?"

"What's in Peru?"

"I think you can go skiing there during August."

"Okay."

He wasn't going to engage; I could plan to have the baby in a hut on the Amazon and he'd go along with it at this point. He wasn't going to get excited. He wasn't going to help plan. He was just going to carry the luggage from Thailand to wherever I chose because right now that was all he could handle thinking about. I knew when he got like this he just needed time. He couldn't process all the change—most of all leaving Beirut so suddenly—so he packed it all away for later. Instead he caught up on episodes of *The Walking Dead* and ate plate after plate of *pad kra pao gai*, a super spicy chicken stir-fry with basil served over jasmine rice—his favorite Thai comfort food.

Finally, I started thinking about Mexico. A friend put me in touch with a couple who'd had their two children in Puerto Vallarta, a beach town on the Pacific coast of Mexico, with a doctor they loved. I e-mailed them. They gushed. The doctor was great, the hospital was top-notch, and the whole birth cost less than $3,000. I was sold.

"Drew, what about Mexico?" I tried again.

"Okay," he said, with the same minimal enthusiasm.

"No, really this time. It will be super easy, we'll get six months as tourists so we won't have to constantly make visa runs, and it's cheap!"

"I like cheap," he said cautiously.

"They have tacos!"

"I like tacos." He looked up from his screen finally, and smiled.

WE FINALLY TOLD DREW'S PARENTS about the baby. Drew's relationship with them had been fading for years, but I was stubbornly trying to keep them in the loop. I would remind Drew about birthdays, Mother's Day, and anniversaries. Even then, he seemed reluctant to reach out to them, and the silence grew longer and longer. His mother sent a daily e-mail to Drew with a piece of scripture in it, but other than that they had little contact. They never asked about his life, and the only time they made contact with me was to ask why Drew hadn't responded to their latest e-mail.

When I mentioned that we'd be having the baby in Mexico, Drew's mother wrote back immediately: "PLEASE don't go to Mexico." I was a little shocked—we had just been in Beirut! Was Mexico really more dangerous than the Middle East?—but Drew just shrugged. Still, I told his mom that the area we were moving to, Puerto Vallarta, was one of the safest in Mexico. It had a comparable crime rate to Hartford, Connecticut. It was safer than Miami. However, she was unconvinced. She wrote, "I wish I could show you a clip from the *O'Reilly Factor*. He warns people when they could be in mortal danger. He says, 'Don't drive, don't do anything in the country of Mexico.' If you can get ahold of a clip from this segment, please do."

In response I sent her photos of the sweeping coastline, white sand beaches, blue ocean, the landscape dotted with resorts and beach umbrellas. I tried to explain that Puerto Vallarta was not the same as the borderlands—millions of American tourists went to Puerto Vallarta and Cancún every year without incident. Eventually she stopped bringing it up. We pressed on with our plan to have the baby in Mexico.

From Thailand, Drew flew to Seattle, where it was easy to establish residency, thanks to our mailbox there, to buy a car and take his driver's test (his previous license had expired). He failed the driving test the first time because he forgot for a moment where he was and started to drive on the left side of the road. Oops, too much time spent in Asia! A few weeks later, I would fly with Cole from Thailand to L.A. to meet up with Drew and drive across the border to Mexico together through Arizona.

On the flight over, Cole and I had a six-hour layover in Shanghai. The airport was freezing cold, and I paid $7 for an orange juice. I found a corner of the airport that was empty, and I lay down with Cole to get a little sleep after our long flight from Thailand. Two Chinese women came over and sat next to us. There were twelve rows of empty seats on all sides, but instead of picking a spot anywhere else in the nearly empty gate, they plopped down next to Cole and me. After watching us for a few moments, they offered some advice in Mandarin. I didn't understand them, but their miming made their meaning clear: *Hey, lady, put your child's shoes back on.* One of them reached over and grabbed Cole's foot and frowned. Cold. My baby's feet were cold. What kind of mother was I? (The kind that has a son who already kicked off his shoes three times in a row before I gave up.) I stared at them blankly. They stared back.

Oh, China.

I was too pregnant, tired, and achy to argue, so I did it. Cole immediately kicked his shoes off again. *See!* I thought, and walked off with Cole to the gift shop to buy him a tiny stuffed panda bear. We ran into a couple with a son about Cole's age, and they were very excited to tell me that they were teaching him English. "It's a very important language," they told me.

I smiled. How bizarre is the world when there's a doppel-ganger family just like mine, but also the opposite. It was so easy to be annoyed by things like the price of orange juice or curious old ladies, but then you were reminded: Everything was a miracle. I was in Shanghai, pregnant, traveling with my tod-dler son, and talking to a Chinese couple about their child learn-ing English. This was my life.

Their child was adorable. I leaned down and said, "Ni hao."

DREW PICKED ME UP at LAX after a customs officer took pity on me, a pregnant lady with a squirming toddler, and let me skirt the line (a long line of Chinese nationals pushing carts filled with foodstuffs from home). I stretched out in the front seat of our new-to-us minivan, a 1994 Dodge Caravan, that de-spite being old as dirt ran fairly well. Cole was in the back, in a car seat, something he hadn't experienced since we left the United States after he was born. He fell asleep almost instantly.

We drove south and crossed Arizona, heading for Nogales,

the border check that we had heard was one of the safest. The entire way, I monitored every baby kick, ache, and headache with a silent prayer: *Please do not go into labor before we get into Mexico.* I was still two months away from my due date, but my lack of U.S. insurance meant that an emergency before the border could bankrupt us. I felt feverish just before we crossed into Mexico, so we stayed an extra night in Arizona. *No, no, no,* I thought. But the extra sleep helped. I just couldn't travel as fast and hard when pregnant, even though I was just sitting. The long days in the car were taking their toll.

The next day we crossed the border. We drove straight through, waved into the country without so much as a word. Drew and I just looked at each other. Huh. There were ten miles of border town, packed with shopping, seedy and dirty. We kept driving. In Sonora we crossed the Mexican side of the border, where we were waved through once again. Beyond that it was just open scrub desert, with cactus and sage bushes, mountains in the background, yellow grass, and green bushes. It was beautiful.

We got lunch at a taco place with an asada restaurant on the side of the highway. It featured a large barbecue grill with wood chips laid over the coals, sending up plumes of fragrant smoke. We paid $1.25 for two large orders of tacos, complete with slices of lime and grilled green onions, and balanced our plates on the dashboard and ate as we drove.

That night we stayed in a cute town called Hermosillo. It reminded me of a smaller Dallas. We rested in an extra-large hotel room, where I collapsed into bed and Drew brought me tortilla soup from the restaurant next door, with fresh avocados—so deliciously ripe and vibrantly green that I almost forgot my sore legs and swollen ankles.

The next morning we had chilaquiles for breakfast, and Drew officially fell in love with Mexico. Chilaquiles are fried strips of tortillas covered in salsa, cheese, and crema, served with a side of scrambled eggs or grilled meat.

"Oh my God," Drew said, scraping his plate down with his fork. "You're going to make this for me every day, right?"

"Absolutely. If nothing else, we will eat well in Mexico, that's for sure."

The next day we landed in San Blas, after a dreary twelve-hour drive. The scenery was beautiful, and the beach looked ripe for development. Did we find a hidden treasure in Mexico? After we checked out of our hotel room, we walked the beach, carrying our flip-flops in our hands. Within five minutes, I understood why San Blas was a relative ghost town. We were being eaten alive.

I reached down and scratched my ankles. There were a dozen red bite marks.

"Drew, are you getting bitten?"

"Nope."

He never got bitten. I was always the one being attacked by mosquitoes, sand fleas, or whatever the hell was munching on me now.

"What is that? I can't see anything. What's biting me?"

"Let me see," he said, and bent down to inspect my legs.

"Holy crap, Christine," he said, rubbing my ankle as if he could erase the damage.

"Okay, let's go."

"Right."

We drove the twisting jungle road down the coast until it broke open just north of Puerto Vallarta. There it was, Banderas Bay, the sweeping shoreline of so many postcards. It was Christmas morning. We had made it.

Drew gazed at the gorgeous scenery for a moment. "Okay, so now I'm excited," he said.

"Good!" I took his hand. "Merry Christmas, honey."

PART 3

MEXICO

Mexico is about the size of the lower forty-eight states in the United States, if you chop off the West Coast. Good-bye, California, Oregon, and Washington. The vastness of the country is important to note, because while my mother-in-law was deeply concerned about our travel in Mexico, there is a lot of distance between, say, Tijuana and Mexico City. It was the equivalent of being worried about Texas wildfires when you lived in New Jersey. Yes, it was all the same country, but just like the United States, in a way, it wasn't. The different regions varied as much in their food, culture, and history as New York City did from Atlanta.

We were staying in the Puerto Vallarta area, a part of Mexico that first crossed into American pop culture with Elizabeth Taylor's 1964 film *The Night of the Iguana*, based on the Tennessee Williams play. Richard Burton bought Taylor a home in a part of town known as Gringo Gulch, perched above the bay near the Río Cuale. Burton bought the house across the street for himself, which made sense, since the couple was famous for fighting. They constructed a bridge to communicate the two buildings, allowing them to reach each other's homes without entering the street and facing the paparazzi. The homes had since been sold, but the bridge was still there, known as the Lover's Arch. After the film came out, Puerto Vallarta went from small fishing village to solidified tourist zone. It has never been the same since.

We spent the week between Christmas and New Year's Eve in the Romantic Zone, the old town, a strange juxtaposition between quaint cobblestone streets, hotels, and shops selling the traditional Jalisco *escaramuza* dress and obnoxious tequila hawkers who accosted you as you walked the Malecón. The other people in the Romantic Zone were mostly other tourists, holding up their iPads to take pictures and sporting the bright pink sunburns of those who had only recently arrived. We drove around with a real estate agent who pointed out apartments above storefronts and gave us tours of massive condominiums. We ate tacos. So many tacos, from the *birria*-filled tacos served only in the morning (a hangover cure, we were told) to tacos al pastor (notably the same cooking technique as in Lebanon) to fish tacos breaded and deep-fried to order, while a woman used a heavy wooden press to flatten out masa in the shape of tortillas. We found the *tortillería* (literally the tortilla shop), which was a small storefront that ground masa and toasted fresh tortillas on a conveyor belt. For $1 you could get a dozen tortillas. There were also butchers; most interesting to us were the ones that butchered whole pigs and deep fried them bit by bit, making *carnitas* that you could buy by the kilo or *chicharrón* (fried pig skin) that you could dip in guacamole. We ate and ate, and we looked for a place to live.

Beyond Puerto Vallarta, there was Nuevo Vallarta, the expat haven, and farther from that were Bucerías, La Cruz de Huanacaxtle, Punta de Mita, Sayulita, and San Francisco (known locally as San Pancho—Pancho is the Spanish nickname for Francisco). The expat scene was strong throughout, but it changed in each place. There were retirees, sailors, hippies, dropouts, and volunteers. Cirque de Soleil cocreator Gilles Ste-Croix started a community and volunteer program in San Pancho that taught local kids everything from English to how to do trapeze. Each place had its own feel.

The biggest challenge was to figure out where we belonged, with a keen eye on picking a place that best supported our aim of learning Spanish. In Puerto Vallarta, despite its charms—and the food—I figured we'd get annoyed with the constant flow of tourists, even if we tucked ourselves far away from the beach. Plus everyone spoke English. One day at lunch, I swore our waiter was American. He had a California accent.

"Where are you from?" I asked.

"Here," he said.

"Always? You grew up here?"

"Yup."

But, I reminded myself, this was not China or Lebanon. We weren't learning Mandarin or Arabic, difficulty level 5 languages where we'd need 24/7 immersion. This was Spanish, a level 1 language, among the easiest to learn for English speakers. Spanish is phonetic. What you read is what you say. It uses the Roman alphabet. There's no split between the written and spoken language, and it's not tonal. After Mandarin and Arabic, I felt a certain calm. *I've got this. I can do this.*

After so many months of studying languages, now it seemed crystal clear what my approach would be: Speak it as much as possible. Hire a tutor. Write in Spanish. Read in Spanish. Spend as much of my time using the language as possible, because while I had a huge "comprehensible input" curve to overcome at first in Mandarin and Arabic, getting to the point where I could speak some Spanish, have it spoken back to me, and understand it seemed like child's play.

Nonetheless, we fired our real estate agent, who seemed obsessed with putting us as close to the tourist zone as possible. His English was flawless but—maybe from so many years of filling vacation homes—he couldn't understand why we'd want to live somewhere more remote, with the locals. The locals didn't live in the *nice* areas, he told us as we showed him the door.

One morning, I sat on our hotel bed with my laptop, the early-morning sunlight cutting across the dark room, and refreshed the online listings yet again. Cole slept next to me, his body so long now, his baby fat melting away. He looked more like a toddler than ever. His hair was sticking to his forehead a little; he always sweated when sleeping. Drew was out hunting down breakfast, queso fresco and fresh tortillas. Just then I noticed a new listing, maybe fifteen minutes old, just published, for a three-bedroom house north of Puerto Vallarta in Bucerías. It was so cheap, $425 a month, that I doubted it would be any good, but I clicked the link anyway. The ad was filled with pictures of a teal-colored one-story home, made out of concrete in the traditional Mexican style. It had a gate around the property and a garden that was even bigger than the house.

Drew walked in the door, quietly placing his bags on the table by the door so as to not wake Cole.

"Drew," I whispered, "come here."

He looked at the photos on the screen. "Oooh, that looks good."

"I know." I wrote the phone number for the listing on a sticky note and handed it to Drew. "Go call him and drive up there now."

"Right now?" Drew looked longingly at the bags of food.

"Yes! He just posted it. We can't lose it. Go see it and sign the contract."

He took the note out of my hand. "Okay!"

Later that day, signed contract and keys in hand, we drove up the coast to Bucerías. The highway that runs through Bucerías divides the town in two. On the left are the ocean and resorts, with cobblestone streets like in the Romantic Zone, but also vacation rentals and souvenir shops. On the right is a neighborhood with dirt roads. We took a right turn into our new neighborhood with a thud as the minivan bottomed out. We inched along, issuing up plumes of dust behind us. It was a ghost town. There were no tourists here, just the homes of locals, all one- or two-story buildings with a large gate around each one. There were *tiendas*, little backyard bars. A paddock with an ancient-looking horse. We continued driving, navigating over a small bridge that crossed a dry ditch. A school. Signs for an orphanage. More houses.

Finally we arrived at our new home, lined with a redbrick fence and several massive bougainvillea trees pouring fuchsia, white, and yellow flowers over the wall from within the garden. The owner, Pablo, opened the gate and we drove in.

"¡Hola!" he said in a thick American accent.

We learned that his real name was Paul, but since moving to Mexico two decades ago and marrying a Mexican woman, he had adopted the Spanish version of his name.

"Here, let me show you the garden," he said, and I rubbed my belly while following him. "These are the mango trees. That's avocado over there. There's guayaba, I forget what it's called in English, it's really good in smoothies, though, and this is jaka—which is—"

"Jackfruit?" I offered, recognizing the brown spiky fruit from Asia. These were bigger than footballs, but I had seen them the size of a large dog when fully grown.

"Yeah, yeah, probably," said Pablo. He showed us more—there were cherries and limes, hibiscus flowers, and the ever-present bougainvilleas that framed the entire yard. Then, "Come inside!"

The interior was dim. There were no lights on, just slowly spinning fans overhead. The floor was laid with cool tile, and the kitchen had a massive bar for prepping food. There was just one bathroom that was fed warm water from the propane water heater outside. There was a separate house, a little bodega for doing laundry, and a third little house for storage.

"I call the house La Casa de las Ollas de Frijoles," said Pablo, showing us around. "I built it myself. It was my first house with my wife, but she wanted something bigger, so now we live on the other side of the highway."

"Why is it called La Casa de las Ollas de Frijoles?" Drew asked.

"Here, let me show you. See those? The bean pots on the corners of the gate? I put those there. It's the bean pot house. Ollas de Frijoles."

Pablo eyed my belly. "When are you due?"

"In two months."

"Oh, I should introduce you to Rosa," he said. "She can help you with the house."

Before I could answer, he led us out of the gate and rang the neighbor's doorbell. "¡Buenos días! ¿Está Rosa aquí?" he shouted into the house, then turned to me, "Rosa doesn't speak English, but she has been looking after the house while I fixed it up for renting."

Rosa came downstairs, smiling, and greeted Pablo. She had dark curly hair and was one of those beautiful women who could be anywhere between thirty and fifty years old.

"Er, Rosa, ella necesita ayudar con el jardín and para limpiar la casa," he said, and then not realizing I knew at least a little Spanish, he translated, "I told her you need help with the cleaning."

Rosa started talking in rapid Spanish, and I could pick out a few things: "Okay, bueno. ¿Cuántos días a la semana? ¿Cuántas horas? ¿Qué día? No puedo trabajar los viernes."

Pablo paused. "Er . . ."

Wait, he's been in Mexico for twenty years and he doesn't speak Spanish fluently? I thought. *He has a Mexican wife!*

"Ella va a tener un bebé," Pablo said. *She's going to have a baby.*

He could say Spanish words to Rosa, but he wasn't understanding what she was saying back. It seemed like every experience I had in Beijing. I could say things but never had a clue what people were saying to me. But this time something else was happening for me: I was suddenly remembering Spanish. I hadn't studied it in years, but hearing the word *viernes* and remembering that that meant Friday unlocked some days-of-the-week memory I had stored deep in my brain from high school Spanish, or maybe my time in Guatemala.

I took an uncertain step forward. "¿Lunes, miércoles y jueves?" I asked. *Monday, Wednesday, and Thursday?*

"Sí," Rosa said, addressing me with relief.

"¿Cuatro horas cada día?" I offered meekly, not sure if I had it right (*four hours each day*).

"Sí."

"Y ¿cuánto cuesta?" I said. *How much?*

"Em . . . tres cientos," Rosa replied after a moment.

"Okay."

Pablo looked pleased. We said our good-byes and I tried to quickly calculate how much three hundred pesos would be . . .

was that $24 a week? Did I just hire a helper for $2 an hour? It seemed impossible.

We headed back inside and Pablo spent the next three hours showing Drew how everything worked. He didn't want to say good-bye. This house was his baby. On the front of the house were two doves, hand-painted by Pablo, a gesture to his wife. "They are her favorite."

Finally he left. Drew and I sank into the couch with glee while Cole played contentedly in the garden. We had done it. A little house on the coast in Mexico, in a neighborhood where our neighbors didn't speak English and there wasn't a tourist to be found.

Now we just had to have this baby.

Twenty-two

D r. Laura wore a white lab coat over her skinny jeans and fitted top. Her high heels clicked on the tile floor as she led us to her office.

We were back in the Romantic Zone, where Dr. Laura's practice was located. While we picked a house in Bucerías, there was no hospital, so we wanted to give birth at one of the two private hospitals in Puerto Vallarta. Dr. Laura had privileges at both. It took us an hour in traffic to drive the palm-tree-lined highway that runs along the coast and past the hotel zone. Once we hit cobblestones, we knew we were close, but it was a bumpy ride and even though we stayed in the area for a week when we arrived, we still got lost. *Do we turn on Calle Aguacate (Avocado Road) or Calle Naranja (Orange Tree Road)?* The stacked houses with orange tile all started to look the same. Eventually we found the *lavandería* (laundry shop) that we recognized from our days of apartment hunting, and were able to find our bearings.

Dr. Laura's practice was behind a single tinted glass door that slid open to the side. It was a small, narrow space, but there was a long hallway that brought you deeper into the building past the offices of the other doctors. I read the doctors' names and specialties as we passed and noticed she was the only ob-gyn. She stopped and turned effortlessly on the ball of one foot and waved us into a room. There was a desk with a large, sweating iced coffee sitting next to a computer monitor and a few medical charts. Other than the charts, it felt like a home office, lightly decorated with some personal effects. The only truly medical aspect was the brightly lit adjoining room with a paper-covered table and stirrups.

She called across the office to her receptionist in the lobby in Spanish, then crossed the room, took her two cell phones and placed them on her desk, sat down, and pulled out a file.

There was a pause and I briefly panicked. *Wait, are we going to do this in Spanish?*

But Dr. Laura said in English, "So you are going to have a baby! Congratulations!"

"Yes!" I breathed a sigh of relief.

She started writing. "So how many pregnancies have you had?"

"One."

"Em, what about him?" she asked, pointing to Cole, who was sitting on Drew's lap.

"Oh right, *right*, yes, two. Sorry, I'm still adjusting to the idea that I'm pregnant again." Drew and I laughed.

"And how was his birth?"

"It was fine. Well, I went over my dates; I went to forty weeks, five days, and then my blood pressure went up. I had preeclampsia, so we did a C-section. They did a biophysical profile and he wasn't moving, so they rushed us to surgery." I paused on the phrase *biophysical profile* . . . would she know what I meant? Was there a difference between American and Mexican medical terms? I hadn't even thought of that.

But Dr. Laura was unfazed. "Okay, we will have to keep an eye on that," she said, taking notes.

"I would like to try for a VBAC," I told her, shifting Cole onto my lap. I stopped to see if she'd understood the term, which stood for *vaginal birth after C-section*, but she didn't even flinch.

"I am okay with that. We will keep an eye on it, but if there are too many red lights, then we will stop and do a C-section. I won't let it go too far." I noticed her use the phrase "red lights" instead of "red flags"—even though her English seemed terrific, she hadn't quite nailed that idiom.

She took down more of my medical history, asked about my diet, vitamins, all the usual things, and then said, "Okay, let's go see your baby!" and we clicked our way deeper into the warren of offices and anterooms.

The ultrasound machine was impressive. It filled most of the room, and on the wall was a large flat-screen TV where the images were shown. It was all much bigger, more advanced, and

more impressive than what I'd experienced when I'd been pregnant with Cole in Seattle. I lay down and she covered my belly
in goop, then moved the wand around until she found the baby.
After she did the measurements, she switched to 4-D mode,
which gave me a 3-D view of what my baby looked like inside
me, like a little sepia snapshot taken inside my womb.

"Do you want to know the gender?"

"Yes, it's a girl, right?"

"Yes, you're going to have a little girl," she told me, and even
though I already knew, I teared up.

"Look, Cole, you're going to have a sister," Drew said.

"That's the baby, look," I said, turning my head so I could
make eye contact while lying on the ultrasound table. But Cole
was playing with a model uterus and didn't look up.

At the end of the appointment, Dr. Laura instructed us to
schedule a follow-up with her receptionist, then gave me a kiss
on each cheek as we said good-bye. She squeezed my hand. I
liked her. She was so professional, thorough, and warm. It was
the most comfortable I had ever felt with a health provider.

My friends back home were a little surprised that I was having the baby in Mexico. "Wow" was the polite version, "Ooh, I
could never do that" was a little more direct, and they said
"What?!" if they were feeling particularly bold. If I didn't
know, I would feel the same way. They were probably imagin-
ing some dusty Mexican town with a free clinic that was dirty
and ill equipped. But so far my experience was far from that. It
wasn't the same massive practice I was used to, with dozens of
chairs in the waiting room and wall-to-wall carpet. And cer-

tainly there were free clinics in Mexico that are not the same as my experience with Dr. Laura. But when it came down to what mattered—the care I received, the doctor's manner, the quality of the equipment—I felt more like one of those Park Slope moms in New York City who could afford to hire a doctor out of pocket, getting the high-end attention and treatment that simply wasn't available to those using health insurance and providers rushing from patient to patient.

As we paid and scheduled our next visit, Dr. Laura came out to the lobby to meet us.

"I almost forgot. Here is my cell phone number. Call me anytime."

As we walked back to the car, Drew said to me, "Whoa."

"I know, right? She's awesome."

"Unbelievable."

We were going to have our baby in Mexico.

EVERYTHING WAS FALLING into place with such ease it felt unreal. We had rented the three-bedroom bean pot house. The hibiscus plants and flowering bougainvillea attracted hummingbirds, which darted past me as I sat out on the veranda to write and watched Cole pedal around on his new tricycle. The sweet smell of fruit and flowers suffused the air, and little geckos climbed the walls.

All my old knowledge of Spanish was flooding back. It felt exactly like running into an old friend and reminiscing about the old days, and they remind you of something and you say,

"Oh right, we went to that three-day festival that year, I had totally forgotten that." Things I hadn't thought about in years became fresh in my mind. The more words I remembered, the more they unlocked other vocabulary.

Plus, in many ways, being in Mexico was just easier than being in China or Lebanon had been. In part, that was because I had relaxed my ideas about the idea of "authentic travel." In Beijing, I had avoided the websites and expat groups that would have made my transition easier. I hadn't wanted to be one of those Americans who moved overseas and sequestered themselves in the American bubble wherever they lived. I had heard stories of Americans living in China for a decade and still not speaking Mandarin.

But I decided I had been wrong about it being a binary choice. My options weren't either "eat McDonald's and only speak English" or "pretend I am thirteenth-century explorer Marco Polo with no access to familiar things or people from my own culture." There was a middle way. In Mexico, I could focus on speaking Spanish and still shop at Walmart. I could get to know the owner of the little vegetable stand near my house and inquire in Spanish about whether the avocados were ripe yet, but also get a reference from the expat group on where to find a good dentist.

I went from being a travel purist, trying to find meaning in the aesthetic of unassisted travel, to being a travel realist, using the tools at my disposal to get the logistics out of the way so I could get to the important stuff—speaking the language, adapting to local life—faster. The less time I spent bumbling around looking in all the wrong places for allergy medicine, instead of just asking friends about which pharmacies sold my brand, the more time I could focus on what really mattered.

In essence, I gave up on getting style points. Sure, it was romantic to think about going to Mexico and furnishing my new house with things bought at the Saturday market from an old woman with a weathered face and a selection of hand-crafted brooms—or I could just go to the local big-box mega-store, pick up a broom (made in China), mop (also made in China), and some cleaning products (imported from the United States), and be done with it. After all, that's what the locals did, too.

Still, it was surreal to drive down the highway, leaving our dusty Mexican neighborhood behind, and choose between several giant grocery stores—a Costco, three Walmarts, or three Sam's Clubs—all within a thirty-minute radius of one another. And while the street-food culture was strong, so was the fast-food one. There were American brands like McDonald's, Burger King, Subway, KFC, and Church's Chicken, but there were also Mexican brands like Pollo Feliz, El Pechugón, El Pollo Pepe, and OXXO (a convenience store that also sold fast food). We didn't eat in those places. We didn't even feel the temptation to do so, not when we could walk out of our house and find a small army of taco stands, small restaurants, and street-food vendors serving freshly made tacos, soups, and more sit-down-style meals featuring chiles rellenos (stuffed peppers) or pollo asado (chicken cooked over charcoal).

Living where we lived, we could spend our time in either a

Mexican bubble or an American bubble. If we kept to our neighborhood, the portion of town we lived in, it was exactly the life we were looking for: local, authentic, and tourist-free. When we ventured back toward Puerto Vallarta, we had to travel through the hinterlands of strip malls, casinos, American fast food, and endless hotels and resorts. You could have any kind of life you wanted here, and we knew which kind we wanted.

IT BEGAN JUST BEFORE DAWN. The roosters in our neighbor's yard would wake up, stretch their legs, and sing out their morning song at a volume that cut straight through our windows, as if the birds were in the room with us. I know that in English, the sound-word is "cock-a-doodle-do," but in reality it sounded more like "CAAH CAHHH CAHHH CAAAAAAAAAH!"

Then Rosa's dogs would bark. She kept them on her roof at night, a half-dozen chihuahuas that kept perfectly quiet unless there was a car, a person, a horse, a sound, or a whisper of wind. Then they leapt to the end of the roof and barked down in the direction of the offense. All six tiny dogs would bark in unison for a few minutes, then quiet down and stand guard, alert, for a few moments longer until satisfied, and then they would collapse on the cool tile until their next call to action.

"Good morning," Drew said to me sleepily.

Our room was dim, with just the faintest light filtering through the flower-patterned curtains. The sun came up on the other side of the house. It was cool, chilly almost, and we were wrapped in a thick comforter we'd bought at Costco.

"What time is it?" I asked, not really wanting to know the answer.

"Uh," Drew said, searching under his pillow for the phone. "It's almost seven."

"Oh God, okay," I said, rolling over to my other side. My belly was round and warm. I could feel the baby's little feet in my ribs. I wanted to sleep more, but suddenly my bladder was calling.

"Help me get out of bed," I said, and Drew jumped out of bed and came over to my side. I grabbed his hand and pulled myself up with some effort. My ab muscles were stretched beyond recognition; I felt like a turtle on its back, unable to do half the things that came so effortlessly in my prepregnancy days.

"I have to pee," I said.

"I know," Drew said, turning on the light in the hallway for me. He was always like this when I was pregnant, so attentive and helpful. It was easy to get used to, to have a glass of water delivered without asking, to be offered a seat before you realized you wanted one.

Cole came out of the bedroom, hair mussed, and rubbing his eyes.

"Water?" he inquired.

"Daddy will get you some water, sweetie; go in the living room."

I walked into the bathroom and just as I finished peeing I heard it, the telltale sound of a *vendedor* coming up the street. He would drive slowly down the street and either shout out his wares or more likely play a jingle from a small speaker attached to the roof of his car. This one sounded like this: "*Vita*. ¡Vita! *Vita gas*." But it was so muffled and tinny I could only guess at the words. Was that the propane guy? We were almost out.

I hopped up, as much as a nine-months-pregnant woman can hop, and called out:

"Drew! Go see!"

"What? What?" he yelled back.

I hurried over to the kitchen where he was cutting pomegranates (*granadas*) and picking out the ruby red seeds one by one.

"Is that the propane guy?" I pointed out the window.

"Oh crap! Okay, hold on," Drew said, then ran out of the house barefoot, unlocked the gate, closed it behind him, and hobbled painfully over rocks and dirt to chase the maybe-propane guy.

Five minutes later Drew came back.

"Was it him?" I asked as he crossed the courtyard.

"I don't know, I couldn't catch him. I was yelling and waving at him, but he just kept driving." Drew walked over to me and touched my belly.

"How's the baby?" he asked.

I moved his hand to where she was kicking. "There. Feel that?"

"Ooh, yes. Wow. How does that feel?"

"Like I have a very small ninja in my belly who is trying to get out by stomping on my spleen."

Drew laughed and kissed me.

"It's okay about the propane guy, he'll be back. You just have to be quicker!"

"I know, I should just wear my shoes all the time."

Fifteen minutes later another *vendedor* came. Drew and I ran out into the courtyard to listen. Cole came bounding behind us.

"What is that? Tortillas? I can't even hear what he's saying." Drew said.

"Go look!" I said, pushing him toward the gate.

Five minutes later Drew came back with a handful of empanadas.

"Holy crap, I could get used to this," Drew said, stuffing one in his mouth. "Mm-hmmm," I said, rubbing my belly absentmindedly. I wanted to take a shower, but without a new propane tank it was unlikely we had enough gas to heat the water.

Mooooooooooooooo! came a new noise from the street.

"What was that?" Drew asked, looking around.

Moooooooooooooooo!

"Go look!"

Drew ran out the gate again and had a hasty conversation with the driver in front of our house. He was driving a small pickup truck and in the back was a large silver container that looked somewhat like a giant propane tank.

When Drew returned, he was empty-handed. "Raw milk, I think." He sat down.

The weather was so agreeable that we had moved our couch to the outside of the house, along with our kitchen table. There was a large outdoor room with tile floors and a roof that opened up into the garden and courtyard. We could work and watch

Cole as he played at the same time. Plus we could keep an eye out for more *vendedores*.

There were so many. The *vendedores* would come down the street, playing their song. The roosters would crow, the dogs would bark hysterically, and we'd listen intently to try to make out what was being sold. Corn. Tortillas. Water. Tacos. Newspapers.

Then someone on a horse would ride by. At least twice a day. He was most likely taking his horse down to the beach to sell rides to the tourists, then returning to his house for lunch or a siesta. It wasn't always the same guy, but the outfit was the same: the straw cowboy hat, denim jeans no matter how hot it was, and a thick belt buckle. The dogs would lose their minds, barking and climbing over one another trying to get as close to the horse as possible.

Every day around noon, Rosa turned on her music. It drifted out of her courtyard into ours. The vocal stylings of Celine Dion were on heavy rotation. I couldn't be sure, but sometimes I thought I heard her singing along, "My heart will go on. . . ."

Finally, the gas guy. I heard it better this time. It wasn't Vita Gas, it was Zeta. "*Zeta.* ¡Zeta! *Zeta Gas.*"

"Drew! Quick!"

Drew ran outside the gate and waved the guy down. He had already passed our house, but no bother, the driver just put the truck in reverse and drove backward down our street. Drew talked to the guy and soon the *vendedor* came into our yard with a giant yellow cylinder, walked expertly to the back of the house, pulled out the special wrench that fits the propane tank bolt, and swapped out the tank, taking the old one with him. $25. Done.

"That wasn't too bad," Drew said, and joined me on the couch, where I was curled up with my laptop.

I gave him a kiss and returned to my writing.

Rosa turned off Celine. Our other neighbors, the ones to the left of us, was having a party and turned up their ranchero music. A rooster crowed. The dogs barked. Cole ran around the yard with his *Star Wars* light saber yelling, "Arrrrrgggggghhhh!"

Whatever you could say about this place, we definitely weren't in China anymore.

Twenty-three

Jorge, wearing a button-down shirt and khakis, wrote on the whiteboard, in his tiny office space. He was giving me a group Spanish lesson, but I was the only one who arrived on time. The group changed constantly but was mostly women in their forties or early fifties who had moved to Mexico from the United States or Canada to retire young, live cheaply, and enjoy the beautiful Pacific coast. When the group was all there, we focused on basic things like prepositions: on top of, behind, in front of, next to, and across (*encima*, *detrás*, *delante*, *al lado*, and *a través*). But when it was just the two of us, he focused on my pronunciation.

Today he was writing out all the vowel sounds. Vowels were my sticking point in Spanish. I was always saying them wrong. In English, we have long and short vowel sounds. For example, the *a* in *cake* is long and the *a* in *hat* is short. It's the silent *e* at the end of *cake* that tells us to not pronounce it like *cak* but instead to draw it out as *caaaake*. In Spanish, however, each vowel is pronounced exactly one way—and it doesn't matter what follows later in the word.

Unwittingly, and often despite my best intentions, my internalized English rules were interfering with my Spanish pronunciation. I kept amending my pronunciation based on the letters later in the word. I was having a hard time suppressing whatever underlying system made those on-the-fly decisions, and it kept bubbling up, even though on a conscious, logical level, I knew how to pronounce things in Spanish.

On top of that, I also have a regional accent in English, perhaps not totally detectable to everyone, but there's something of a Boston accent hidden in there, which makes it even more difficult (I grew up dropping my *r*'s and saying things like "Pahk the cah in Hahvad Yahd"—and if it wasn't clear, that's "Park the car in Harvard Yard"). The accent is mostly gone, I think, but I still mumble and swallow syllables.

What a mess.

In Spanish, this meant when I said *para* (which is pronounced *pah-rah*, I was actually saying something closer to *pair-a*. The Spanish *pa* and *ra* sounds are short and the same length. *Pa. Ra.* Big wide open mouth for each. My brain was sloppily insisting that I utter instead a long *pair* sound with a short *a*. *Pair-a*. The sounds were wrong, the cadence was wrong, it was all just wrong, wrong, wrong. I knew it, and I would catch it sometimes, but on new words? I would slip into old habits.

The kicker was that it also changed the meaning. *Para* in

Spanish means "for." *Pera*, the word I was actually saying, means "pear."

Poor Jorge. If I said, "Este libro es para ti" (*This book is for you*), it came out sounding like *This book is pear you.*

I could just imagine Jorge's thought process: *Pear? Pear? What pear?*

What other monstrosities had I cooked up with my poor pronunciation? It must have been pretty bad because Jorge was once again stopping to do a vowel drill.

He wrote the word LALA on the board.

"LA-LA," he said, emphasizing the wide-open mouth of each syllable.

Then he wrote the full list:

LALA
LELA
LILA
LOLA
LULA

For each of those, he also changed the second vowel:

LALA
LALE
LALI
LALO
LALU

At the end, he had a five-by-five grid on the whiteboard of every combination of vowel sounds. He had me say them all out loud, and I struggled to hold back my urge to pronounce LALE with the silent *e* at the end (like my English-trained brain assumed) and with a long *a*.

"LA-LE," I said with some effort.

It was like having mental hiccups, going over the list and finding the rough spots. The faster I said them, the more those errant English controls would take over and steer me off course. I felt like I was trying to block out club music blaring in one ear while trying to read a book. It could be done, but I was constantly distracted and had to spend so much energy to suppress the noise.

But like sandpaper over rough wood, with practice, I was wearing down the rough spots. I needed that Spanish reflex, the unthinking, unquestioned response to a Spanish word that just made the right sound tumble out of my mouth. I needed muscle memory. Jorge was helping me get it.

Just then, two students walked in. One was in her late sixties and wearing a sundress; the other was in her forties, blond, wearing a tank top and bejeweled flip-flops.

"¡*Hola*, Jorge! Sorry we're late," the younger woman sang as they took their seats.

"Buenas tardes. ¿Ustedes traen su tarea?" *Do you have your homework?* Jorge asked.

"Um . . ." The blond woman shuffled through her papers.

"Sí, pero no tuve mucho tiempo para estudiar y . . . um . . .

entonces . . . no tengo todo," *Yes, but I didn't have much time to study, and, um, so, I don't have it all*, she said as she flattened out half a piece of paper on the table.

Nonplussed, Jorge smoothed back his jet-black hair and started the lesson. Today we would be learning about Spanish idioms.

"'Echar agua al mar,'" he began. "¿Qué crees que eso significa?" *What do you think this means?*

"To hit? To strike? Water at the sea?" the older woman offered.

"Close. 'To throw water at the sea,'" he said. "Pero ¿qué signfica eso?" *But what does that mean?*

"Para hacer algo cualquier no tiene un cambio?" I said, not totally sure about my word order. *To do something that doesn't create a change?*

"Sí, muy bien, Cristina," he said, changing my name to the Spanish. "Significa hacer algo que no tiene ningún efecto. No tiene sentido." *It means to do something that has no effect. It makes no sense.*

Was that what I was doing? Was I dumping bucket after bucket of water into the sea? Could I ever change my brain to slide into Spanish a little easier, to stop this feeling of running through mud? Or would I be like the other students in my group, treading water for months, maybe years, inching along the vast highway of language learning, the end nowhere in sight, finding myself a year from now, or two, or three, sitting in a classroom like this, with these same students, or students just like them, learning the textbook expressions and canned vocabulary of some other teacher, who had taught and failed dozens of identical students like us before?

Did Jorge have a single fluent student? I wondered. I didn't ask. I didn't want to know. I put my head down and wrote the words *Echar agua al mar* in my notebook. Next to it I wrote: *To throw water into the sea. Pointless.*

WHILE I WAS AT CLASS, Drew would stay home with Cole, who went a little stir-crazy during the day. The sun got so hot from midmorning until evening that the streets would empty. Cole would find things to do. He'd ride his bike around the house, play with bubbles on the cool tile of the veranda, or chase Drew around with a sword. Then Drew and Cole would come in the creaky old Dodge Caravan and pick me up at school.

"¡Hola, Cole!" I said, trying to use Spanish with him so he'd start picking it up.

"Mama! Park!"

There was a small park near our house, and every evening we'd walk over. It was Cole's absolute favorite thing in the world. There was a basketball court, an outdoor exercise area, and a gazebo. He'd ride his bike around and around the perimeter for as long as we'd let him. He was obsessed with riding his bike, and the only flat, paved area to do it was there. But right now it was midday and dead hot. Even the dogs were sleeping.

"Cole, no hay niños en el parque ahorita." *Cole, there're no kids in the park right now,* I said, hoping to dissuade him.

He didn't believe me. When we got back to the house, he asked again, so I walked down to the park and showed him.

"Mira, no hay niños."

"Where are the kids?"

"Colegio." *School.*

He just looked at me.

"School," I repeated in English.

"Okay, Mama," he said, and took my hand to walk back to the house.

Inside it was barely lit. We kept all the lights off, the doors wide-open, and the fans turned up to high. A soft current of air ran through the house and kept us cool enough so that we didn't need AC. Every afternoon I made lunch in the kitchen, mixing equal parts of corn flour and water to make masa, the dough used for tortillas. It was meditative to make fresh tortillas. I wrapped my tortilla press with plastic wrap, the same way I saw the ladies at the taco stand do it, so the dough wouldn't stick. I took the dough in my hand, rolled it into a ball, placed it in the middle of the press, brought down the heavy wooden block, and pressed on the lever until there was no more give. If the water and flour mixture was correct, when I lifted the handle, there would be a perfectly formed tortilla. If not, it would stick or crumble and break. I adjusted the mixture as I went until it was perfect, and then I slipped into the repetitive task of rolling, squeezing, and peeling tortillas, then toasting them on a flat skillet, known in Spanish as a *comal*.

If I was making regular tacos, I used no oil. But if I had some leftover *cochinita pibil* (slow-roasted pork with achiote), I could make *huaraches* (Spanish for "sandals"), which are oval-shaped discs topped with meat. For those, I cooked the dough in lard (known as *manteca de cerdo* or literally "pork butter"), which was sold in the supermarket in two sizes: small (about the size of a pound of butter) and large (a tub the size of a large popcorn in a movie theater). Then there was always pico de gallo, although it was known here as salsa mexicana. Though at first I'd made individual batches of pico at every mealtime, I soon bought a set of large red Tupperware buckets, not too different from what kids play with at the beach, but with plastic covers, and made giant vats of it. It was how I saw all the local women doing it, and it quickly made sense. I could chop a few dozen roma tomatoes, some onions, a bunch or two of cilantro, and some garlic, then cover it in fresh-squeezed lime juice and make enough for the week. It went on everything. An omelet for breakfast? Add some pico. Tacos? Grilled meat, fish, sandwiches, or soup? Pico, pico, pico.

We loved the combination so much that we made it every day: fresh tortillas, grilled meat, sliced avocado, pico de gallo, shredded lettuce, lime, and a little bit of habanero sauce.

It was easy to start using Spanish with Cole during these lunches. He understood everything based on the context.

"¿Más pico?" I would say, pointing to the pico de gallo.

He would nod.

"¿Quieres sandía?" I would ask, showing him watermelon.

Another nod.

For the first while he clearly understood the Spanish words

I was saying at mealtime—*agua*, *pico*, *sandía*—but he wouldn't say any of them himself. Then, one day—

"Mama, agua," Cole said to me. I just looked at Drew.

"¡Agua!" Cole said again when I didn't respond.

"¿Sí, sí, claro, un momentito, okay?" I said as I went to the fridge to get the water pitcher and fill up a cup. I handed it to Cole and he gulped it down, then handed the cup back to me and padded off to the courtyard. Drew and I just stared at each other.

"Wow, that was awesome," Drew said finally.

"He's learning Spanish! Holy crap."

We walked outside and settled on the couch. I put my feet up on Drew's lap and he absentmindedly stroked my shin.

"Well, so, what should we do? Do you think he's still learning English?" I asked him as he stared off into the garden.

"I don't know. It's great, though. It's working," he said, turning to me, "but, and no offense here, is it bad that he is going to hear most of his Spanish from someone who isn't fluent? Is he going to have an accent?"

"I don't think so," I said. "I mean, from what I've read, as long as we're in a Spanish culture, then any accent he gets from me will work itself out. Think of it like this—if someone moves to the United States from Puerto Rico at a young age, even if their parents speak absolutely terrible English, they always grow up to speak English just fine, and even have an American accent. Always. I mean you never see someone who moved there as a little kid, talking like their parents." I watched Cole dig under the jaka tree with a beach shovel. He was meticulously removing soil and placing it in a pile on the cement courtyard.

"So does that mean we have to live in Mexico forever?" Drew asked.

"I don't know. It would help, that's for sure."

The dogs started barking next door. The Jehovah's Witnesses were back, canvassing the neighborhood. It was too hot to be out walking around, but even in this heat they were dressed in crisp long-sleeve shirts and dark slacks. Drew waved to them as they passed.

"Drew! Don't wave at them! They will come visit us again!" I whisper-yelled at him.

"It's fine, they know we're not on the market. Besides, they are not here for us. They want to save Mexicans; no one goes to Mexico to save American tourists," he responded, picking up my foot and rubbing the arch.

"Anyway, when the baby comes, what should we do? Should we teach her Spanish, too?" I asked, offering him my other foot when he finished.

"Yes, I think so. Besides, she will be Mexican, after all."

He got up to check on Cole. Cole's handiwork was impressive. He was now moving the small paving stones from the retaining wall of the garden into a big pile in the middle of the courtyard.

"Hey, buddy, let's put these back, okay?" he said, picking up rocks. Then he addressed me again, "Christine, our kids are going to be bilingual! Our daughter is going to be Mexican! Stop worrying!"

It was true about the Mexican citizenship part. One of the advantages to having the baby in Mexico was that she'd pick up dual citizenship: Mexican by place of birth and American from her parents. If we wanted, she could have two passports. It also streamlined our path to permanent residency if we ever wanted to stay long-term.

Though I still struggled a bit with my vowel pronunciation, on the whole my Spanish was improving at an amazing pace. And as our language project neared completion, my thoughts kept jumping ahead to what was next. Where would we live? What languages would the kids speak? What languages would they be educated in?

"Hey, Mama!" Drew yelled to me, holding a running hose in his hand menacingly.

"No!" I said, and dove for cover. Cole cackled and ran over to me.

"Mama, Mama, Mama!" he said, crawling up on me.

"¿Qué quieres?" I asked.

"¡Agua!"

Twenty-four

I opened my eyes and looked at Cole sleeping next to me. It was one of those rare quiet moments, just after the roosters stopped crowing their early-morning wake-up call, and before the vendors started hawking their wares on the street, agitating the neighborhood watchdogs, the little *perritos* who spent their days barking from the roof of Rosa's house. My belly rested heavily on its side, and the baby was wedged so tightly in my rib cage that I had almost never-ending heartburn. I stroked Cole's hair back and kissed his forehead. The baby would be coming soon. These were some of Cole's last moments as an only child and I wanted to soak them up.

After a bit, I gingerly rolled over and swung my legs out of the bed. Using my arms as my sole support, I pushed my rotund torso upright and began the hobble to the bathroom. I could hear Rosa in the kitchen, singing under her breath as she cleaned the house. She didn't talk to us much, just focused on her work, scrubbing the house down, mopping the nearly two thousand square feet of tile and sweeping the even larger courtyard and garden of the never-ending supply of fallen bougainvillea flowers. In the days she had off, the house collected dust like nothing I had seen before, the clouds of fine dirt kicked up by passing trucks floating up above our garden wall and settling everywhere. Even the windows needed to be wiped down with a wet cloth every couple of days. Combined with tending the garden, she squeezed everything she could into her weekly twelve hours, just barely getting it all done.

Thank God for Rosa, I thought every time she was there.

I made my breakfast, a fruit smoothie with milk and oatmeal. I had sworn off salt for the last trimester, in an attempt to keep my blood pressure low and avoid preeclampsia if that was possible. Still, my blood pressure was slowly rising each week at my weekly appointment with Dr. Laura. My hands and feet were swelling with edema. My face looked puffy and moon-shaped. I had started gaining weight at a rapid clip, even though I had kept my diet as clean as possible. I was eating all the glorious fruits and vegetables that Mexico produced, making all my meals from scratch, and yet my body kept ballooning. I knew what that meant. There was only one cure for preeclampsia—to have the baby. However, I wanted to avoid a second C-section if I could, and going into labor naturally would be better than inducing on that front.

Our friend Pam had flown down from Canada a few days

earlier. She was staying in our extra bedroom for the month, to watch Cole during the birth and to help out after the baby came.

Pam was already on the veranda working on her laptop when I finished blending my smoothie. Her reddish hair was pulled up into a messy bun on top of her head and she was frowning at her computer screen.

"I can't get this photo to upload," she said as I sat next to her with my strawberry concoction.

"We're going to Dr. Laura's office today," I said, sipping on my shake and looking over at her screen. She was editing a photo essay for a Canadian travel magazine she sometimes wrote for.

"Cool," she said. "So do you think you will have the baby soon?"

"I don't know. We'll see," I replied.

"Are you excited?" she asked, leaning back from the computer.

"Yes. I mean, I can't wait to finally see her, but I'm nervous about the birth," I said, and put down my cup. "Look at this belly!"

"I know, you are huge, it's so adorable," she said, and laughed. Pam and I had known each other for a long time after meeting in Thailand years before. We were both avid travelers and writers, and we'd kept in touch over the years. The last time we got together, Cole was just a baby.

"I have to practice my Spanish medical terms more; I am not even prepared for this," I said.

"Yes, but they speak English, too, right?"

"In theory, I hope. Dr. Laura speaks good English, at least. As for the others, we'll see."

Drew and I packed up the car and headed down to the city. In Dr. Laura's air-conditioned office we sat like students waiting to get test results on an exam they weren't sure they'd passed. The nurse weighed me, clucked at the uptick in my weight, and took me into the doctor. Dr. Laura kissed me on each cheek, then sat me down to take my blood pressure.

"Okay," she said, and returned to sit behind her desk. She took a breath, then addressed us: "So are you ready to induce this baby today?"

No! my heart screamed. I decided to take a more measured tack.

"Yes, if necessary—but what about waiting to see if it can happen naturally?" I asked, and Drew reached over and held my hand.

"Yes, well, I think we have reached that point." Dr. Laura leaned in. "Remember I told you we would keep an eye on your chances of developing preeclampsia? Well, your blood pressure is right on the line, and you have a lot of edema. I am concerned that if we wait any more we won't have any options." She folded her hands in front of her calmly.

"And if we don't induce, if we try to wait and it doesn't work—then we'd have to go straight to a C-section?" I asked, putting together what she was saying.

"Yes, and I am not sure this will work. But we can try. Or we can schedule the C-section right now, it's up to you. But you said you wanted to try for a VBAC, so if that's what you want, then we should induce you now."

I looked at Drew and smiled.

"We're going to have our baby today!" I said, trying not to cry.

"Come on, let's get started," Dr. Laura said, and led me into her adjoining examination room. Drew came with me, and Dr. Laura explained that she would be applying a light dose of induction cream to my cervix, and then she'd send me home to see what happened.

"If you start seeing little spots in your vision or hearing noises, or if you get a headache or anything at all out of the ordinary, I want you to come to the hospital *immediately* and call me on my cell from the road."

"Okay, because that means my preeclampsia has gotten worse?" I asked, suddenly realizing how much we were really risking.

"Yes," Dr. Laura said seriously.

Drew and I walked out of her office a little stunned and giddy. Before driving back to the house, we got some lunch, and I mentally kept checking my body for any signs of labor. Was that a contraction? Did I feel different? I never went into labor with Cole, so I had no idea what to expect.

Back at the house, I rushed to tell Pam.

"We're inducing!" I called out as soon as we entered the house.

"Wait, what, right now?" she said, jumping up as I burst into the room.

"Yes! She gave me some meds at her office and now we just wait. I could have this baby at any moment."

"Wow, that's amazing! How do you feel?" she said as she came around the table to greet us.

"Great! I mean I don't feel anything yet, but we'll see."

Drew was nervously smiling too much and had dashed off into the house to start preparing for the baby. We still hadn't cut off the tags on the new baby clothes, and there was so much we hadn't purchased yet. I was just over thirty-nine weeks pregnant. We'd been so sure that we had another week.

Pam picked up Cole and followed me into the house. Drew was already packing the overnight bag, and I turned toward them and gave Cole a kiss.

"Cole, the baby is coming. Are you ready to see the baby?" I asked, and we both looked at my belly.

"Baby?" he asked, wiggling down out of Pam's arms. He put his hands on my belly and spoke into it, "Baby come out!"

You heard your brother, little one.

THAT NIGHT AFTER DINNER, still not in labor, we went to the park, which was packed. The day had finally cooled down and a man was grilling corn on a mobile food stand. The *tienda* was open, selling popcorn, lotus-shaped fried chips, and ice cream. The basketball court had been taken over by a game of soccer and a dozen young men were kicking a soccer ball up and down its length. Pam and Drew sat on a bench while Cole rode his bike around the perimeter, chasing the local kids on their bikes. Another family sat next to us, playing with a remote control car. I waved to them and sat briefly with Drew and Pam, then stood back up.

"I think I have to walk," I said.

"Are you feeling something?" Pam asked.

"I don't know. Maybe. Dr. Laura said walking might help it start."

"Do you want me to come with you?" Drew asked.

"No, it's fine, I am just going to walk around the edge of the park. Stay here, you can see me the whole time."

I spent the next two hours making slow laps around the park, my huge belly drawing the eyes of everyone each time I passed. I felt sort of crampy but nothing like the labor pains I had read about. *Come on, come on, come on*, I thought as I walked, my hips burning and lower back clenched, willing myself to go into labor. But I only felt regular pregnancy discomfort, the aches that come with adding so much weight and shifting the balance so far forward.

That night I fell asleep thinking about the baby, trying to will myself to sleep so I would be rested for labor later. In my dreams, I spoke perfect Spanish, talking with Dr. Laura about the baby when she said, "Usted va a tener una niña." *You are going to have a baby girl.*

"Ya sé, pero ¿qué tan grande es ella? ¿Cuánto pesa?" *I know, but how big is she? How much does she weigh?*

I wasn't translating, it just bubbled out of me. Dr. Laura melted away, the way people do in a dream, and now I was trying to buy something at the store, but I couldn't find it. I kept asking people if they had seen it. They kept shaking their heads. I circled around and around the store, looking and asking.

Then I woke up. I whispered to Drew, "What time is it?" and he bolted up, "Baby?"

"No, what time is it?"

He fished under his pillow for his phone and squinted at it.

"Five thirty a.m. Is the baby coming?" he said in a rush.

"No, not yet." My body was quiet. I put my hands on my belly and it was soft, not tight and hard like it had been when I was walking around the park. I closed my eyes and started counting, waiting for a baby kick. One, two, three, four . . . After fifteen seconds I felt it, her little feet pushing against me, the space so limited that it didn't even make my belly bulge when she did it.

She was okay, but the induction hadn't worked. Yet.

WE KNEW THAT LIGHT EXERCISE might help jog the baby down into position, so the next morning Drew and I headed to the *Malecón* in Puerto Vallarta, the town's iconic oceanside boardwalk that runs along the beach looking out at the deep blue Banderas Bay. The waves looked rough against the cool blue expanse of ocean and sky. Giant sand art installations dotted the beach, and string lined the perimeter, keeping the tourists back while the artists worked, smoothing sand with their hands, then spraying a fine mist of water with a canister mounted on their backs to keep the sand wet enough to continue working. A mermaid, a castle, a pirate ship.

We walked away from the Old Town, up into the hills of Puerto Vallarta. This had been my idea in order to jiggle the baby down. In practice, this was exactly what it sounded like: me walking up every set of stairs, doing covert sets of little lunges behind bushes when no one was looking, rolling my hips and massive baby bump, trying to feel for some position that would finally force this baby down and send me into labor.

I. will. have. this. baby. today.

Drew trailed behind me on the dozens of steps, carrying freshly squeezed orange juice (the energy drink of choice for labor day). We stood on a balcony and watched the ocean for a bit, the wind whipping wildly around us and cooling off the sweat from the long climb. It was something of a date, since Cole was home with Pam. We were so rarely without Cole that I felt like we were a couple of tourists on their honeymoon, except we were nine months pregnant and instead of getting drunk at lunch and having sex in our hotel room, we were trying to hustle up staircases so my cervix would open. It sounds strange, but it was one of the most romantic days of my life.

We returned downhill toward the Old Town, then across a wobbly foot bridge over the Río Cuale, and skirted the blazing afternoon sun in the shade of the double-story buildings that lined the streets, each one with a downstairs shop and upstairs apartment. Flowers and overgrown potted plants dangled off balconies overhead, with fat hibiscus flowers drooping from between iron railings. The pressure in my lower abdomen was sharp, and I was now convinced the baby was well lodged in my pelvis. I was preparing myself for the next steps of labor: the hospital admission, the pitocin drip, the mandatory epidural for my VBAC, the vaginal birth I felt certain I was about to have.

When we returned to Dr. Laura's office for more tests, I tried to relax as the fetal heart rate monitor dug into my swollen belly, Drew doing his ad hoc (and as typical, completely inaccurate) reading of the printout. I was having mild contractions now, apparently, although I couldn't feel them. The machine recorded each subtle movement and shift. The baby's heart rate sounded good, Drew and I thought.

After the test, we sat in Dr. Laura's office, a little smug. Drew had studied the printouts and we were both prepared for the good news.

"The baby's heart rate is too low," Dr. Laura said, reading from the printout and not looking at us. "She's not handling it well."

I let the news wash over me, the finality of that statement. I knew what it meant. Dr. Laura confirmed what I was thinking, saying, "Unless she has really progressed, I think we have no choice but to do a C-section now."

Drew piped up. "Can we check?"

She took me into her examination room and asked me to undress as she was standing there. I did it, stripping off my pants and underwear with her watching, which I'd gathered was custom here in Mexico (unlike back home, where you undress privately, as if that makes a difference). As gracefully as possible

I climbed half naked onto the table. I stared at the overhead light and waited for the news, my heart in my throat.

"Okay," the doctor said. "You are one point five centimeters dilated." *Yay!* I suppressed a smile, just barely, but I was ecstatic.

"But . . . the baby hasn't moved down at all." *Oh.*

"I'm sorry," Dr. Laura said. "I can tell you really walked around and tried to get that baby down, but sometimes it doesn't work."

She stopped the examination. Drew teared up. I loved him so much in that moment, for how much he wanted this for me, even in the face of unavoidable circumstances.

Just like that, a phase of my life closed. I had always wondered what the labor of childbirth would be like, what contractions felt like, if I'd be able to handle the pain, how I'd feel in the last moments. It turned out that childbirth just wasn't in my story. But I felt surprisingly calm. After all, at the end of this journey was a baby.

Twenty-five

In case you didn't know, pregnant women are notorious for Googling scary crap about their pregnancies. I was no exception. I spent the entire night before my C-section terrifying myself with birth stories of babies born with the cord wrapped around their necks (which was what Dr. Laura feared the issue was with our baby). Drew kept yelling at me about it ("Why are you *crying*? Wait, don't read that! Stop! *Are you crazy*, don't even talk to me, I don't want to know!"), so I made him read a few of the stories, which of course made him sob as well. Eventually Drew fell asleep while I stayed up clicking link after awful link.

We rolled into the hospital the next morning, a private hotel-esque space just north of the upscale Puerto Vallarta marina area. We had paid our hospital fees in advance ($1,100), and we were told we'd square away our bill with the *doctora* privately. It was incredibly cheap compared to U.S. hospitals, but for most

Mexicans the fees were prohibitively expensive, so the place catered to a few wealthy locals and a majority of tourists and expats who were visiting Mexico temporarily. Because of this, the hospital didn't have a lot of births. In fact, we were the only birth that day. When we arrived, the nursery was empty.

The room was nicer than the room I had for Cole's birth in Oregon. It had a full suite attached, with a living room area beyond the standard bedroom and bathroom setup. We had cable and room service, and the bed was surprisingly soft with a big white duvet. Drew settled in on a spacious couch next to my bed.

I met my nurses, who started by speaking to me in Spanish but then quickly switched to English. They wheeled me into the surgery theater and faded away into the preparations. My anesthesiologist gently rolled me on my side and started his work to put the epidural in. Another nurse held my shoulders and I whimpered a little as the needle went in, even though I tried my best to be silent. I felt the rush of painkillers going down my legs and had a charley horse in my calf for about ten seconds—and then I felt nothing, but only for a moment.

Suddenly a wave of nausea hit me so hard that I lost my ability to talk. I watched them moving busily around me, chatting in Spanish, and I grappled with trying to say anything, English or otherwise.

I could hear my heartbeat on the monitors. The volume was turned up and the *thump, thump* of my heart was like a kind of soundtrack to the moment. I was underwater, fighting to battle back the seasick feeling long enough to say something, when I heard my own heart rate drop precipitously. The nurse came over. "Christine, what's wrong?"

I pulled up out of the sickness long enough to say, "I feel sick."

They rushed to give me oxygen and tilted the operating table to the left to remove the weight of the baby from my inferior vena cava, a major artery that gets squished when a pregnant woman lies on her back.

Slowly, I felt better, and soon the surgery started. They brought Drew in, cap, gown, and all. He held my hand and said, "You're doing so good, sweetie."

I mustered a smile.

In my first C-section, the doctors had talked about golf while they operated. About weekend plans. About things they had to finish around the house. This time comforting Spanish syllables rolled over me like a wave. Despite my growing proficiency, I regressed to a point of complete lack of understanding. It felt like complete and total language amnesia.

The surgery seemed to go so fast. I wasn't aware of anything that was going on. I was told about the birth later, as if I hadn't been in the same room, a story that was related back to me, that seemed to have happened to someone else. When they did pull her out, I held my breath until she let out a scream. It sounded gurgled like she had some fluid in there, which made me nervous. I gave Drew a look that I hoped signaled, *Go, check her*, and without a word he rushed off to greet her. When they brought her over to me, I kissed her messy face and she was whisked away again. She was bright red and breathing normally.

Okay, she's fine, I thought, and relaxed.

I spent another hour or so in surgery while Drew left with the baby. I wasn't nauseated anymore, but the Spanish continued to be impenetrable. I let the soft rolling sounds of the language go untranslated. When they finished, they wheeled me into an anteroom for "observation." The doctors disappeared, and a single nurse checked my blood pressure from time to time. I wanted to see my baby. How long would I have to wait? I was getting emotional. I watched the clock, the second hand moving painfully slowly: one, two, three, four, five . . . I closed my eyes and willed myself to be patient. I would see her soon enough. How long had it been? Fifteen minutes? An hour? How much longer?

Finally, they wheeled me back to my room, where Drew and some of the nurses awaited me. My first question was, "Where's the baby?"

"No, not yet," the nurse said in broken English.

"Drew, where's the baby?" I asked.

"Uh, she's in the nursery, but they say she can't come out for three hours."

"Why? Is something wrong?" I panicked and my heart started beating fast.

Drew rushed to answer. "No, nothing is wrong, they just said that's policy."

"Well, that's not okay!" I needed to see the baby *right now*. "Go get our baby!"

Drew ran out to the nursery. He talked to the nurses, then demanded to see the pediatrician. They told him again: Nothing is wrong, and we could see her, but not for an hour. Because, well, because they said so. So Drew called Dr. Laura, who by that point had already left the hospital. Drew rather frantically told her we needed to see the baby right now, like right this second, not in an hour. He hung up and we heard the phone ring in the nursery and the sounds of them talking to Dr. Laura. A nurse came rushing in.

"Oh! You want to see the baby? Why didn't you say so! Just let us get her dressed."

"Drew, go with her!" I said. He was already following her out the door.

I could hear some conversation, then a loud bang.

"No!" Drew.

"NO!" Again, Drew. What could possibly be going on? I waited, almost hyperventilating.

Eventually, the nurses came into the room with the baby and placed her in my arms. Finally. My sweet little one. She was so impossibly small. That panicked feeling I had of not seeing her melted away. I had my baby.

I breastfed her right away, and she latched on so perfectly that the nurses (who were a little touchy over being bossed around) had to admit, "Okay, she's got this covered," and left.

It was just me, Drew, and our baby. This soft, warm, little baby was so alert and gentle and sweet. Pure love.

Later I asked Drew, "What happened? Why were you yelling?"

"They were trying to give her formula. I don't think any of them spoke English, not really anyway. So I said no the first time as they were putting the bottle up to her mouth and they just smiled and nodded and kept doing it, so I really yelled."

"Thank you," I said. "Thank you so much."

"I love you." Drew kissed me on the forehead and put his arm around me.

"I love you, too," I told him. We both looked at our brand-new baby girl. "Look at her, Drew. Little Stella."

"Stella Lucia Gilbert. She's perfect."

WE KEPT STELLA in our room for the entire two-day stay, and although we had many more fights with the nurses—mostly miscommunications because of the language barrier, because my Spanish skills continued to inexplicably regress at key moments—thankfully Dr. Laura was a rock star. She answered all of our calls, day and night, and triaged issues with the nurses for us, way more than we could have ever imagined. At one point, Drew came back to the room with food for himself, and the nurses came rushing into the room to take it away.

"No, no food."

"No es para mí, es para mi marido," I said. *It's not for me, it's for my husband.* They looked at me suspiciously. Did they really think I was going to break my postsurgery fast by chomping down on a hamburger? I could barely walk to the bathroom, never mind digest a giant hunk of meat.

They slowly relented and left the room. I burst into tears. It was so frustrating dealing with the nurses, between the language issues and cultural ones. On the first day they had dressed

Stella in all three of the outfits we had brought with us, layered on top of each other, and gave me a dirty look when I said there weren't any more clothes (I honestly didn't expect them to put her in so many layers). They wouldn't let us use the AC, so the room was sweltering hot, something of a Latino tradition to keep the baby as warm as possible. No doubt Stella was quite comfortable at ninety-eight degrees since exiting my womb, but I was cooking.

I had prepared all these Spanish medical terms that we didn't end up needing, but I hadn't even thought of how much the culture would impact the experience, from formula feeding, to bathing schedules (they gave her at least two baths per day—I think they just liked playing with her), to room temperature, to how they treated me in general. They were bossy and totally ignored my requests. I was emotionally tender and not ready for it. My postbirth hormones didn't help either. I cried a lot in those two days.

Slowly, I got to know our little *bella*. She was very strong, and even quieter than Cole, who had been a very quiet baby. She didn't cry, she loved to be held, and she nursed every few hours. I had forgotten how truly *little* babies are, and how utterly divine they smell, especially the crown of their head.

Bliss.

When Cole came to visit, he smiled so much I swear he instantly fell in love with his sister, too. He asked if he could touch her and I said yes, to which he jabbed a big fat toddler finger right into her forehead. Then he licked her. Because why not?

The pain from my C-section was unrelenting, and when

Dr. Laura came to visit us on our last day, I cried again. She made me walk around the room, half hunched over and in searing pain, then hugged me and told me I was strong. I asked for more pain meds. She wrote a prescription, but we found out that in Mexico that was just a note to remind us what to buy at the pharmacy. We didn't need a prescription at all, we just had to know *what* to buy.

As Dr. Laura took out her credit card machine so we could pay her portion of the bill (it felt strange to put a birth on a credit card, but there you go), she talked about the surgery.

"There was a lot of scar tissue, so I cleaned that up. Also the previous doctors folded all the layers of skin together, but I stitched each layer separately, so now you won't have that little bump; it will lie flatter."

Drew handed over his credit card and she charged us the remaining $1,650, which covered all her care, the surgery, the anesthesiologist, and the induction.

"And this one," she said to Stella as she picked her up and cradled her in her arms. "She had the cord wrapped around her neck so many times that I had to flip her and untangle her to get her out. There wasn't even enough cord to get her out the natural way. There was no way she was ever going to descend."

I hadn't even felt her flip the baby. That's how out of it I was during the surgery.

"Did you name her?" she asked.

"Yes, Stella Lucia."

"Oh, that's a beautiful name for a beautiful little girl."

Then so quickly, we went home. The four of us.

On the ride home, Drew and I kept saying to each other, "Whoa, we have kids. Kids. With an *s*. Kidsssss." Then we laughed and laughed.

THANK GOD FOR PAM, who had dropped everything to come stay with us for a month. We didn't have our families there, but it was so nice having my friend with us. She took care of Cole while we were in the hospital, and they bonded right away. While I was still in the hospital, she called me and said, "Cole wants me to sleep with him, in his bed, is that okay?"

"Yes, of course, he probably just misses sleeping next to me."

"Okay, good, I wanted to check."

Stella loved Pam, too, falling asleep on her chest, so impossibly tiny and lovely. Through travel and persistence, I had built us a family, a patchwork of Drew, our kids, and our friends and community.

Around this time Drew and I started seriously talking about staying in Mexico. It was perfect in so many ways. There was a six-month tourist visa that could be renewed by leaving the country for one day—or if we wanted to apply for permanent residency, Stella's birth in Mexico streamlined the process for the rest of the family. Because Drew and I were freelancers, working on writing, photography, and film projects, we had a long-documented history of income without a direct employer (exactly what the immigration officials in any country want to see—you can support yourself and will not take a local job).

I didn't know how we'd fit Arabic and Mandarin into our

lives here (because I was still set on studying them), but Drew was happy here, and Cole was fitting in so well and learning new Spanish words every day. It was unbelievably beautiful and the food was fantastic. We could live here on $2,000 a month and have a three-bedroom house next to the beach, put our children in private schools and eat like kings (kings who loved tacos). The people were family-oriented, the community was welcoming, and the neighborhood we were in, while extremely noisy, was also full of fun and music. My kids could learn how to ride horses here, they could be surfers, they could sail boats. We could open a business or continue to work online. We'd be able to spend most of our time with our kids while they were little, instead of constantly working.

Was this the new-baby honeymoon period or had we found a home?

Twenty-six

Pam left. My heart ached as I watched her walk away at the airport, her messy bun bouncing gently as she dragged her suitcase behind her. Cole asked on the ride home, "Where is Pam?" He had gotten so used to her living with us—we all had—that it had been easy to forget that she was only staying for the month. She did leave a small bag of clothes and shoes behind with the promise that she'd return soon enough.

I started my Spanish lessons again. The kids were well on their way to learning the language. Stella had been learning all along, of course, although she didn't speak yet and wouldn't for a while. Babies are born understanding the cadence and melody of their mother's tongue, and so she must have heard months of English and Spanish while renting out my womb.

Stella, like all babies, was born a "universal listener" with the ability to learn any language. Her newborn brain was equally receptive to the sounds of Mandarin or Arabic or Spanish. Janet Werker at the University of British Columbia famously studied this when she tested Japanese infants. In Japanese the *l* and *r* sounds are indistinguishable. They sound exactly alike. If you played the *l* and *r* sounds for a native Japanese speaker who did not know English, he or she would not be able to hear the difference—just like I couldn't hear the difference in tones in Mandarin; my brain just ignored it as unneeded information, unless I seriously trained myself to listen. But for babies it's completely different. In Werker's experiment, Japanese babies could identify the difference between *l* and *r* at six months. But by age twelve months they started to ignore the difference, just like all Japanese speakers do.

What this tells us about language is that as babies we are open and able to learn anything, but as our young brain develops we map those patterns we see in our environment as hard rules. Our brains are changed forever by the languages we hear as an infant.

At six months old, Stella spoke her first words. *Mama. Dada. Agua.* (What can I say, we really like water in our house.) But Drew and I knew we weren't going to be able to keep up Cole and Stella's Spanish study on our own. Already I was slipping on my Spanish with the kids. It happened slowly, without deliberate thought; at first it felt strange to speak to Stella and Cole in Spanish when we had English-speaking guests (because unlike China and Beirut, where no one visited us, now that we lived on the beach in Mexico, we had a nearly constant stream of friends coming by for a visit). I was self-conscious about my Spanish because I knew it wasn't perfect, but even more so when hosting English-speaking guests, who no doubt felt left out when I would switch to Spanish with my kids. Was I being ob-noxious? Did they think I was showing off? I wondered.

It was a bit of a cultural identity crisis. If I had married a Mexican man, then I might feel differently about it. Or if I were Latina, even if I didn't grow up speaking Spanish, then com-ing home to Mexico to learn the language would feel more nat-ural. However, I didn't have a cultural link to Spanish culture, and I hadn't lived in the country long enough to feel I had staked a claim in it. So speaking Spanish still felt like a mask I was putting on. In my worst moments of doubt I wondered if it was a kind of cultural appropriation. I worried about how my speaking accented Spanish to my kids would be perceived by a Mexican insider.

I knew that parents teaching their children English as a second language probably didn't feel this same way, that the benefits of kids learning English were plain enough to see, and there was nothing cultural about it. And after all, it's not like I was playing the tourist while learning the language. I wasn't adopting just the romantic bits and ignoring the rest. I was liv-ing among Mexicans, not secluded in my American bubble. But it didn't feel like enough, at least not yet. I felt like I still needed to earn my place in this culture.

This internal debate bubbled away in the background, but I still continued to speak Spanish to the kids, while Drew spoke to them in English. We reasoned that that way they'd progress equally quickly in each language. But two things in particular happened that ultimately ended my experiment in "one parent, one language" (OPOL). The first was having Cole slowly begin to speak Spanish in public and hearing people laugh at him. I'm sure that part of it was that, yes, of course it's adorable that my blond-haired, blue-eyed American little boy was saying "Gracias." But I heard something else. He was speaking with my American accent. His "gracias" didn't sound like the Mexican kids on our block; it sounded like an exaggeration of my accent. I knew that the more he spoke Spanish in public and the more native Spanish speakers conversed with him, the more natural his accent would become, but for now, he was embarrassed every time he used Spanish in public, and my heart broke to see him feeling like that.

Then a second thing happened. I was reading Cole a bedtime story in Spanish and he curled up in a ball and withdrew. He didn't want me to speak in Spanish to him. It became worse over the next few days. He would laugh or shy away if I spoke in Spanish. Eventually he started telling me to stop. Quite plainly, in fact. He just said: "Stop."

I had traveled all the way around the world to learn languages to teach them to my son, and now, at a bold three and a half years old, he had asked me to knock it off.

You know what? I did.

I stopped. I wasn't sure if it was forever, but I started speaking English again. He still understood Spanish, but I wasn't going to force it on him. I didn't think about it, but I stopped speaking to Stella in Spanish, too. I let it go. Drew and I sat down and talked about it.

"It doesn't matter if I speak Spanish to the kids," I said as we ate dinner beneath the canopy of our favorite taco stand in downtown Bucerías. Stella was curled up on my lap and Cole was sitting next to Drew, poking at his quesadilla, which he prounounced "kiss-a-dilla."

"You don't think? I thought it was working," he said, chewing. "The whole I-speak-English, you-speak-Spanish thing."

"Sí, pero no es importante porque they are getting plenty of exposure, plus we should just send them to school in Spanish," I said, picking at my chorizo with my fork.

The waitress came over and asked, "¿Está todo bien? ¿Nada más?" *Everything okay? Anything else?*

Drew reflexively said, "Nada más. Gracias." *Nothing more. Thanks.* He turned back to his taco, dumping more hot sauce on it than seemed advisable. "So we'll send the kids to school in Spanish and speak English at home?"

"Well, here's my thinking. Cole will learn English because it's our language, but also it's a world language. And he will grow up in our culture. But we can't give him Spanish culture at home. And without Spanish school he's not going to learn enough about the history, culture, and language to ever be fully bilingual. I think sending them to school in Spanish is our best shot at them being both bilingual and bicultural," I said.

Drew looked over at Cole, who was munching away happily on his kiss-a-dilla and asked him, "Cole, do you want to go to school?"

"Yes!" he said without hesitating. Drew and I looked at each other.

"You know it won't be just like playing, right?" I asked Cole. He nodded yes, but of course he had no idea. I had never planned to put him in school so early. After all, Drew and I worked from home; we had the golden ticket—careers that allowed us to work from anywhere in the world. All we had to do was upload our work and communicate via e-mail. We were two stay-at-home parents and we wanted to enjoy our children and take care of them ourselves.

But Cole was desperate to spend more time with other kids. He wanted to go to school. He had his heart set on it.

"Okay," Drew said, and finished off the rest of his taco, then wiped his mouth with a napkin and tossed it onto his plate, "Looks like we're sending the kids to school in Spanish."

"Yay!" Cole and I sang out in unison.

Later, Drew and I looked into public schools, but the enrollment period had already passed. There was a private bilingual school in our neighborhood, though, and they had open admissions. We took a tour of the facility, and they had a big playground, daily snack time, and lots of play-based learning. The teachers spoke English, but barely. It was bilingual enough that Cole could communicate in English, but he'd mostly be learning in Spanish.

We signed him up. The first day of school he filled his Spider-Man backpack with a spare set of clothes, a toothbrush, and a toy for show-and-tell. He picked his Woody doll from *Toy Story,* and we dropped him off at school. Drew walked him to the gate because I was afraid I would cry. Cole walked in and never looked back. Drew returned to the car and I asked him, "Are we doing the right thing?"

"Did you see him? He practically skipped into the school. He will be fine. This is only hard for us." Drew took my hand.

He was right. Cole didn't just like school, he loved it. In the following weeks his Spanish took off. For all the time I spent speaking in Spanish to him, suddenly being in school meant he had to use the language and he was busting out vocabulary I had no idea he knew.

"I have a *novia*," Cole confided in me one evening.

"You have a girlfriend?" I asked.

"Two." He held up two fingers.

"Really."

"Valentina and Sophia." He looked smug.

"How do you know they are your girlfriends?"

He shrugged.

Each day the teacher left a note in Cole's backpack for me about how school had gone. One day there was a reminder to parents about Mexican Independence Day the next day. Cole was supposed to dress up. I searched online for clues as to what he should wear, and found a bunch of photos of little kids in sombreros, fake mustaches, and checkered shirts with handkerchiefs around their necks.

I bit my lip. "Drew, do you think . . ."

"What?" Drew said, looking at the photos.

"I mean is this maybe . . ."

"What?" He looked at me uncomprehendingly.

"I don't know, if we send him to school with a sombrero and a fake mustache, is that like a parody of Mexican culture?"

"Like he shows up and the teachers are mortified because we've just misinterpreted the whole thing?"

"Exactly. I mean, this seems like if I did this in the States it would be pretty racist." I looked again at the giant sombreros.

"Right, in the States it would be weird," Drew agreed. "But here it's Pancho Villa; he's a national hero."

"Okay, I don't know." I thought about where to find a good costume. "Let's go to Walmart."

So we headed to Walmart and—surprise!—there was an entire section dedicated to children's costumes for the holiday. Just in case, I e-mailed my friend who had lived in Mexico City for years and she confirmed, "Yup, that's what they do."

So I dressed Cole up with his fake mustache and giant sombrero, and tied a colorful handkerchief around his neck, then sent him off. We found out later, as kids dressed as famous Mexican heroes streamed into the school gates, that we'd picked the exact right outfit. At this moment I realized what we were really doing was raising a bicultural child. From my childhood growing up in the United States, I had a certain frame of reference for new experiences. Cole's frame of reference would be completely different. I could read textbooks and studies all day about raising bilingual children, but it was little things like this, sending our toddler off to preschool dressed as Pancho Villa, that made me realize what we'd signed up for. And while Cole wouldn't necessarily appreciate the difference, it felt like a gift to me to understand a culture enough to know that Mexican Independence Day comes in September, not on Cinco de Mayo.

. . .

EVERY NIGHT AFTER DUSK, we'd take Cole and Stella and walk over to the little park next to our house. I'd drag Cole's bike for him over the dirt road. There was one little boy there he really loved, named Alejandro—but the kids didn't know each other's names. When they saw each other, they ran toward each other.

"Boy!" Cole yelled.

"Niño," Alejandro yelled.

Then they smashed into each other, arms outstretched like they were about to hug but couldn't figure out how to put on the brakes. They fell to the ground and embraced.

They'd spend the next few hours riding their tricycles as fast as they could around and around the park until Alejandro's mom waved to him and gestured for him to go home. At ten p.m. sharp the park cleared out, the invisible tug of mothers and curfews.

"Where did the kids go?" Cole asked me.

"Home. They have to go to school tomorrow."

"Oh."

"¿Listo?" *Ready?*

He nodded and we walked back to the house. In the courtyard, Cole pointed up at the sky.

"Look, Mama! It's the moon! *La luna!*"

"Sí, muy bien. Y las estrellas también." *Very good. And the stars, too.*

"Las estrellas," he repeated reverently. We smiled at each other.

Twenty-seven

It had been a year and a half since we'd left Beijing, but for a long time I'd continued to spend a few hours each week dutifully plugging away at the textbooks Drew so thoughtfully rescued from the trash when we fled the country. I decided to take an online quiz to test my Mandarin skills and gauge how well my solo study, far from China, was working for Mandarin. The quiz was a placement test for an online course. If you had asked me cold to say something in Mandarin, the best I could have mustered was "Wo shi Christine" (*I am Christine*) and "Ni hao" (*Hello*). In context, though, I could make out simple spoken phrases, remembering as I went, the pronunciation and tones still buried deep in my brain. With the *hanzi*, the written characters, I was less successful. I had a vague memory of most of the ones on the test (like the character for "woman," 女, which I had remembered because it reminded me of a person doing a curtsy), but I couldn't recall the meaning for most. I tested as a midlevel beginner.

I couldn't find a test to take for the Lebanese Arabic dialect I'd studied, but I knew I couldn't read the script anymore. If I sat for a long time with a word, going letter by letter, counting the dots from right to left and concentrating, I could slowly jog my memory enough to untangle it, but my fluency was gone. There had been a time when I could sight-read in Arabic, when I could write in the script as quickly as in English. But a transcontinental move, a pregnancy, a birth, a new baby, and life had all gotten in the way, and with it, my Arabic skill had deteriorated rapidly. There wasn't a way to measure it, but it felt like I had lost Mandarin and Arabic more quickly and more completely than I'd learned them. It took a long time to push that boulder up the hill and when I let go, it rolled back down at a rapid clip.

I thought about the polyglots I'd researched who spoke twenty-some languages but didn't speak them all the time. Maybe I hadn't gone deep enough with each language to prevent language loss, but it seemed, for me anyway, that I wasn't the kind of person who could study Arabic for four months, move on to something else, and retain anything of use. Maybe if I had spent two to five years on each language, that would work. Or if I had attended college-level classes in each language. If I had achieved professional-level fluency. If I had worked or taught or lived in the language long enough. But I didn't do any of those things.

I spent two years learning three languages, two of which were the hardest for English speakers to learn. What I found was that while you could cram enough to pass a quiz, the thing that really mattered for language retention long-term was time. You could learn Spanish to conversational fluency in six months, I had no doubt, but most people need a deeper level of fluency to keep from losing it as soon as they stop speaking it every day. For Arabic and Mandarin, given that the writing system for each is different than the spoken language, it could hypothetically be possible to be fluent in one or the other in two years, but from what I saw, it was more like five years. Looking back at my original notes on the Foreign Service Institute rating of difficulty for each language, there was a direct correlation between the level of the language and how long you'd have to study:

Level 1 (Spanish, French): one year
Level 3 (German): three years
Level 5 (Arabic, Mandarin, Japanese): five years

I did a two-year experiment to attempt mastery of two level 5 languages and one level 1 language; I worked my ass off, but what I really needed was eleven years. If I had reached this understanding in a way that I would have accepted in the beginning (and, given my stubbornness and ambition, the way I would have accepted would have been the angel of language learning descending from the sky to hand me a scroll saying, "Don't rush"), then my next question would have been: Do I want to spend the next eleven years studying just to say I can speak these languages?

It's hard to say.

I could do anything in eleven years: I could learn to run a marathon in under four hours, get my PhD in political science, become a world-class salsa dancer, or start a dozen startups. Being realistic about the time it takes to really, truly learn the language was crystallizing. What did I want? Did I really need or want to learn all three languages? It was so simple: If you didn't have a burning desire and a real-world application for the language, then you could only hold open the space for an exercise in futility for so long. Your arms get tired. You relax. The whole thing falls down.

Drew and I started talking about what came next. What did we really want from our lives and how did we want to raise our kids? A few things had become obvious to us. We wanted our children to be bilingual. Definitely. And a more recent realization: We also wanted to raise them to be aware of other cultures. The bilingual part would be relatively easy to achieve in the United States if we found an area that had bilingual schools. The cultural part was trickier, although not impossible.

I learned in Beirut that we all have an *us and them* mentality. The Middle East had previously always been "them" to me, but learning Arabic and living in Lebanon made me have empathy for a group of people I used to think of as on the other side of some invisible line that I couldn't approach. In the 1970s and 1980s, Henri Tajfel wrote about this phenomenon and called it social identity theory. We think of people in our social circles more favorably; we inherently apply the most positive motivations to the actions of those people we see as "in our group." We can see this play out in how some people in the West talk about the Middle East—assuming, wrongly, that those who live in the Middle East are fundamentally different, perhaps more violent or unable to get it together, or unwilling to change. Living there, what I saw was a group of people struggling with the same politics and cultural forces we struggle with in the West.

So my social group got larger. I didn't just identify with New Englanders anymore, or Americans, or the Western world. Beirut had shifted my perspective and I now thought of the Lebanese as my people, too. So when there was a car bombing in my Ashrafieh neighborhood, I was just as shaken as when the Boston Marathon bombing later happened back home.

Language brought me to the Middle East, and language let me get close enough to erase those social lines. The gift of language is not just the ability to speak another language (which, let's face it, is less important than ever for English speakers as the world adopts English). The real gift, the life-changing part, is opening up your worldview. If we want to prepare our children for the future—one that will no doubt be more globalized than ever—then that broadened sense of identity is the most useful tool a young person can have. It makes them adaptable, it helps them think about issues across cultures, and it will be a required skill for the next generation of workers. You can't sit in a corporate office in Chicago and dream up ads for a campaign in Beijing without having cultural awareness. How can you sell something to someone if you don't even know what they want? What motivates them? What do they think is cool?

I started this experiment thinking that bilingualism was the goal, but ended more convinced that biculturalism—or at least multicultural awareness and appreciation—was more important. Knowing this, feeling this in our hearts, one thing became clear: We weren't moving back to the States. We had traveled too far outside the bubble. How could we ever go back?

DREW HAD PICKED UP SPANISH without any lessons. It had been a year since we first arrived in Mexico, when he'd tentatively ordered a beer as "una cerveza, por favor" because it was the only phrase he had memorized (so he drank a lot of beers those first few months), rather than tangle with the menu, which seemed overwhelming. One year later, things were totally different.

Pam was flying back to Bucerías to join me on a ten-day road trip and we were taking the breaking-down, busted-up old 1994 Dodge Caravan across Mexico for a girls-only road trip. In advance of our trip, Drew headed out to find a *taller mecánico* to replace two of the tires and the rear brake light. One year before, he wouldn't even have considered such a task—since he'd need to speak Spanish to lots of people—let alone just driven out the door with little to no plan. When he came back a few hours later, he was flushed and animated.

"It was awesome!" he said as he got out of the van and slammed the door shut. I was sitting on the veranda with Stella while Cole rode his bike around the house in rapid circles.

"What happened?" I asked, confused by his sudden ebullience.

"Oh my God." He grinned. "So I went to that place, the one on the highway? And I was all like, 'Hola, pues, tengo que comprar nuevos neumáticos,' right? And he's like, 'Okay, dude, well we don't do that here, you need the tire place.' In Spanish. All in Spanish. And I totally understood him."

"That's awesome!" I said as he came over and sat down next to me.

"Hello, Bella," he said to Stella, kissing her on the top of the head, and then he said to me, "I know, right? So then he's like, 'Go down there, straight ahead, take a left, that's the place,' and so I did."

"Did you find a tire place?" I asked.

"No, that place was closed. So I asked another guy, '¿Dónde puedo encontrar los neumáticos?'—you know, just some guy walking down the street—and he directed me to another place."

"And you got tires there?"

"Yes, and it was so cheap. It was so awesome, though. I was just talking to everyone. They told me I probably need new front tires, too, but I think we'll be fine for now."

"I'm so impressed!" Drew took Stella off my lap and cradled her. I watched for a moment, then asked, "So what do you think did it? What helped your Spanish?"

Drew thought about it. "Honestly, I think it was just having to use it all the time, plus watching cartoons in Spanish with the kids. Mostly, though, it's just hearing it. I go into the market, I overhear someone else asking for something, I see what they are getting, and then next time I can use the same phrase. That's how I figured out the *carnicería* offered *adobada* seasoning on the meat, or that you could ask for meat for stew as *carne para guisar*—or meat for grilling as *carne para asar*—and they'd just give you the right cut, you don't have to say flank or skirt steak or whatever."

"Right," I said. "And the nice thing is that since we have the kids with us, everyone always wants to talk to us."

"Yeah, any time I am out with Stella, I end up having a conversation. Is the baby a boy or a girl? Where are her earrings? Don't you know they will do that free at the hospital? Go to the *clínica*! Or do it at home. With an ice cube. Ha!" Drew said.

"So much vocabulary!"

"I know, it's great," he said. "I mean, there's no way to live here like we do and *not* learn the language, really. I feel bad for those people who stay here and just speak English all the time, no matter what. It's almost like they are blocking out the Spanish, like 'I don't want to hear that.'"

"I was afraid that would be us, *como un par de gringos*," I said.

"We are a couple of gringos, but our daughter is Mexican."

We both smiled. Then I said, "Okay, Señor Hispanohablante, ¿quieres asar un poco de carne para el almuerzo o no?" *Do you want to grill a little steak for lunch or what?*

"Sí, mi amor, claro que sí." *Yes, my love, of course.*

"Genial, quiero usar la salsa de piña que hice ayer." *Great, I want to use the pineapple salsa I made yesterday.*

"¡Ag-wa!" Stella yelled out. She had worked her way off Drew's lap on the couch and was holding herself up in a standing position.

"¡Agua!" Cole also yelled out, reminded by his sister's request that he too was thirsty.

"Okay, I will get you some water! Hold on!"

Drew and I headed to the kitchen. It never stopped thrilling us to hear the kids use any Spanish.

PAM ARRIVED FROM CANADA a few days later. We stayed up late catching up and listening to music.

"I can't believe how big Stella is," she told me.

"I know, she's a little Viking, too, tough as nails. She'll be walking any day now," I said.

"Unbelievable. When I left, she was so tiny, she would sleep on my chest. So have you guys decided where you're going to go next? What's the plan?"

"I don't know. I want to take this trip with you, then we'll make a decision."

"It's the end of an era."

"I know! I can't believe how fast everything has happened."

"Well, I can't wait to see where you end up next."

"Me too, Pam! Seriously. Me too."

Twenty-eight

You know when the Mexican *policía* laughs when you tell them, "We're going to Mexico City," that you're not on the tourist trail anymore. Pam and I had begun our road trip and the adventure was just beginning.

So far, we had traveled from Puerto Vallarta on the Pacific coast to outside Guadalajara then to Guanajuato, and now we were making our way to Mexico City in our beat-up van that Drew had bought in Seattle and driven down to Bucerías when we first arrived. When I suggested this road trip with Pam, Drew had nearly pushed me out the door, saying, "Yes, you should definitely go. Please go!"

I might have taken this as a not-too-subtle hint except I knew he had been exasperated by my reluctance to ever leave the kids. At ten days, this trip was by far the longest I would be away from the children. It would be good for me, I told myself as I kissed my babies and husband good-bye.

It felt strange to be unfettered, but Pam and I were making the most of our adventure. Instead of taking the bland toll highway into the city, which would get us there in five or so hours, we decided to take the rural route winding through mountain roads into the city.

On the side of the road people with carts sold strawberries and cream, waving us down as we drove by, but soon they became less frequent and the small towns faded away until we were driving through green fields with blue-tinted mountains in the distance. As the sun set, I turned to Pam and said, "I'm really glad we took this route."

"Me too," she replied. Then, "What time is it?"

"It's six ten, why?"

"We need to write this down for later—so we remember we both agreed this was a good plan."

We laughed. We had been approached twice already on this leg of the trip by police officers. The first pulled us over because of our foreign license plates, and the second was at a traffic checkpoint. Each time they asked, "Where are you going?" in a tone that seemed to imply we were quite far from anything at all.

"Mexico City!" we cheered.

Blank stare. A small laugh. Head shake.

"Adelante." (*Okay, off you go.*)

For dinner, we ate *pollo asado* from a four-table roadside operation that had a massive rotisserie over charcoal. The sun set. We took pictures. Night fell and we continued to drive, catching glimpses of city lights between the trees but moving slowly.

At the *centro histórico*, we pulled over at the first hotel, handed the valet our keys, booked a room with a view, and collapsed in our beds. We had spent the day laughing and talking through the long drive, enjoying a part of Mexico we would have missed if we rushed, a part of the trip that made it feel more like an adventure than just a self-led tour. But still, the cool, crisp white sheets after a shower were a revelation.

For me, Mexico City's biggest draw was the food. Our first full day we ate lunch at Pujol, a five-star restaurant that offers an eleven-course tasting menu with a focus on modern Mexican cuisine. It was voted one of the world's fifty best restaurants, and at $79 USD per person, it was also one of the most affordable on that list. The dishes came out with meticulous care over two hours. Shaved ice with chili powder and lime, appetizers of sashimi tuna on a blue corn tostadita, aguachile with chia seeds covered in a smooth layer of avocado. The waiter brought out a massive hollowed-out gourd the size of a pumpkin that was filled with aromatic smoke, baby corn with chiles, coffee, and cream. It was all presented in Spanish. Dishes like "Botanas Elote con mayonesa de hormiga chicatana, café, chile costeño—Infusión de maíz rojo, pericón, raíz de cilantro—Chicharrón de col rizada" included words I couldn't guess at, like "chicatana" or "pericón," so my translations for Pam sounded like this: "Corn and some kind of ant mayonnaise, coffee, some kind of chile . . . uh . . . an infusion of red corn and cilantro? Um . . . plus chicharrón and cabbage, I think." The ingredients on the plate were all recognizable to me after a year of living in Mexico, but I didn't know the high-end foodie names for some of these things.

Other dishes were easier. "Taco de barbacoa, adobo de chile guajillo, hoja de aguacate, guacamole" was barbecue tacos with a guajillo chile marinade (the same guajillo chiles I routinely bought at the grocery store for my own *adobada* recipes) with avocado leaves and guacamole. Most of these words weren't taught to me in school when I studied Spanish in high school or college—in fact, for years I thought the Spanish word for sandwich was "bocadillo" (most people in Mexico use "torta" instead) or that drinks were "bebidas" (like the English equivalent, "Would you like a drink?" but in Spanish it's usually asked, "¿Qué quieres tomar?" (literally, "*What do you want to drink?*"). It was only through living in Mexico, shopping for these ingredients, cooking with them, going to restaurants with locals, that I had begun to learn the vocabulary that Mexicans actually used. My lunch at Pujol was reminding me that it didn't end there. Even in English new culinary terms and techniques are being invented; the sources of ingredients involve an expanding backstory that is increasingly told in restaurants.

Of course, the meal was delicious; there wasn't a course we didn't love. One of my favorite dishes was a very simple cauliflower with *almendrado*, an almond sauce—I was completely caught off guard at how good it was. Next there was the suckling lamb taco with poblano chile, then fresh fish with an elote cream sauce. By this point we were swooning over our dishes—the mole madre, the fermented banana covered in macadamia nuts and chamomile petals, a dollop of guava and sweet potato purée, and brioche with Mexican cheeses and fruit. We sipped an infusion of corn hairs, lime, and star anise while finishing our final course: candied pumpkin with cream.

We spent the rest of the day touring the city and taking photos, but I was anxious to get to the next morning's street food tour. This would serve as a culinary counterpoint to Pujol and would give us a chance to consider the difference and relative merits of two very different ways to approach Mexican ingredients.

The thing about street food in Mexico is that it's powered by the people. As we walked out of Pujol, down the street we saw a very impressive-looking but nearly empty restaurant. Just outside the restaurant was a modest carnita stand with a line around the corner, selling tacos as fast as they could prepare them. I realized: If it tastes good, it wins.

The next morning, bouncing from street cart to street cart, Pam and I tried to figure out the culinary influences on the food as we wolfed it down. The carnitas were from Michoacán, where they cook pork, all of it, in pork fat, making an insanely crispy and delicious shredded pork taco that's then usually covered with cilantro, onions, a slice of pineapple, and salsa. From the Lebanese came *tacos al pastor*, slow-roasted meat similar to *shawarma*, but instead of the lamb used in *shawarma*, using pork that's covered in Mexican spices. The spices vary, depending on the recipe, but almost always include dried chiles like ancho, cascabel, or guajillo. Then there's the tamale, corn masa steamed in banana, corn, or avocado leaf and filled with a little cream, mole, or cheese with some chicken or maybe raisins.

In a way this was part of my language education. I knew now that it was not enough to just study out of a book, to perfect your accent, or to write endless essays. You have to fall a little in love with the culture to learn it. In my case, on this day, that meant knowing that carnitas are pork cooked in pork fat, but that they also come in a variety of cuts, that if you just ask for a "carnita, por favor," they'd give you a mix. But you're missing out if you don't know about the other parts of the pig (and yes, they cook them all), including the stomach, calf, leg, testicles, skin, braided intestines, regular intestines, uterus, just meat, ribs, ear, snout, or penis. My favorite was *chamorro*—leg meat that's slightly fatty and perfect.

Then, at the next cart, I discovered my newest taco obsession: the *tlacoyo*. On the Pacific coast, they don't have these very often, but they're divine. It's an oval-shaped taco that's stuffed, in this case, with cheese, and mine was topped with *nopales* (strips of grilled cactus that has the consistency of green bell peppers when cooked but tastes milder). I covered it in *salsa verde*, a green salsa made with tomatillos. So good. I closed my eyes for a second to taste it better.

Mexico City was like a large version of Madrid, but the food alone was enough to make you want to stay. We only had ten days on our road trip to make it as far south as Chiapas, so we couldn't stay here long. We hit the road again, still a little high on the experience in Mexico City.

Then the trusty Dodge Caravan started to break down. Going around corners, the electric door locks would click on and off, the interior light would flash, and the door chime would go off. Within a few hours it was happening every few minutes. We pulled into a gas station, and I popped the hood.

The guy who had checked our oil when we left Puerto Vallarta had forgotten to replace the oil cap, so there was oil all over the engine. Nothing to be done about that, so I took a look at the fuses. I had no idea how to fix electrical things, but I did know that if you remove the fuse for something, you could effectively shut it off. I removed three fuses based on the little chart: the airbags (ha! we don't need those), the electric locks, and the interior light. When we turned the car back on, all the annoying things had stopped except the door chime.

I told Pam that I was a genius. She was not convinced. I drove around the parking lot. *Ding, ding, ding,* chimed the door.

I couldn't find anything online via my cell phone about which fuse shuts off the door chime, but I did figure out that the door-ajar sensor for the driver's-side door was setting it off. I read a post online about how to fix that: Remove the door panel and spray it with WD-40. I had neither WD-40 nor any tools, so I took a spare bottle of engine oil from the trunk and a pair of tweezers and tried to oil the lock, the little hook on the inside of the door that grabs the loop on the door frame when it closes. I pushed it down and rotated it and it clicked into place.

Locked. Which was great! Except the door was hanging open still, while the lock was now closed. I tried to unrotate the lock with my tweezers, but it wouldn't budge. So I couldn't close my door. I put the fuse for the door locks back in—nothing. The auto locks for my door no longer worked. So I did the best thing I could think of: I slammed the door as hard as possible.

The door bounced back open. I inspected the locking hook that I'd been proud of pushing into position. It was now bent beyond use. The whole thing was totally, utterly screwed.

Then suddenly I was surrounded by five guys who took turns slamming the door as hard as they could to get it to close. I explained what I had done in Spanish, but they focused on showing off their brute strength, slamming my poor busted door over and over again.

Pam looked concerned, but I was too pleased with myself to feel much worry, for I was talking in Spanish about car parts with a bunch of guys who didn't speak English. The guys and I were having rapid-fire Spanish conversations. I felt as fluent as I had ever felt. Even though I don't know all the vocabulary for the individual car parts, I understood enough to pick up the new words on the fly.

One of the guys called his friend who was a mechanic. The mechanic showed up driving the most banged-up car I had seen since we left Puerto Vallarta. It wasn't until he checked out my door that I believed that he was in fact a mechanic—his butt crack was exposed above his pants and it was the most magnificent leathery brown skin I had ever seen. Only a lifetime of having your ass up in the air with ill-fitting jeans would produce such a glorious effect.

The mechanic had the same (brilliant) idea as me, but instead of slamming the door over and over, he had actual tools. So he banged the hell out of my latch with a mallet and pried up the lock until he could then slam the door closed. He told me in

Spanish, "Okay, you can get someone to fix this door, later, or you know, you can just never open the door again. Just don't open it. Ever."

Okay, sounds good to me. I offered to pay him for his time, the hour of master craftsmanship with a rubber mallet. He asked for 100 pesos, about $7.50. Done.

An hour later, when we got a flat tire, I opened the door. I had totally forgotten. I stopped the car and jumped out, opening the busted door without thinking, and ran to the other side to look at the tire. It was really bad.

I opened the back of the van and pulled out the jack and got to work. It took me about ten minutes of cranking to get the car up, and another ten minutes to wrestle the lug nuts free with Pam's help, and as I was about to put the new tire on, a police officer drove up.

The officer strode over to us confidently, and asked, "Where are your husbands?"

Hah.

Pam answered him in English, "Our husbands are at home, with the kids." She smiled.

He looked at her for a beat, decided not to press the issue further, and crouched next to the tire. He cranked the jack up a few times, then tried the tire, but announced that it wasn't working. I pointed to the back of the jack, saying "mire" (*look*)—there was still plenty of length for it to go up—but he ignored me and wandered off to his car.

"Pam, I am just going to do it," I said.

"Do it!" she encouraged me, still holding the lug nuts.

So I started cranking the car up as fast as I could. A few minutes later he came back, shooed me out of the way, and tried the tire again. Oh. It worked. Was that a flash of embarrassment I caught on his face?

No matter, we thanked him and were off again.

WE SPENT A FEW DAYS high in the mountains in San Cristóbal de las Casas, where it was so cold that we shivered under our blankets at night. I called Drew and talked to the kids on video chat, while Pam downloaded her photos and checked e-mail. Then we continued back toward the Pacific coast, planning to loop through Oaxaca on our way back to Puerto Vallarta. I read off the signs in the towns we passed through, translating the Spanish for Pam: "Children have the right to school." "We love you Chiapas, we're on your side." "Keep the streets clean." There was one sign for a local politician who had just won re-election and had also won a rock through his grinning paper face.

Then, between two towns, we smelled oil. Burning oil. I pulled into a gas station and thankfully knew enough Spanish to work out what was going on. I quickly learned that the word *tapón* was the simplified expression for the oil plug—and I learned that we didn't have one. The one that was missing from Puerto Vallarta, the one that kept the oil inside the car, the one I knew we needed to replace but had survived a thousand miles without, well, it was gone. And after a day of driving bumpy roads, we had splashed out nearly all our oil. The engine was hot. The *tapón* was missing, but even worse, when I revved the engine, the valve that regulated the coolant was spraying gushes of the stuff before it ever reached the engine.

They found a new oil stopper, but for the coolant hose we would need a *taller mecánico*.

"Do you know one?" I asked the now-familiar group of men who were standing around my steaming engine debating what I should do.

"Sí. Soy mecánico," one of the men offered.

We followed him to his house, something I wouldn't normally do, except that since we were in such a small town, it was likely that all the mechanics worked out of their front yards.

The mechanic didn't have the part, he said, but for 200 pesos, he'd fix it. That was only about $15, but after counting our change, we barely had it. We hadn't seen an ATM since San Cristóbal and, due to not wanting to carry excessive cash, we were now almost broke.

The fix was a PVC pipe, forced into place. They refilled the coolant for us and closed the hood. *It'll hold*, they told me. *We have to go to church soon, it's getting dark. Good-bye.*

An hour later, the PVC pipe was broken and all of our brand-new coolant was in the parking lot of a convenience store. We crawled into the next town, Tapachula, with the engine temperature gauge in the red zone. I came up with a plan: Get money from an ATM, leave the car overnight in this lot, take a taxi one hour into the jungle to the coffee plantation where we have reservations, come back in the morning and find a mechanic.

Our taxi driver recommended his dad for the job, speaking to me in a really fast and difficult Spanish accent. He spent the entire drive to the Argovia Finca telling me to trust him, while Pam and I sat in silence. When we arrived, the plantation staff came down to meet us. Pam had texted them about our late arrival, and the marketing director talked to the mechanic in Spanish, telling him imperiously, "These are very important clients. They are journalists from the United States. Please do a good job and not too expensive." I handed the keys over to the taxi driver to bring to his mechanic father, and we headed up to our rooms to shower. It had been a long day, so after dinner I called Drew and the kids and then we headed straight to bed.

The next day the car didn't come back. The day after that, the taxi driver and his mechanic father returned, sheepishly, with the fixed minivan, which had also been detailed, repaired, and tuned up. They had to travel to Guatemala, they said, to get car parts. They fixed the valve. And replaced the radiator. In fact, they replaced everything that wasn't bolted down, from the timing belt to all the tubes and valves. It looked great. I started the car, and it practically purred. This seventeen-year-old beast had never run so well. Great! Where was the bill?

It took him a good fifteen minutes to carefully run through a handwritten invoice of everything they did. It didn't include line item prices, and he hadn't told me the total yet. He was stalling. Finally he told me: Thirteen thousand pesos. About $1,000.

That was just *slightly* higher than the 250 pesos I paid the other mechanic to fix it, and while I appreciated that he'd done such a good job, we'd only paid $1,500 for the car in the first place, and now he wanted almost that much for repairs? Who would put that much money into an old clunker? Then I remembered: The night he dropped me off at the resort, the staff had come out and the marketing director had told him we were three things: important, American, and journalists. Aka, *cha-ching!*

I spent two hours negotiating the price down, using every trick I knew. I walked away, I came back and made an impassioned plea in Spanish, I asked them to price each item on the list, and I told them I'd only pay for the work I asked for: replacing the one valve. But I realized, too, that they were actually in a bit of trouble. They had purchased parts, hired labor, and they had to cover their expenses. I offered $200, then $250, and then $275. I showed them the contents of my wallet. It seemed demeaning and somehow entitled to engage in this kind of tough negotiation, wearing each other down. It was certainly not in my culture to be so aggressive. Finally the resort owner pulled me aside and tutored me on technique.

"I have an idea," he said. He was Mexican, and also the manager of a large team of employees. The resort was a working coffee plantation and had as many as two hundred workers in the high season, plus he sold his coffee all over Mexico. I was sure he had plenty of experience with negotiation.

"Tell him he can keep your car, that you won't pay anything but he can try to sell it himself to get the money back," he advised.

It was a ploy. I knew it was nearly impossible to legalize an American car in Mexico, but it showed a level of desperation on my part that was rather convincing. They rejected the offer but suddenly were willing to drop the price significantly. They offered $400. I paid it.

We started driving north. And one hour outside Tapachula, on the only highway going north to Oaxaca, we ran into Aduana, the agency that handles vehicle imports. We were stuck in an internal border check. I spent another two hours talking in Spanish, this time with customs officers. They were relentless with questions: The car was in my husband's name, so where was my husband? If I was really crossing into Mexico from another country, the owner of the car should be there or I should have a notarized letter or something. I didn't have any of those things.

Thankfully, they let us go. Sort of. They escorted us back onto the highway, sending us back in the direction we just came from. We took our chances of running into them again, and simply chose a different route. Two days later we were finally in Oaxaca.

In Oaxaca we stayed at the lovely Azul hotel, in which each room was decorated by a different Mexican artist. I picked up some mole paste for Drew, took a cooking class with Pam, and declared my road-tested Spanish a success. I was practically floating. I had never been so challenged to use the language before, and if I could make it through all those interactions in Spanish, then I had succeeded. I had argued with a customs officer in Spanish for *two hours*!

I started out this experiment just wanting to converse in another language. Now I was battling bureaucrats. I was calling it, I told Pam: I was *fluent*. My Spanish wasn't perfect, and I would have a lifetime of learning to perfect it, but I could speak with fluidity, I could handle situations where I had to think fast and talk even faster. There's no finish line in language learning, but this felt like a major milestone: I could make myself understood and I could understand what was said to me. I had gone from dabbling to knowing a language. Maybe even to being bilingual.

Twenty-nine

It was time to leave. Pam and I returned to Puerto Vallarta, and she flew home to Canada. Drew and I had decided to leave Mexico, too. But we didn't want to move home to the United States. I needed the incentive of living in a foreign culture—a non-English-speaking culture—to keep my bilingualism up. Otherwise I'd do what I did the last time I learned Spanish and returned to the United States: I'd stop speaking it. It would fade. And as for the kids—they would speak Spanish if we enrolled them in bilingual schools, but how long would they keep it up after graduation if it had been only an academic exercise? If we didn't form our life, our family, our friends, and our community around the new language, was there any point in even learning it? If there was no practical need for the language, it would become nothing but a time-consuming parlor trick that I'd taught my children—impressive, perhaps, but the exact thing I wanted to avoid in the first place. I didn't want to raise prodigy children solely for the sake of loading up their college applications; I wanted this to be part of their identity. Of our identity.

Without strong family ties in the United States, and to avoid raising bilingual kids in a largely monolingual culture, we knew we wanted to continue living overseas. Spanish seemed like the natural choice for us, but Latin America was so far geographically from the Middle East, and I wasn't ready to give up my Arabic studies, even if I wasn't sure it was something my kids needed to learn. We started to look at Spain, which had reasonable residency visa laws. After five years, we could get a permanent residency visa for Spain, and five years after that, we could apply for naturalization and the entire family could get Spanish passports.

That would mean my kids could go to college in the EU or the U.S. We could have the kids in Spanish school and then transfer to an English school for high school, so the kids would be balanced in their Spanish and English, able to write and read at a high level in both languages. I spoke with some friends who grew up as so-called third-culture kids—kids raised outside their parents' country, belonging neither 100 percent to their parents' culture nor 100 percent to their new culture—and one of the things I was told by my friend Meriah, who grew up as a missionary kid and still spoke Japanese, was that the faster you can adopt the local culture, the better. It could be isolating to be different from everyone else, so living in a country, like Spain, where we would be comfortable fully adopting the local parenting style, the traditions, the holidays, and so on, would make our children's childhoods less stressful. Of course Cole and Stella would always have parents who spoke English, but the more we could create a typical Spanish home for them, the better.

So, Spain, then. But where in Spain? Well, Barcelona seemed like the perfect choice. It was a big city, but not too big. We had visited there before and loved it. Also, Barcelonians spoke Catalan, and educated their kids in both Spanish and Catalan. So our kids would grow up as trilinguals. I talked to another friend who was Spanish but lived in Madrid. He said, "Why Catalan? What's the point? No one speaks it." But I reasoned: The people in Barcelona speak it, so my kids' friends will speak it. That was incentive enough.

After studying the most common languages in the world, I knew firsthand that there was no point in speaking any language—even if billions of other people speak it—if you don't actually know any of those people. Over nine million people speak Catalan (which, granted, is nothing compared to a language like Mandarin, which has over a billion speakers). But even if only 100,000 people spoke it, but that number included everyone we knew, then it would make sense to learn it. Besides, Catalan was a Romance language with roots in French and Italian, so knowing Catalan would give our kids a leg up if they ever wanted to learn French, Portuguese, Italian, Romanian, or any other Latin-based language.

Plus, everyone is bilingual in Barcelona. It was like Beirut in that way. In Barcelona (and Catalunya), the unique cultural identity is very important, and speakers work hard to keep their language and culture alive. In a way, I had a lot in common with them; I was working hard to give my children languages and cultural awareness. It was a priority not held everywhere in the world.

I still had a deep interest in the Middle East and Arabic, so I would be glad to be just a short flight away from Morocco, Egypt, Beirut, or Jordan. There was a large Muslim population in Barcelona, and plenty of Arabic learning centers. I would have a lot of resources if and when I returned to consistently studying Arabic. For Mandarin, on the other hand, I came to a realization that should have been obvious long before I started this project. I didn't love China like I thought I would, and I think that's okay. I love lots of places, but China and I don't click—but I do love Thailand. Every time we go to Asia or anywhere near it, we find some excuse to stop there. We love the country and the people. We have friends there. Thai was a tonal language—why hadn't I picked Thai from the start? Why? Because I wanted to pick the most *useful* languages—and I blindly used the total number of speakers to measure that. But if we weren't committing to living in or visiting China regularly, then knowing Chinese wasn't useful to us. Not at all. It would be much more practical to learn Thai because we actually visited the country at least once a year.

So I altered my plan. I'd stop studying Chinese, and start with Thai. My goals for Thai were small; I just wanted some basic conversation skills. There was no need for my children to be educated formally in the language because they were unlikely to go to college in Thailand or to need to read Thai books or write essays in Thai. When we visited the country, we'd speak the language. The kids would pick it up and forget it, over and over again. Some words would stick and when we returned the next year, the exposure would reactivate the language, and they'd slowly build their base. For us, that was plenty.

Drew would keep practicing Spanish and maybe learn a little Catalan, but he'd probably always be a reluctant language learner. The kids would speak Spanish, Catalan, English, and a little Thai. I would, too, and I'd also be able to read a little Arabic. This plan finally made sense, and I knew it would work because it mirrored our lives and how we'd use the languages. We were structuring our lives in such a way that for the children the languages would not be something they were forced to learn, or a chore they had to complete, but instead, just "the way we talk."

WE TOOK A SHORT TRIP to Mexico City to get Stella's U.S. birth certificate (which is actually called a consulate report of birth abroad, since she was not born in the United States) so we could apply for her passport. It came two weeks later, and we could officially leave the country just after Stella's first birthday. We did end up having to get the car door fixed after all, since the "repairs" the mallet-happy mechanic did in Mexico City didn't really fix the problem. Luckily, in Puerto Vallarta, where we have friends, we didn't have to negotiate on the price. Everyone knew we were just normal Americans, not super-rich, important, traveling journalists as the mechanics in Tapachula believed. Drew and I took turns behind the wheel of the Dodge

Caravan on the drive north, across the border and into Texas. Our Mexican baby Stella entered the United States for the first time.

We stayed with my friend Kayt in Houston as we tried to sell the car (we ended up having to drive to New Orleans to finally get rid of it because no one in Houston wanted our beat-up minivan). I was completely culture-shocked after so much time away from home; I walked around the grocery store in a daze. Meat was so cheap. You could get *anything*; there were so many options. I looked at the Mexican food section. There were the same spices I would find in my local market in Puerto Vallarta, except there were actually even *more* of them. You could get anything from dried chiles to bags of Jamaica tea. There was an entire aisle dedicated just to cereal. Another for shampoo and conditioner. I was frozen with all the choices thrown at me by the American grocery store. How could you ever decide?

Our host, Kayt, was a science writer. She started telling me about the research on learning music at a young age. "It doesn't even matter if you like it or not; taking music lessons has huge cognitive benefits." Her young son was learning the piano from their home in suburban Houston. I thought to myself, "Well, jeez, that would have been easier."

WE FLEW TO BARCELONA. I visited the market right away. There was organic local produce, and tons of cherries, which were in season. We made the Catalan dish *conejo al aioli*, a garlicky rabbit dish grilled on the barbecue. The Spanish here was harder for me to understand, the vocabulary slightly different. When I ordered a beer, it was a *caña*, for a small glass, rather than just ordering a *cerveza* or *chela* in Mexico. But it was immediately clear to me that we'd made the right call moving here. Life was lived outdoors in this city. People went for walks, hung out in the plazas, had a drink in a café with a friend. It was so social and friendly, and kids could be seen everywhere you went. There were playgrounds everywhere. So many young families, and it was easy to make friends. In our first week, we were introduced to several moms who wanted their kids to learn English and were eager to have play dates with us. It seemed like everyone we encountered was our age and had kids. We were in parenting heaven.

We arranged to take some bikes up the coast to Girona and tour around the beach towns north of Barcelona. This area was the best of all worlds. A beautiful city, full of amazing culture and food and architecture, and just one hour north was the Costa Brava, full of spacious beaches and world-class cycling routes. If we wanted to go to Paris, we could take the high-speed train and get there in a few hours.

"We are never, ever leaving," Drew told me.

Okay, deal.

Thirty

Drew and I walk with Stella and Cole through the Gothic quarter, the same place we stayed during our honeymoon ten years earlier. I have Stella in a wrap, Drew is holding Cole's hand, and I am holding Cole's other hand.

I'd set out on this quest to better understand the world, to improve myself, to give my children a brighter future. I don't know if I accomplished any of those things, but surely it can't hurt to be bilingual. But I have some peace now about the world and my place in it. I have my priorities set. When we started, we had completed a year of fast travel with a toddler and I was sitting in a hotel room in Egypt trying to figure out what was next. I was chasing, seeking, running, stretching myself because I had to know.

I wanted a deeper connection with my grandfather before he died because I longed for family. Maybe it was the absence of a healthy home and family in my childhood that meant I had to search the globe to find my place in the world. In the end, I decided the most exciting and meaningful thing I could do with my life was to settle down in a thriving city by the sea, become part of the community, and raise my kids. Almost all of my adult friends with kids had already figured this out, but I like to take the long route. I needed to explore a bit first. I had had no framework for what a happy family even looked like. Somehow through luck, providence, and the limitless patience of my husband, I seem to have gotten all those things.

Here we are strolling through the same winding streets that we had held hands and walked through as newlyweds. Back then, it was the most romantic time of my life. I was intoxicated with travel, thrilled with every public fountain and outdoor café, exhilarated by the sound of foreign words rolling off foreign tongues on the street. Now I am full of a different feeling. It's this quiet happiness that infects your life when your children are cheerful, your spouse is relaxed, your family is together. These two moments in time reach across the expanse of ten years and touch each other. It was the happiest moment of my life then, and having my children with us in this same spot is even more than happy. It is peace.

I lean over and kiss Drew on the cheek.

"Welcome home."

NOTES

....

INTRODUCTION

In a report commissioned by the EU on English speaking, only 20 percent of Spain residents spoke English well enough to hold a conversation (compared to nearly 95 percent of Norway, where fluency in English is so common, it might as well be an official second language). Directorate-General for Education and Culture, Directorate-General for Translation and Directorate-General for Interpretation, "Europeans and their languages—Special Eurobarometer 386," European Commission, June 2012. http://ec.europa.eu/public_opinion/archives/ebs/ebs_386_en.pdf.

CHAPTER 1

Her research showed that there was a cognitive benefit to being bilingual, that speaking a second or third language could stave off the effects of dementia by four to five years. E. Bialystok et al., "Bilingualism as a protection against the onset of symptoms of dementia," *Neuropsychologia* (2007): 459–464.

F. Craik et al., "Delaying the onset of Alzheimer disease: bilingualism as a form of cognitive reserve," *Neurology* 75 (2010): 1726–1729.

E. Bialystok, "Reshaping the mind: the benefits of bilingualism," *Canadian Journal of Experimental Psychology* 65 (2011): 229–235.

R. K. Olsen et al., "The effect of lifelong bilingualism on regional grey and white matter volume," *Brain Research* (2015): 128–139.

Bialystok's interview from the *New York Times* . . . C. Dreifus, "The bilingual advantage," *New York Times*, May 30, 2011.

The Foreign Service Institute, the branch of the U.S. government that trains diplomats in many things, including foreign languages, rates Arabic as a level 5 language on a scale of 1 to 5—in other words, one of the hardest for a native English speaker to learn. Interagency Language Roundtable, "An overview of the history of the ILR Language proficiency skill level descriptions and scale by Dr. Martha Herzog." http://www.govtilr.org/Skills/IRL%20Scale%20History.htm.

CHAPTER 2

I read a number of books in preparation for this project. Here is a list of some of the more useful ones:

N. Chomsky and J. McGilvray, *The Science of Language: Interviews with James McGilvray* (Cambridge, UK: Cambridge University Press, 2012).

V. Cook and B. Bassetti, *Language and Bilingual Cognition* (New York: Psychology Press, 2010).

G. Deutscher, *Through the Language Glass: Why the World Looks Different in Other Languages* (New York: Picador, 2011).

R. Ellis, *Language Teaching Research and Language Pedagogy* (Hoboken, NJ: Wiley-Blackwell, 2012).

M. Erard, *Babel No More: The Search for the World's Most Extraordinary Language Learners* (New York: Free Press, 2012).

D. L. Everett, *Don't Sleep, There Are Snakes: Life and Language in the Amazonian Jungle* (New York: Vintage, 2009).

D. L. Everett, *Language: The Cultural Tool* (New York: Vintage, 2012).

A.M.B. de Groot, *Language and Cognition in Bilinguals and Multilinguals: An Introduction* (New York: Psychology Press, 2010).

F. Grosjean, *Bilingual: Life and Reality* (Cambridge, MA: Harvard University Press, 2012).

F. Grosjean, *The Psycholinguistics of Bilingualism* (Hoboken, NJ: Wiley-Blackwell, 2013).

E. Harding-Esch, *The Bilingual Family: A Handbook for Parents* (Cambridge, UK: Cambridge University Press, 2003).

A. E. Hernandez, *The Bilingual Brain* (Oxford, UK: Oxford University Press, 2013).

K. King, *The Bilingual Edge: The Ultimate Guide to Why, When, and How* (New York: HarperCollins, 2009).

B. Z. Pearson, *Raising a Bilingual Child (Living Language Series)* (New York: Living Language, 2008).

S. Pinker, *The Language Instinct: How the Mind Creates Language* (New York: Harper Perennial, 2007).

V. Raguenaud, *Bilingual by Choice: Raising Kids in Two (or More!) Languages* (Boston: Nicholas Brealey America, 2009).

N. Steiner, *7 Steps to Raising a Bilingual Child* (New York: AMACOM, 2008).

X. L. Wang, *Growing Up with Three Languages: Birth to Eleven (Parents' and Teachers' Guides)* (Bristol, UK: Multilingual Matters, 2008).

CHAPTER 3

Krashen, a linguist and second-language acquisition expert who wrote several papers on the topic in the 1980s, most notably his 1982 paper, "Second Language Acquisition . . . " S. D. Krashen, "Second language acquisition," *Second Language Learning* (1981): 19–39.

He also wrote two books about the subject:

S. D. Krashen, *Principles and Practice in Second Language Acquisition* (Oxford, UK: Pergamon, 1982).

S. D. Krashen, *Second Language Acquisition and Second Language Learning* (Oxford, UK: Oxford University Press, 1981).

CHAPTER 4

Who was the first foreigner to become fluent in Mandarin? It was most likely Matteo Ricci, and while I didn't get to write about him in the book, his biography is worth a read: R. P. C. Hsia, *A Jesuit in the Forbidden City: Matteo Ricci 1552–1610* (Oxford, UK: Oxford University Press, 2012).

CHAPTER 7

The U.S. Environmental Protection Agency issued a report stating that on some days as much as 25 percent of the pollution in Los Angeles comes from China.

The EPA's report was issued in 2006. Here is the Chinese response:
"US Report on Pollution 'unfair,' 'unreliable,'" August 4, 2006. http://
www.gov.cn/english////2006-08/04/content_354164.htm.

In 2010, researchers did a follow-up study in the Bay Area and found that
29 percent of the pollution came from China in their sample:
E. J. Gertz, "Lead isotopes tag the origins of particulate air pollutants," November 10, 2010. http://pubs.acs.org/cen/news/88/i46/8846news3.htm.

Additionally, the World Health Organization reported that around the
world, seven million people in 2012 died from the effects of pollution:
D. Pennise and K. Smith, "Biomass pollution basics," WHO. http://www
.who.int/indoorair/interventions/antiguamod21.pdf

The *New York Times* also published an in-depth piece about the pollution
in China:
J. Kahn and J. Yardley, "As China roars, pollution reaches deadly extre-
mes," *New York Times*, August 26, 2007. http://www.nytimes.com
/2007/08/26/world/asia/26china.html.

CHAPTER 8

I read quite a bit of Diana Deutsch's work, and although not all of it made
it into the book, this piece in particular shaped my thinking:

D. Deutsch, "Speaking in tones," *Scientific American*, July/August 2010, 36.

In 2009, she performed an experiment that tested two groups of music
students—one group from the United States and another from East
Asia—to determine how many of them had perfect pitch (the ability to
accurately identify a musical note from a sound). D. Deutsch et al.,
"Absolute pitch among students in an American music conservatory:
association with tone language fluency," *Journal of the Acoustical
Society of America* 125 (2009): 2398–2403.

D. Deutsch et al., "Absolute pitch among students at the Shanghai Conservatory of Music: a large-scale direct-test study," *Journal of the Acoustical Society of America* 134 (2013): 3853–3859.

Perfect pitch is still rare, but in 2004, Deutsch did a study of speakers of
Mandarin and Vietnamese (both tone languages) and recorded them
saying the same word over several days. D. Deutsch et al., "Absolute
pitch, speech, and tone language: some experiments and a proposed
framework," *Music Perception* 21 (2004): 339–356.

Researchers from Northwestern University published a study in *Nature Neuroscience* in 2012 that showed that hearing a piece of music while you sleep can improve your performance of that same piece of music when you're awake. J. W. Antony et al., "Cued memory reactivation during sleep influences skill learning," *Nature Neuroscience* 15, no. 8 (2012): 1114–1116.

CHAPTER 11

University of Haifa. "Literary Arabic Is Expressed in Brain of Arabic Speakers as a Second Language." ScienceDaily. ScienceDaily, 5 November 2009. http://www.sciencedaily.com/releases/2009/11/091104091724.htm.

The acquisition-learning distinction is the underpinning of the entire foreign-language-by-immersion movement, and it's the principle by which I organized our lives in Beijing: I lived in an environment where the language was used constantly, I created situations where I was forced to use the language, and voilà, I planned to become fluent. K. Morgan-Short et al., "Second language processing shows increased native-like neural responses after months of no exposure," *PLoS ONE*, March 28, 2012.

S. N. Bhanoo, "How immersion helps to learn a language," *New York Times*, April 2, 2012. http://www.nytimes.com/2012/04/03/science /how-immersion-helps-to-learn-a-new-language.html.

CHAPTER 13

Grosjean said that most bilinguals are not, in fact, bicultural, writing that "there is the misconception that all bilinguals are bicultural (they are not) and that they have double personalities (as a bilingual myself, and with a sigh of relief, I can tell you that this is not the case)." F. Grosjean, "What bilingualism is NOT," August 2010. http://www .francoisgrosjean.ch/bilingualism_is_not_en.html.

CHAPTER 14

Researcher Arturo E. Hernandez shared his experience of learning multiple languages in his book *The Bilingual Brain*. A. E. Hernandez, *The Bilingual Brain* (Oxford, UK: Oxford University Press, 2013).

In his 1881 book *Les maladies de la mémoire,* the father of French psychology, Théodule-Armand Ribot, wrote of a forester living on the border of Poland who grew up speaking Polish and later in life moved to a German-speaking area. While in this town, he didn't hear or speak Polish for more than thirty years. T.A. Ribot, *Les maladies de la mémoire* (Paris: Bailliere, 1881).

Patricia Kuhl studied Catalan and Spanish bilingual infants and found that they could detect subtle differences between the two languages as early as age four months, even though they are both Romance languages and have shared word sounds and vocabulary and a similar cadence (linguists call this *prosody).* P. K. Kuhl et al., "Infants show a facilitation effect for native language phonetic perception between 6 and 12 months," *Developmental Science* 9 (2006): F13–F21.

A. Garcia-Sierra et al., "Bilingual language learning: an ERP study relating early brain responses to speech, language input, and later word production," *Journal of Phonetics* (2011).

In a 2004 study, researcher M. Rosario Rueda tested bilingual children using a task-switching game . . . M. R. Rueda et al., "Development of attentional networks in childhood," *Neuropsychologia* 42 (2004): 1029–1040.

More specifically: if you're like the rest of us, after your twenties you'll slowly start losing brain mass. That loss accelerates when you get into your fifties. By the time you hit your seventies, you will have lost 5 to 6 percent of your total brain mass compared to what you had at age thirty. By age eighty, you can lose as much as 25 percent. R. Peters, "Ageing and the Brain," *Postgraduate Medical Journal* 82, no. 964 (2006): 84–88.

R. Scahill et al., "A longitudinal study of brain volume changes in normal ageing using serial registered magnetic resonance imaging," *Archives of Neurology* 60, no. 7 (2003): 989–994.

L. Svennerholm et al., "Changes in weight and compositions of major membrane components of human brain during the span of adult human life of Swedes," *Acta Neuropathologica* 94, no. 4 (1997): 345–352.

Bialystok's research showed that even in bilinguals with significant impairment from dementia, the rest of their brain seemed to compensate for the loss, allowing them to stave off the effects of dementia for much longer than their monolingual peers (four to five years before symptoms begin to show), even when their fMRI scans showed similar

loss. Dr. Bialystok has researched the topic of aging and bilingualism extensively:

E. Bialystok et al., "Effects of bilingualism and aging on executive function and working memory," *Psychology and Aging* 29 (2014): 696–705.

E. Bialystok et al., "Effects of bilingualism on the age of onset and progression of MCI and AD: Evidence from executive function tests," *Neuropsychology* 28 (2014): 290–304.

E. Bialystok, "Reshaping the mind: the benefits of bilingualism," *Canadian Journal of Experimental Psychology* 65 (2011): 229–235.

F. Craik et al., "Delaying the onset of Alzheimer disease: bilingualism as a form of cognitive reserve," *Neurology* 75 (2010): 1726–1729.

M. Freedman et al., "Delaying onset of dementia: are two languages enough?" *Behavioural Neurology* 2014 (2014): 808137.

J. F. Kroll and E. Bialystok, "Understanding the consequences of bilingualism for language processing and cognition," *Journal of Cognitive Psychology* 25 (2013): 497–514.

G. Luk et al., "Is there a relation between onset age of bilingualism and enhancement of cognitive control?" *Bilingualism: Language and Cognition* 14 (2011): 588–595.

G. Luk et al., "Lifelong bilingualism maintains white matter integrity in older adults," *Journal of Neuroscience* 31 (2011): 16808–16813.

L. Luo et al., "Bilingualism interacts with domain in a working memory task: evidence from aging," *Psychology and Aging* 28 (2013): 28–34.

L. Ossher et al., "The effect of bilingualism on amnestic mild cognitive impairment," *Journals of Gerontology Series B: Psychological Sciences and Social Sciences* 68 (2013): 8–12.

CHAPTER 15

As I discovered these aspects of Arabic, I became more interested in the history of Islam, and bought the book *Destiny Disrupted* by Tamim Ansary, an American historian who grew up in Afghanistan and now lives in San Francisco. T. Ansary, *Destiny Disrupted: A History of the World Through Islamic Eyes* (New York: Public Affairs, 2010).

CHAPTER 16

Linguists Virginia Volterra and Traute Taeschner studied two Italian-German bilinguals and found that one girl had a vocabulary of eighty-seven words with just three words that matched in both languages. V. Volterra and T. Taeschner, "The acquisition and development of language by bilingual children," *Journal of Child Language* 5 (1978): 311–326.

One study examined Korean children who were adopted between ages one and three years and moved to the United States to join non-Korean-speaking families. D. Birdsong, "Introduction: whys and why nots of the critical period hypothesis for second language acquisition," in D. Birdsong (ed.), *Second Language Acquisition and the Critical Period Hypothesis* (Mahwah, NJ: Erlbaum, 1999), pp. 1–22.

J. E. Flege, "Age of learning and second language speech," in D. Birdsong (ed.), *Second Language Acquisition and the Critical Period Hypothesis* (Mahwah, NJ: Erlbaum, 1999), pp. 101–131.

In François Grosjean's book *Bilingual: Life and Reality,* he tells the story of two brothers who are acquiring French . . . F. Grosjean, *Bilingual: Life and Reality* (Cambridge, MA: Harvard University Press, 2012), chapter 15.

If an fMRI scan were done of me speaking Mandarin or Arabic compared to speaking my native English, it would show activity in different areas, not the same areas that it would show if I were natively bilingual. G. Vingerhoets et al., "Multilingualism: an fMRI study," *Neuro-Image* 20 (2003): 2181–2196.

By the way, this brain development is so important that if you don't learn any language by the time you're about thirteen years old, it's probably impossible for you to ever fully use any language correctly. S. Pinker, *The Language Instinct: How the Mind Creates Language* (New York: Morrow, 1994).

In another case, a six-and-a-half-year-old child named Isabelle was found having spent her life locked up in a darkened room with her deaf-mute mother. After they escaped, she was first tested at a mental age of nineteen months with no language skills at all. S. Pinker, *The Language Instinct: How the Mind Creates Language* (New York: Morrow, 1994).

CHAPTER 19

A study by the American University of Beirut in 1999 showed that at one point most twenty-somethings in Beirut were suffering from PTSD. M. B. Abu-Saba, "War-related trauma and stress characteristics of

American University of Beirut students," *Journal of Traumatic Stress* (January 1999): 201–207.

CHAPTER 26

Janet Werker at the University of British Columbia famously studied this when she tested Japanese infants. . . . "I had traveled all the way around the world to learn languages to teach them to my son, and now, at a bold three and a half years old, he had asked me to knock it off. You know what? I did." A similar story from the *New Republic* that I found after the fact: N. Scheiber, "For Three Years, I Spoke Only Hebrew to My Daughter. I Just Gave It Up. Here's Why," *New Republic*, April 21, 2014. http://www.newrepublic.com/article/117469/why-i-stopped-speaking-my-daughter-hebrew.

CHAPTER 27

In the 1970s and 1980s, Henri Tajfel wrote about this phenomenon and called it social identity theory. For more on his theories, here is his latest book on the topic: H. Tajfel, *Social Identity and Intergroup Relations* (Cambridge, UK: Cambridge University Press, 2010).

ACKNOWLEDGMENTS

I am very grateful and humbled to have had so much help and guidance in the creation of this book. To my agent, Joy Tutela, you made this book possible, working as a partner and mentor each step of the way. Thank you for lending me your experience and being the calm center in the storm. To my editor, Gigi Campo, you are amazing. I always felt like you understood where this book was meant to go, even from the very beginning. You have my utmost gratitude for helping to shape this book.

There were so many academics and researchers who fielded my questions, but to Daniel Everett, Vivian Cook, and Diane Deutsch, I'm especially thankful for your generosity and patience.

I'd also like to thank my friends and family who have weathered many late nights, long discussions, and uncertainty along this journey. Love and gratitude to the Gilbert family, Kayt Sukel, the Lozano family, and all my friends in Chiang Mai, Beijing, Beirut, Bucerías, and Barcelona.

Finally, Drew, you make my whole life possible. Thank you for supporting all my crazy schemes, picking me up when I fall down, and joyfully leaping with me into the next big adventure.